IRELAND

Hippocrene Companion Guide to
IRELAND
Travel, Culture, Society, Politics and History

Henry Weisser

HIPPOCRENE BOOKS
New York

For information, address:
Hippocrene Books, Inc.
171 Madison Avenue
New York, NY 10016

Library of Congress Cataloging-in-Publication Data

Weisser, Henry, 1935–
  Hippocrene companion guide to Ireland : travel, culture, society,
politics, and history / Henry Weisser.
    p. cm.
  ISBN 0-87052-633-2
  1. Ireland—Description and travel—1981– 2. Northern Ireland—
Description and travel—1981– 3. Northern Ireland—
Civilization.
  4. Ireland—Civilization. I. Title.
  DA978.2.W45 1990
  914.1504′824—dc20   89-77459
                                                                          CIP

Editorial design, development and production by
Combined Books, Inc., 26 Summit Grove Ave., Suite 207,
Bryn Mawr, PA 19010,
(215) 527-9276

CONTENTS

A WORD OF THANKS

Countless persons contributed to this book: scholars, students in Ireland, students in America, colleagues with an Irish interest or connection at Colorado State University, and a great variety of people all over Ireland who share that wonderful Irish characteristic of being willing to talk at length with someone recently met.

A few people must be singled out by name for special thanks. Mr. Paddy Tutty of the Irish Tourist Board in Dublin kindly supplied illustrations for this book.

While I lived in Dublin recently, Dr. Cyril White and his wife, Lil White, welcomed me into their home with truly legendary Irish hospitality. Lil White must be one of the greatest cooks in the western hemisphere. Cyril White is a Dubliner descended from generations of Dubliners who loves his native city. Since part of his formal education was at American universities, he also understands and appreciates America and Americans. A sociologist at University College, Dublin, he has generously shared countless insights with me, and answered what must have seemed like barrages of questions. When I expressed concern that I might distort some of his viewpoints in this book, he responded, "So what? When you write it, it is going to be all your opinion anyway." So these warm and kindly Irish people have also provided me with a disclaimer for the errors and mistakes that may inadvertently appear in these pages.

Last, my daughter, Jeanette Weisser, deserves credit for editing the manuscript and suffering through long expostulations on the phone. When she graduated from college she owed me a debt for overseas travel. I wisely urged her not to repay me, declaring that I should rather have her edit my future publications. I wonder if I have ever made a more worthwhile investment.

I also wish to thank the History Department and the College of Arts, Humanities and Social Sciences of Colorado State University for granting me a sabbatical leave so that this book could be written.

INTRODUCTION

This book is for Americans who want to be well informed about Ireland: travelers, business people, officials, students and those with a special interest in the country. It can also serve as supplemental reading in college Irish studies classes or Irish history survey classes.

The book explains the basic facts and circumstances about the culture and history of Ireland as well as the topics that concern contemporary Irish people. Someone experienced in the Irish tourist industry once remarked to the author that German tourists tend to arrive in Ireland so well prepared that they can impart new information to Irish people about their own heritage. Americans, by contrast, have a reputation for arriving much less prepared, but eager to learn everything on the spot. This book hopes to enable some Americans to counteract that stereotype. It is always better to arrive forearmed with information and forewarned of potential difficulties.

This book is based upon an almost lifelong interest in Ireland, nurtured at first by Irish-American neighbors in Brooklyn and Long Island, New York, and deepened in recent years by conducting five study tours to Ireland for students and teachers. Most recently the author lived in Dublin for an academic semester. I regularly teach Irish history at Colorado State University, where many of my students are Irish Americans who are looking for their roots.

The fact that this study is written by an American for Americans offers some advantages. Irish authors can lose their readers in thickets of detail when they write about aspects of their own country, or they may hold a certain conviction or point of view with passionate commitment. Since the author does not have a single known Irish ancestor, he is spared any family connection to any of the groups or religions that have contested for control in Ireland, and thereby contributed to the many tragedies that scar Irish history. It is hoped that this lack of Irish ancestry has helped to create an unbiased and impartial account. Even so, the controversial nature of some issues discussed in these pages may lead some readers to think that on some points the author is opinionated or shooting from the hip. Others may regard some generalizations as too sweeping or may accuse the author of presenting stereotypes. Such is the price of attempting to present a succinct account of a culture and history thousands of years old which continues to suffer from violent controversies and heated disputes.

The book concentrates upon the Republic of Ireland, a sovereign, independent state. Northern Ireland, a substantial portion of the province of Ulster, is governed by Britain and is not treated as fully in these pages.

Many accounts of Ireland are highly romantic and sentimental. This book strives for a cold, hard look at the realities of contemporary Ireland without a sweet gloss of any kind.

This book was designed to be useful. The chapters

are structured to convey important information efficiently, so that the person who wants to be prepared to deal with Ireland and the Irish need not plow through a shelf of books.

The first chapter deals with a few practical matters but concentrates on travel highlights. It omits minor attractions and the usual hotel and restaurant recommendations that fill up most travel books. Chapter Two discusses the social and psychological aspects at play when Americans confront Ireland and the Irish, candidly explaining the best and the worst features of many situations. Chapter Three takes up language and aspects of the arts and also provides a handy dictionary of Irish English terms translated into American English. Chapter Four deals with important aspects of Irish society, including geography, education, wealth, poverty, religion, the family, crime and sport. Chapter Five takes up politics by discussing the nature of democracy in the Republic, relations with Britain, and the ongoing problem of Northern Ireland. The concluding chapter presents the highlights and main themes of Irish history and suggests the most interesting sites from each era to visit.

CHAPTER ONE

Travel

SOME BASICS: CLOTHES, FOOD, MONEY AND ACCOMMODATION

Ireland is one of the easiest places in the world for Americans to visit. English is spoken everywhere, the climate is temperate, and the food is familiar. Few nations of the world accept and understand Americans more readily than Ireland, where the warmth, hospitality, humor and friendliness of ordinary Irish people toward Americans are outstanding characteristics. The simple fact that several million Irish people became Americans over the centuries and that the Irish economy depends upon gaining dollars from tourism help explain this situation.

Irish society and history are complex, and subsequent chapters will delve into various topics so that

1

American visitors can sharpen their perceptions, mini-
mize misunderstandings and enhance appreciations.
This chapter will consider basic topics and places to see.

Clothes

All travel literature declares that dress in Ireland is
casual. Nevertheless casual in Ireland seems to have a
different meaning from casual in America. Colors worn
in Ireland are more subdued. Black and dark blue are
prominent. The bright primary and secondary colors of
American casual clothes stand out boldly, indicating that
the wearer is a tourist. So do some of the American
clothes designed for ski slopes or visits to southern California. It is far better to try to blend into the environment and be less conspicuous. For the same reasons, do
not purchase bright green articles of clothing in anticipation of a trip to Ireland. The casual clothes worn by
most Irish people generally appear to be more sober
and of higher quality than those worn in America.

Ireland is cool and wet all year round; more so in
winter than in summer. Summer and winter temperatures do not diverge as far as they do in most
regions of the United States. The best way to select
clothes for Ireland is to choose what would be appropriate for a fall vacation in New England when rains are
forecast. Sweaters, windbreakers and overshoes can be
very useful in Ireland in July and August.

A few items of light clothes can be taken for those
rare and exceptional hot muggy days when temperatures might soar all the way up to the low 70's
Fahrenheit. Ordinarily temperatures hover in the high
50's or low 60's in the summer months. A sturdy um-

brella and a waterproof raincoat and hat and waterproof foot gear should be taken. Keeping dry from head to foot is important.

Most Americans bring along far too much luggage, packed with too many clothes and too many gadgets. No matter how often this admonition is proclaimed, people continue to subject themselves to dragging unnecessary goods along with them. Take the minimum amount of clothes. All over Ireland there are friendly shopkeepers presiding in well stocked establishments who can supply whatever is needed. It is far better to meet needs on the spot than to take along extra items in anticipation of needs. Try to be a loose packer, leaving extra space for those inevitable items which will be picked up along the way.

Food

Irish food should be very familiar to Americans. In fact, some of it is American because McDonald's, Burger King, Godfather's Pizza, Seven Eleven and other American fast-food or convenience food outlets have made their appearance. Dublin even has at least one Tex-Mex restaurant. Most ordinary Irish food is similar to British food, which is similar to ordinary American food.

Jokes about Irish food abound, such as: "It is the best food in the world until it is cooked." Some gastronomic horrors do exist: perfectly luscious salmon can be drowned in thick, gooey sauces; greasy fried foods are widely prepared without any regard for cholesterol or calories whatsoever, often in lard; starchy pasta and egg combinations appear in stark incongruity; and mysterious meats are disguised in thick gravies called curries. On the other hand, the author has enjoyed absolutely superb meals in Irish homes and very good ones in Irish restaurants.

Historically, classic Irish cooking was simple compared to the Continental cuisines. Fresh meats, fish, butter, eggs and potatoes were and are the main ingredients for the best of Ireland's roasted and baked dishes. American visitors might appreciate the particular variety and freshness of Irish seafood. They might also be surprised to learn that corned beef and cabbage is a featured dish around St. Patrick's day only in the United States.

One of the most advantageous features of the British legacy for contemporary Ireland is the presence of food from the distant realms of what was the British Empire. Indian and Chinese restaurants flourish in Dublin and other Irish cities. Many of the Chinese establishments and some of the Indian ones offer relatively low cost takeaway meals. Food in Ireland in stores and supermarkets is expensive compared to costs in the United States.

Money

The Irish pound, called the punt in Irish, has been lower in value than the British pound, to which it was once tied. The British pound sterling is still used in Northern Ireland, of course. Irish coins are easy to become familiar with because the pound is divided into 100 pence, and written IR£. Irish bills have a great advantage over American currency because different denominations have different colors and sizes. It is harder to give away the wrong Irish bills by mistake, although Irish business people can be depended upon to give the right change in any case. The disadvantage of dealing with Irish money is that the pound is worth more than the dollar, usually around $1.50. Many feel tempted to spend more when the unit is larger than the dollar, even when they know, rationally, that an item marked with a 5 on sale really costs $7.50 or so.

Accommodation

Accommodation in Ireland is abundant, easy to arrange, relatively inexpensive and very varied. For people on a tight budget, this is a boon. On the other hand, visitors who demand and expect the uniform convenience and predictability of good American hotels and motels can lurch through a series of disappointments in Ireland unless they are willing to pay top prices.

The Irish Tourist Board is very helpful in arranging accommodations. Each major city, each area attractive to tourists and each international airport has an Irish Tourist Board office which willingly expends effort to place visitors in appropriate accommodations. The Tourist Board also publishes booklets giving lists of approved hotels and bed-and-breakfast locations along with their amenities and prices. It also has information on youth hostels.

The major inconvenience of most of the inexpensive bed-and-breakfast rooms is that the toilet and the bath are usually shared and elsewhere, sometimes mysteriously hidden down corridors or under stairs. There are no standards for the size, shape, furnishings and quietness of individual rooms beyond basic parameters set by the Irish Tourist Board. Most of the buildings that are now bed and breakfast locations served other purposes originally, most having been homes of large families. When they were converted for tourists, improvization was the rule, sometimes with most curious results. The unapproved, informal bed-and-breakfast spots, which are found everywhere in Ireland, may be even more irregular.

A few Irish hotels cater to the American or European or Asian big spenders by trying to imitate large American operations. While all of the conveniences might be provided in near American style, the price will be astounding. Most Irish hotels tend to be quaint and cheap and somewhat seedy, which can be charming. Sometimes standards of cleanliness and freshness detract from the charm by falling short of American expectations. Yet where in the United States today can a room in one of the best hotels in town cost the equivalent of only between two and four ten dollar bills? On the other hand, after a sojourn in Ireland, the standardized, built for the 20th century American motel chains, with their clean, convenient, ample and utterly predictable facilities will look like a bargain also.

DRIVING IN IRELAND

Why Drive?

Driving in Ireland is hazardous. Visitors who are there for only a few weeks in the tourist season can get to the most significant places by relying on trains and bus tours. Renting a car may be more logical for those who stay longer or who are there during the offseason. Americans tend to find it difficult to spend time anywhere without a car because driving is an integral part of the American way of life. Yet the high cost, inconvenience, frustration and outright danger of driving make it advisable to avoid renting a car in Ireland.

Drivers in Ireland have to face too many hazards because of the conditions of the roads and what is on them. Any car rental is almost guaranteed to result in at least a few heart-stopping close calls. It is so much easier, so much simpler and cheaper to take the extensively developed public transportation and use public tourism facilities. Of course, there are always those distant cousins far up in Donegal and that exquisite little town in western County Cork that cannot be visited without a car. Such temptations might lead to an expensive and risky adventure behind the wheel.

Planning a trip from an Irish road map almost invariably leads to underestimating the time it takes to get around. A fifty-mile span on an Irish road map can become the equivalent of a three- or four-hundred-mile trip in the United States, measured both in time and in wear and tear on the driver's nerves.

While it is fairly easy to rent a car in any major city or airport, it is costly. An American driver's license from any state is all that is needed. Because Ireland is reputed to have the highest fatality and accident rate per miles driven in the European Economic Community, the bill reflects steep insurance fees. Petrol, as gasoline is known in Ireland, is leaded only and exorbitant. For example, filling the tank of a tiny rented Japanese mini-sedan cost about $37.50 in 1988.

Hazardous Roads

Not too long ago, Ireland was praised for its un-crowded roads. The number of vehicles on them has increased dramatically in recent years, jumping from 300,000 to 900,000 between 1960 to 1983. It has be-come very important for a family to own a car, and according to recent government publications, half of Ireland's households have acquired one. Only 10% of these households have more than one. Statistically, the miles of road per capita is still the highest in Europe, but when hundreds of thousands of family cars take to the highways, horrendous traffic situations occur in most of the country. The road system was designed for far fewer vehicles and it has not been upgraded sufficiently.

Most of the roads in Ireland are, in one word, terrible. It is frequently difficult for the driver to tell whether he or she is following the right road because the surface, width and general appearance of even the most important motorways will change frequently. For one stretch a motorway may consist of spacious lanes and adequate shoulders and then it can suddenly be-come a very narrow, shoulderless road hemming the driver in between walls of dense shrubbery or stone. The surfaces are just as varied as the appearances, rang-ing from smooth to badly potholed. Most roads need repairs.

To make matters worse, these irregular roads are usually not well marked. There are small green signs for the major motorways and small white signs for other roads and for major motorways also. Distances are con-fusing because the newer green signs show them in kilometers and the older white ones show them in miles. Big, clear signs, such as those hanging over the American interstate highway system are extremely rare in Ireland.

In some parts of western Ireland the signs are not even bilingual. It is a curious sight to see an American trying to read a map with place names in English while parked by a post bearing a dozen signs in Irish that point to at least half as many directions.

Sometimes the lines painted on the road are clear and sometimes they are worn away. Dotted lines allow passing and a solid line warns the driver to refrain from passing. But as with so many other things in Ireland, these are treated only as rough indicators of what to do. Drivers pass when they can, just as pedestrians cross wherever possible. Orange beacons flashing at a zebra striped crossing indicate that drivers must stop whenever pedestrians use them. The square yellow grids at town intersections mean that drivers must stop short of them so that the intersection can remain clear while cars negotiate turns through them. A double yellow line by the curb means no parking, but cars are parked over them and over their adjoining sidewalks in busy towns.

Unfortunately, main roads go right into the middle of towns, where they are likely to narrow, a condition exacerbated by parked cars, trucks and buses. Loading and unloading trucks seems to take precedence over traffic flow. In towns popular with tourists, enormous buses clog the roads. Private cars seem to park wherever it is convenient, sometimes with the aplomb of diplomats parking in New York City. All of this means that cars on major motorways can come to a crawl going through towns. Passengers are likely to gasp as vehicles inch their way past obstacles with almost no room to spare.

Lack of resources and space means that bypasses around these bottlenecks have not been built. These same circumstances dictate that interchanges are in the form of the roundabout rather than the American-style cloverleaf. Roundabouts funnel traffic into a circle, and roads shoot off the outer rim in different directions, like spokes off of a wheel. These vehicular merry-go-rounds can be breathtaking because traffic roars behind a driver who is straining to see the proper exit marker. Cars cut in and out, some making their own dramatic entrances and exits all the while. In busy roundabouts steering wheels are clenched.

Construction and repair sites are especially hazardous in Ireland because they tend to be poorly marked. For example, when one lane traffic must alternate at an American repair site, workers in hard hats and equipped with radios stand holding "slow" or "stop" signs. In Ireland a simple unattended traffic light might be the sole regulator. In general, beacons, barrels or equipment near the road can suddenly become hazards upon rounding a turn because warnings and signpostings are so sparse.

Sheep, donkeys and cows can also become sudden hazards when they stray on the roads, which is a very frequent occurrence, especially in western Ireland. Sometimes masses of animals show up with a herdsman and sometimes a solitary stray will very suddenly appear. Farm equipment is another common hazard because it can be huge and lumber along slowly and cumbrously. Even people can become hazards when they stand inches from the highway, in dark clothing, either strolling along or hitching a ride.

Hazardous Irish Drivers

Irish drivers seem to reflect the Irish characteristics of patience, unhurriedness and genial politeness most of the time. But there is a startling Celtic unpredictability and impulsiveness that can come into play at anytime, anywhere. A car ahead can brake sharply or veer off suddenly, or a car can zoom up from behind in a fury, as if to push everything off the road in order to race on.

The very worst characteristic of Irish drivers could be called "the Irish pass." It can be observed in America now and then, but while in America it provokes horn blowing and vehement gesticulations, in Ireland it is a normal occurrence. The Irish pass assumes that all two-lane roads can become three-lane roads if one car wants to "overtake" another. So drivers pull out to pass in the face of oncoming vehicles, which are expected to veer to the side, while the car which is being overtaken can help by veering the other way. The results can be simply breathtaking. In one split second a narrow two lane road may be required to accommodate three cars across, two going in one direction and one going in the other. It takes a while for Americans to get used to pulling out to "overtake" right into oncoming traffic. It takes much less time to acquire the habit of veering over when an Irish driver coming the other way launches a passing attempt into the space not far from the driver's windshield.

The Hazard of Driving on the Opposite Site

Driving on the opposite side of the road is a special hazard Americans must endure in Ireland as well as in Britain. By the way, avoid referring to the left side as the "wrong" side of the road, because there is nothing wrong about it for the Irish.

The first few moments of driving on the opposite side can be harrowing. Prior to the first experience, be sure to experiment with the gearshift and turn signals while parked. It takes a while to become comfortable shifting gears with the left hand, and to have the windshield wipers activate instead of an expected turn signal can be disconcerting in heavy traffic.

Once on the road, help resist the temptation to stray into the wrong lane by imaging a white line outside, right next to the steering wheel. In Ireland there may be a yellow line, called a "divider," or no line at all.

Turns are the most difficult feat of all because they must be negotiated just the opposite way from turns in the United States. Left turns in Ireland are short and sharp. Right turns swing wide, out across one lane and into another. Always keep the line, real or imaginary, close to the steering wheel.

When there are two lanes or more going in one direction, unfortunately a condition not found often enough in Ireland, the faster lane is to the right rather than the left. Just the opposite from the "slower traffic keep right" of American Interstates prevails because slower cars should keep to the left.

It takes a while to get used to judging distances on the left, or the passenger's side of the car. Experienced American drivers more or less automatically calculate distances on the passenger's side when this is on the right side, but when it is on the left their perceptions might be far enough off to scrape curbs or worse. This hazard, and all the others associated with driving on the opposite side become much less intimidating after a few days' experience. Most Americans get used to it by then, and can drive fairly normally.

PUBLIC TRANSPORTATION

Regular Bus Services

For visitors who want to avoid driving to the most important places in Ireland, public transportation provides buses and trains. Buses are cheaper and go to many places while train travel costs at least twice as much to the same destination, and serves a much more limited number of locations. Nevertheless, trains have the advantage of being faster, more efficient and more comfortable.

Ordinary bus travel in Ireland can become an ordeal. The bus itself might be old and battered and have to travel over bad road surfaces. Schedules can turn out to be just chancy rough approximations. Journeys that look short on the map can take an unconscionable amount of time because every little hamlet might require a stop to let people on or off and bottlenecks in towns will reduce speed to a crawl. On long journeys, lengthy rest stops also add time. Breakdowns are a real possibility. All too often the traveler on Irish buses emerges exhausted after being crowded into a seat for a long session of shaking and bone rattling, a victim of worn-out shock absorbers clattering on bad roads.

Trains

It is far better to take the train despite the cost. The expense might be mitigated by special rates on weekends or by any other special tickets available. Always ask about these things at the window. Some people prefer to purchase a travel pass so that they can enjoy unlimited travel for a period of time. See what is available from a travel agent in America before departing for Ireland. A pass may be a very worthwhile investment, depending on how the purchaser wishes to spend time in Ireland.

If a destination is a town or village only served by a bus, the best thing to do is take a train to a stop as close to the location as possible, and then try to pick up a bus there. Unlike buses, trains can be relied upon to depart and arrive on time, and they are spacious and usually uncrowded. Their speed saves time for sightseeing. They enable round trips to the main towns in Ireland from Dublin and back on the same day. These trips are called "return" trips in Ireland. Ticket agents will ask, "Single or return?" for one way or round trip tickets, respectively.

Here are some examples of distances in time, one way from Dublin, on the best trains: Galway, three hours; Belfast, two and a quarter hours; Cork, just over three hours; Kilkenny, almost two hours; Wexford, two and a half hours; and Waterford, almost three hours. (See Dublin map.)

Since trains are fairly frequent and run from early morning until late in the evening, day trips to the towns above are quite feasible. This means that a Dublin base can be maintained during a vacation in Ireland and the trouble of shifting to other places can be avoided. On the other hand, visitors might want to change base from Dublin to Cork or Galway or Sligo. Under either circumstance, take the train.

Bus Eireann Day Tours

There is a world of difference between the ordinary buses and the special government tour buses used for day trips. The Bus Eireann day tour vehicles are larger, newer, have plush insides, reliable motors and good shock absorbers. Their ride is infinitely more comfortable than the almost Third World experience on many of the ordinary buses.

There are some disadvantages in taking these tours. It means being cooped up with a large number of bright eyed, cooing tourists. It means listening to drivers who try to be very informal and friendly, using a rich brogue to tell jokes and stories and clever sayings that tourists are supposed to hear. Astute listeners think most of it is a canned spiel pretending at spontaneity, a spiel used countless times before. What is more, much of the material is drawn from old rural traditions and folklore, the very culture that has disappeared from so many parts of Ireland.

If the fellow tourists and the driver can be tolerated or even enjoyed, these Bus Eireann Day Tours are a convenient bargain. They incorporate many sights efficiently, showing the advantage of traveling in a small sized country by incorporating a large area on the map of Ireland in a single day trip. An American in a rented car armed with road maps is no match for the tour buses in finding good roads and shortcuts. The cost can be as little as $15, and the maximum price is not much higher.

Busaras, the main bus station in Dublin, is the best place to pick up these tours. Perhaps the very best of all of them is the Boyne Valley Tour. It travels north of Dublin to a lush countryside that has had a rich history. During a one day sweep, the tour visits prehistoric graves at Newgrange, the important city of Drogheda, the scene of the Battle of the Boyne, where there is not much to see, a famous early monastic settlement at Monasterboice, and the famous hill of Tara, the seat of ancient kings.

Another good bet is the tour to the monastic ruins at Glendalough in the Wicklow Mountains. Although it takes a long time to get there, some of the loveliest scenery in Ireland is passed along the way, including parts of Dublin Bay. Other places that can be reached by day trips from Dublin are the ancient towns of Kilkenny and Waterford, the ancient church sites of Cashel and Clonmacnoise, and the impressive castle of Cahir. Some special trips go to the country around Sligo associated with the poet William Butler Yeats, and some go to Galway and Salthill on the western shore.

Dublin is not the only good embarkation point for day trips. Cork, Waterford, Limerick and Galway host several worthwhile day trips. They go to such impressive places as the Cliffs of Moher, the rugged Connemara region, the scenic Ring of Kerry, Bunratty Castle, Blarney Castle and many other places.

So far only a few of the more than 60 day trips available from Bus Eireann have been mentioned. The best thing to do in Ireland is to request a current schedule from the Tourist Board. It is important to pay close attention to when the trips operate because they vary from a few days per season to every day in the season. Most operate one or two days per week. Knowing the limits of the tourist season is vital, because when it is over almost every tour bus heads for the garage.

THE TOURIST SEASON

Many Irish people claim that the seasons of their country cannot be told apart, a reference to the cool summers and the mild winters. Yet the tourist season remains clear and distinct. When it is on, all of Ireland is open to the visitor. When it is over, a small percentage of places remain open.

In general, the tourist season runs from mid-May to mid-September, with everything open and in high gear from June through August. Some places do open in early May and some stay open until October, but it is easy to experience disappointment outside of the hard core of the tourist season, roughly ten weeks beginning in mid-June. Recently members of the Irish Tourist Board, *Bord Failte,* declared that more effort must be put into making Ireland a year-round attraction for American vacationers. Nevertheless, access to most of Ireland's cultural and historic sights is in the summer only.

Naturally, many places in Dublin and other cities remain open all through the year. A large city does not shut its museums, galleries, cathedrals and historic buildings when the bulk of the tourists leave. A flow of Irish, British and European visitors continues during the off season. Nevertheless, only a very few non-urban tourist attractions outside of Dublin remain open the year round. The Rock of Cashel, Bunratty Castle and Bunratty Folk Park can be mentioned as examples of places that do not close.

HOW TO USE LIMITED TIME IN IRELAND EFFECTIVELY

A trip to Ireland for many people means that much must be pushed into a short time frame of perhaps one, two or three weeks or even just a few days. With so many towns, cathedrals, monastic settlements, castles, museums and historic sites covering Ireland, how can the visitor pick and choose effectively? One of the worst things to do is rush about in a mad haste making a futile attempt to polish off dozens of items from long lists of things to see. This can turn a trip into a high pressure, high stress operation that is just the opposite of what a vacation is supposed to be. Furthermore, such behavior will conflict with the laid back, low pressure style cultivated in Ireland.

Unless months are available for sightseeing, many worthwhile places will have to be omitted. Set priorities at the outset. The top priority should go to any special personal quest in Ireland. This can be seeking out the family's ancestral home, visiting an aged relative, or seeing a special landscape or seascape or castle which has haunted the mind's eye for a long time. For some people, kissing the Blarney Stone or taking a ship to the Aran Islands or seeing a play in Dublin may be of special personal significance. These preoccupations should have the first claim on time.

What should the next priorities be, particularly if the time remaining is limited? Since Dublin has so much of Ireland's historical and cultural heritage on display in a compact area, spending time in the city is guaranteed to be an efficient and enriching experience. It is important to think in terms of categories for places outside of Dublin. For example, Ireland has scores of castles, many of which are well worth a visit, but it is usually better to have a pleasant time scrambling around one of them than to rush to half a dozen of them. Cathedrals, early monastic settlements and colorful historic towns can also be considered as categories from which one very good example can be chosen for a visit and the rest passed by. Of course, there are some places that defy categorization because they are unique, one of a kind, such as the Rock of Cashel, for example. Scenery is another category. There are several stretches of rustic scenery which have been extolled through the centuries in song, story and immigrants' memories. With only a short time to spend, it is better to enjoy one part of Ireland than to be frazzled by a race to see as many scenic regions as possible. Setting out priorities for such varied attractions requires some sorting out.

DUBLIN SIGHTS THAT SHOULD NOT BE MISSED

Dublin's Cathedrals

Dublin's two ancient cathedrals, St. Patrick's and Christ Church, are huge landmarks and should not be missed, no matter how short a time the visitor has in Dublin. Compared to other famous cathedrals, such as

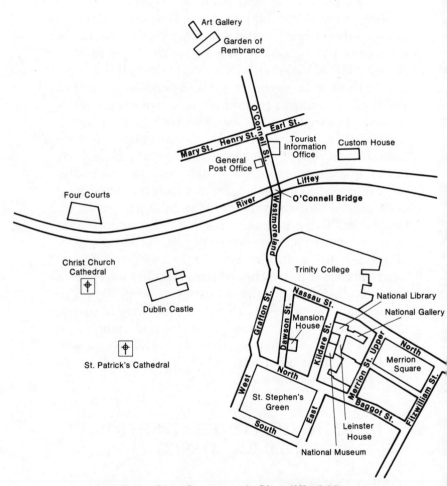

Dublin's City Center: A Simplified Map

Chartres, Cologne, Canterbury, Salisbury, and Durham, Dublin's cathedrals are not so very magnificent, but in their Irish setting they are splendid because of their size and age. Sad to say, both cathedrals underwent heavy-handed Victorian Gothic restoration and "improvement" in the 19th century, so only pieces of the older parts of these buildings can be seen today.

Many Roman Catholic visitors are astounded to learn that St. Patrick's Cathedral in Dublin, Ireland, is a Protestant edifice. When it was built in the 12th century, it was Catholic, and remained so for hundreds of years until the Reformation, when the Church of Ireland was established. The Church of Ireland is similar to the Episcopal Church in America or the Church of England. St. Patrick's connection with the British Empire is amply attested to by all of the mouldering flags, statues to the honored British dead, and patriotic imperial monuments throughout the building. One of St. Patrick's famous dead was a passionate Irish patriot, however, even if he had been a Protestant. Jonathan Swift, author of *Gulliver's Travels* and much more, a man who is a giant in the history of literature, is buried just to the right of the entrance. For a long time, Swift was Dean of St. Patrick's Cathedral.

Christ Church Cathedral, dating back to a small Viking Cathedral, and rebuilt in the 13th century, is also a Protestant cathedral today. It contains a recumbent tomb effigy of a knight that legend proclaims to be Strongbow, the original Norman invader of Ireland.

Some people complain that Dublin's cathedrals are too cold as well as too British, but they really are very friendly places because the people associated with them are eager to point things out and answer questions.

Kilmainham Jail

Kilmainham Jail has become something of a secular cathedral for Irish republicanism. It is as sacred to Irish nationalists as the Alamo is for Texans. The historical atmosphere is so rich that Kilmainham can be cited as one of the best historical exhibits in the whole world.

Kilmainham is an imposing great ugly hulk of a complex of buildings. It took in its first political prisoners in 1796, became derelict in the middle of the 20th century and has been restored in recent decades. The main hall houses an elaborate museum devoted to those who rebelled against British rule over the centuries, but emphasizing the heroes of 1916. Tours of Kilmainham point out where illustrious prisoners were kept as well as the cold, stark, stony yard where executions took place. There is also an audio-visual presentation in the old chapel which is highly nationalistic.

Kilmainham is a considerable distance west of the city center and a lengthy bus ride is required to get there, but it is well worth the trip. Nowhere else can the Irish revolutionary and republican tradition be appreciated so intensely, especially that watershed of modern Irish history which is still highly important to all Irish people today, the Rising of 1916.

Trinity College

Trinity College is in the heart of Dublin, a university founded by Queen Elizabeth I, and for centuries the bastion of Ireland's privileged, Protestant elite. It has been to Ireland what Oxford and Cambridge have been to England.

The grounds are open to the public and well worth a stroll. Old buildings blend in gracefully with the new, but the architectural highlights are a number of graceful 18th century buildings surrounding the main squares. The peace and tranquillity within the college compound are in marked contrast to the roar of traffic and surge of people in the busy streets surrounding it.

The Old Library of Trinity College possesses wonderful ancient illuminated manuscripts, the most famous of which is the Book of Kells. They are situated in the impressive Long Hall of the Old Library, and can be seen after paying an admission fee that is charged only during the tourist season.

Directions to the Old Library can be obtained at the Porter's Office, just inside of the main entrance and to the left. The main entrance faces the juncture of College Green and Westmoreland Streets, just opposite the large Bank of Ireland building that used to house the Parliament of Ireland.

The National Gallery

The collection of paintings in the National Gallery does not measure up to the national collections of Britain, France and Spain, but it is well worth a visit nonetheless. The collection of works by Anglo-Irish artists, British artists and Irish artists offer fascinating insights into Irish history and culture. While the old masters of European art are well represented, there are so many Dutch and Flemish paintings from the 17th and 18th centuries that they tend to overwhelm with so many seascapes, jolly burgers, religious scenes and still lifes of food.

The National Gallery needs another extension or the addition of new wings. It is so overcrowded with exhibits that many of the portraits of famous people in Irish history hang along a circular staircase leading to the toilets. What is more, many exciting 19th- and 20th-century paintings are hung miles away in the Hugh Lane Municipal Gallery of Modern Art at Parnell Square, above the north end of O'Connell Street. An argument can be made that many of these paintings belong with the main collection rather than with the more abstract and experimental art of the latter part of this century.

The National Museum

Ireland's National Museum contains a rich collection of displays that go back to the earliest of times and go up to the 1916 Rising. Recently renovation and rebuilding have closed important sections to the public, but the Museum's very special Celtic art treasures have always been kept on display. Unfortunately, an admission fee has been charged to view them. The Ardagh Chalice and the Tara Brooch, both from the 8th century, have been universally used in a variety of publications to illustrate the golden age of Celtic art. Many other objects from the period in precious metals are on display, including processional crosses and other early Christian art.

When fully open, the National Museum also features prehistoric graves, ancient Egyptian material, crystal, church vestments, ancient musical instruments, Viking material and various memorabilia from the 1916 Rising that rival the displays at Kilmainham Jail. The

Museum also owns an annex building along Merrion Row that houses special exhibits.

Dublin Castle

Dublin Castle does not look like an ordinary castle from the outside. It is so unimposing and unimpressive from its street entrance that it can be missed. It is necessary to go into the courtyard to appreciate its size. Like other castles still in use, it has had additions over the centuries, so that the oldest core, dating from the early 13th century, is completely engulfed by the architecture of subsequent centuries, particularly that of the 18th.

Dublin Castle is one of the most important historic buildings in Ireland. For centuries it was to Irish nationalists what the Bastille was to France, a symbol of oppressive rule. From the 16th century until 1921 it was the citadel of British rule, the home of the Viceroy and the center for British administration. Today it is used for state occasions by the Irish Republic. When not in use, which is most of the time, the State Apartments are open to guided public tours that are highly informative. The aura of the ornate grandeur of royal rule, seen most explicitly in the throne room, is well preserved.

Dublin's Georgian Heritage

What makes Dublin outstanding among the great cities of Europe is its Georgian heritage. Famous buildings, long streets of residences, and charming squares have survived in quantity from the elegant 18th century. Walking around the best preserved parts of Dublin is one of the best ways to spend time in the city.

The Georgian heritage comes from the time when Dublin was the second most important city in the British Empire and expanding from the wealth and trade that this status provided. The brightly painted doors of various colors on Georgian town houses is one of the hallmarks of Dublin. Most of these elegantly austere buildings originally belonged to the Protestant gentry, a good many of whom would have estates in the country as well. One example of a restored Georgian town house is open to the public, free, at the eastern side of Merrion Square. Georgian town houses surviving in good shape and in good neighborhoods tend to become offices for businesses, foundations and institutes.

The longest street of Georgian buildings in the whole world is Fitzwilliam Street, where only a few of the old buildings have been gouged out for modern replacements. Fitzwilliam Street leads to Merrion Square, where everyone who visits Dublin should go for a stroll. It is lovely, green and quiet within the square, and visible over the tops of trees and bushes on all four sides are Georgian buildings. Fitzwilliam Square is nearby, also surrounded by Georgian buildings, but this square is not open to the public.

Several other locations in Dublin have rows of Georgian buildings extant, but nowhere are they as lovely, as numerous and as well preserved as in the area around Fitzwilliam Street. For a contrast, see the buildings around Mountjoy Square north of the Liffey, where the decay and destruction of the Georgian heritage is all too evident. Many Georgian buildings fell derelict in the last hundred years and have been replaced, sometimes with extremely incongruous buildings.

Two gigantic Georgian public buildings along the

River Liffey need to be seen from the outside. The
Custom House is to the east of O'Connell Bridge, along
the north bank of the river. Its magnificent facade,
studded with statues and symbols, gives some idea of the
majesty of British Ireland. Two modern buildings
nearby, the 16 story Liberty Hall and Busarus, the bus
station, enhance appreciation of 18th-century architecture considerably. The Four Courts is upstream, to the
west, along a stretch of the Liffey's shore which is in sad
decay. The Four Courts is a busy Georgian structure,
where Ireland's most important courts function. Its
dome is a famous Dublin landmark from the Georgian
era.

Dublin's Busy City Center

Dublin's city center (spelled *centre* in the Irish English derived from Britain) is a congested, thriving and
compact area inviting exploration on foot. The simplified map of it in this book can be photocopied and
used to supplement the official maps supplied by the
Tourist Board.

The center lies on both sides of the river Liffey, and
O'Connell Bridge is the landmark in the middle of it.
Just to the north of the Liffey, in an area studded with
statues of Irish heroes, is the General Post Office, which
was the main bastion of the heroic and hopeless Rising
of 1916. The Irish Republic was proclaimed on its steps
on that occasion. Despite its historic nature, the building
still functions as a very busy post office. Notice the statue
of Cuchulainn inside, which is a memorial to the dead of
1916. Cuchulainn was a legendary Irish hero who tied

himself to a stake when facing a numerous enemy so that he could never retreat.

A bit further up, and across the street on the eastern side, is the most important Tourist Information Office in Dublin. It offers a wide variety of pamphlets, maps, schedules, announcements, brochures, and booklets, many of them free. Reservations, current travel tips and particular problems can all be handled by the usually friendly staff.

The area around O'Connell Street and O'Connell Street Bridge may pose a few risks. Pickpockets may lurk on the lookout for careless tourists. Some young children who beg will steal if given a chance. Caution should be exercised even though the heavy traffic and throngs tend to allay fears. While mugging is rare in Dublin compared to American cities, deft purse and wallet snatching is a skill some Dubliners ply masterfully.

Earthy, colorful, lively shopping streets go off of O'Connell Street in either direction: Henry Street, Mary Street, Earl Street, Coles Lane and Denmark Street. Shopping areas north of the Liffey tend to cater to poorer Dubliners. Shopping areas south of the Liffey tend to be more upscale.

O'Connell Street turns into Westmoreland Street once the Liffey is crossed. Walking south, past the convenient Thomas Cook's and American Express offices, pedestrians come to the imposing main Bank of Ireland building, which used to be the home of Ireland's own Parliament until it was dissolved in 1800. Right across the street, on its eastern side, is the entrance to Trinity College. After the street bends around the front of Trinity College it becomes Grafton Street, which is now a pedestrian mall and fashionable shopping street re-

sembling many other prosperous pedestrian streets in
Europe. Note the conspicuous American fast-food outlets. Two other shopping streets in this immediate area
are well worth noting. Nassau Street flanks Trinity College to the south, and goes off from the northernmost
part of Grafton Street at right angles. It is noted for
interesting bookstores and quality textile outlets as well
as Dublin's unique Tex-Mex restaurant, which serves as a
refuge for Western Americans addicted to that cuisine.
Dawson Street parallels Grafton Street to the east of it,
and ends at Nassau Street. It too has notable bookstores
and textile outlets. Mansion House, the home of Dublin's Lord Mayor and the scene of various civic exhibi-
tions and activities, is right along busy Dawson Street.

Both Grafton and Dawson Streets terminate to the
south at St. Stephen's Green, a well landscaped, restful
park, an oasis in a busy urban area. Its flowers, duck
ponds, statuary and large numbers of Dubliners make it
a worthwhile place to spend some time. Traffic flows
heavily around the green in one direction, on streets
named St. Stephen's Green North, East, South and
West. Kildare Street goes north from St. Stephen's
Green North, and contains the National Library and
National Museum. St. Stephen's Green North becomes
Baggot Street toward the east and has interesting pubs
and shops. Upper Merrion Street goes north from Baggot Street, paralleling Kildare Street, and passes
Leinster House, the seat of government, and the National Gallery to the west and Merrion Square to the
east. The stately peace that the wealthy enjoyed in the
18th century can be recaptured by a stroll through the
square. Fitzwilliam Street with its long row of Georgian
houses is just on the eastern side of the square. Upon

reaching Baggot Street, a left turn, or a turn eastwards, will lead to the grand canal. It can be followed for miles, but such a hike would lead far from the city center, in a direction down from it and under it.

A Few Other Dublin Sights

Those with more time available in Dublin might want to consider seeing the following places: The Bank of Ireland across the way from Trinity College used to house the Irish Parliament before it was disbanded in 1800. What used to be the Irish House of Commons is entirely taken over by the bank, but the old House of Lords chamber is preserved the way it was, complete with royal mace; and tapestries celebrating Protestant victories covering the walls. Bank porters are pleased to show it to visitors during banking hours.

The Guiness brewery is an enormous plant, said to be the largest in Europe, and is responsible for producing one of Ireland's most important and most famous exports. The Guiness firm is more than a brewery. It is an institution in Dublin, noted for its charitable and civic contributions. The brewery is a very popular place to visit, perhaps more on account of the distribution of samples than because of the free video tape program and museum.

Glasnevin Cemetery, properly called Prospect Cemetery, is very significant for those interested in modern Irish history because it contains the impressive graves of many of Ireland's heroes. The Botanic Gardens are nearby. Along the Liffey to the west, on the north bank, is an entrance to Phoenix Park, a gigantic green area of close to two thousand acres which includes a zoo.

The Hugh Lane Municipal Gallery of Modern Art contains many excellent British and French 19th century paintings as well as some of the varied and experimental works of this century. It is north of O'Connell Street, by Parnell Square. Just across from it is the Garden of Remembrance, dating from the 1960's, featuring impressive sculpture and patriotic inscriptions honoring those who died for Irish nationalism.

St. Michan's Church is a very old, much restored church just northwest of the Four Courts Building. Visitors are treated to an eerie tour of the crypt containing curiously mummified bodies.

Dublin's Pubs

Dublin is justly famous as the world capital of the drinking man and woman. Dublin's pub life is legendary and still thriving, despite exorbitant cost for drink brought on by taxation. On Fridays and Saturdays many famous pubs are so crowded that everybody is congealed into one mass of convivial, conversing humanity. Getting a drink or using the toilet can become a lengthy struggle involving gentle pushing and shoving against a dense mass. Noise and smoke levels become almost intolerable at such times, but somehow wonderful talk gushes forth in all directions.

Pubs are everywhere in Dublin, catering to different clienteles ranging from workers to intellectuals, and they stand forth resplendent in differing decors, from seemingly untouched Victorian or Edwardian charm to garish ultra modern. The Irish Tourist Board provides a list of famous pubs selected by the Guiness brewery. A few deserve mention to illustrate the variety available: O'Donahue's, near St. Stephen's Green, is famous for music by amateurs and it draws hordes of young people. Toner's, in Baggot Street, is noted for its literary associations, its old furnishings and its customers from the world of writers, artists, poets and students. The Brazen Head is the oldest pub in Dublin, located close to the south bank of the Liffey, upriver, on Lower Bridge Street in what is a rundown area undergoing urban renewal. It dates from 1666 and has a unique atmosphere derived from its setting and historical connections.

Everyone visiting Dublin, drinkers and non-drinkers, should treat themselves to a "pub crawl," a nocturnal exploration of one pub after another. Striking characters and conversations are guaranteed to turn up all along the way.

THE GREEN ENVIRONS OF DUBLIN

No matter how historic and exciting a place it is, the noise, traffic, congestion, fume-filled air and fast pace of Dublin can wear down the visitor after a while. Despair not! The green, lovely land depicted in the travel brochures is within easy reach. In fact, it is only minutes away on the Dublin Area Rapid Transit, DART for short. This remarkably fast, efficient and clean train system goes out of the city to the north and to the south, skirting Dublin Bay. It was built at considerable cost, and it still is far from being a profitable operation today. It is a boon to suburbanites who live along the Bay and commute into the city, and it can become a boon for visitors who want to get out of it and yet maintain a Dublin base. What is more, it is inexpensive.

One of the most pleasant places to go for outdoor activities is Howth, a charming seaport town north of Dublin. It has grand seascapes, good hiking trails, an old abbey, a castle and the site where a vessel bringing guns to the revolutionaries of 1916 was unloaded. All of this is on Howth Head, an impressive peninsula that juts into the Atlantic. Many wild, uncrowded stretches of trail trace the outer rim of the peninsula, affording wonderful views of the sea as well as a chance to see some rough and beautiful vegetation up close. Just ask for directions out to the Bailey Lighthouse to get started. While trudging along, observing the distant islands, the splashing waves below, and the colorful, swiftly darting sailboats, Dublin seems so very far away.

The DART system also leads to an interesting castle in an impressive, spacious park setting. Malahide Castle, north of Dublin, can be reached by bus from the city or, better, by a combination of a trip on the DART system and a short connecting bus ride. Ask at the Tourist Board for current bus designations and schedules. Although the interior has been stripped and refurnished, the castle strongly conveys the atmosphere of the 17th and 18th centuries, thanks in part to the dark wood paneling and abundant portraits. Dramatic events associated with the castle are presented by well prepared pre recorded tapes in every major room which can be activated by a push button.

The DART system can also bring the visitor to a stately home built by the Anglo-Irish aristocracy. Kilruddery House is in Bray, a stop at the southern end of the DART system. Bray is an old seaside resort town that is just slightly seedy today. Movie producers could use Bray as a set for the seaside in the 1930s and 1940s, a time before the departure of affluent bathers to sunny Spain. Good hikes can be taken in Bray, either along the boardwalk, called the Esplanade, or up to Bray Head, a hill overlooking the bay that is covered with thick vegetation.

Kilruddery House is some distance from the Esplanade, and some local residents might not know where it is. Be patient in asking directions. A local bus from the Esplanade will cut down the time it takes to get there, but it is within walking distance for vigorous pedestrians. Kilruddery House's vast grounds, gardens, and spacious, ornate interior will all convey the economic and social power of the Protestant Ascendancy in the early 19th century. So do the furnishings, statuary, and treasures of this important aristocratic family from Bray. Other great houses of the 18th and 19th century Protestant Ascendancy are scattered over the country. None of them are as easily accessible by public transportation as Kilruddery House.

On the way back to Dublin from Bray is one of the most famous sites in the history of literature, the James Joyce martello tower. It is the same place featured in the opening of his masterpiece, *Ulysses,* and it is a place where this giant of 20th century literature lived. Martello towers were erected along the coasts of Ireland to thwart the feared invasion of the French under Napoleon Bonaparte. This particular round, squat tower is now a museum dedicated to Joyce. The memorabilia, letters, papers, books and photographs on display are

Places Featured in the Text

interesting even to those who have not previously developed an interest in Joyce. The museum is also of
manageable size, meaning that it can be taken in nicely
on an afternoon visit. It does not daunt or overwhelm
the visitor by being excessively massive.

Surrounding the Joyce tower are lovely seascapes.
There are a few coves with swimming beaches nearby,
including the famous Forty Foot, where hardy swim-
mers plunge into the cold Atlantic all the year round.

To get into the James Joyce Tower and Museum,
take the DART south, just past the ferry port of Dun
Laoghaire (pronounced Dunleary) and get out at the
Sandycove station. Avoid confusing Sandycove with
Sandymount, which is closer to Dublin and also along
the bay. Head east from the Sandycove station to the
ocean shore and then south for a short time toward the
tower which should then be in clear view.

SORTING OUT SCENERY

The Irish Tourist Board provides helpful road
maps that show the routes through the more scenic
parts of Ireland as colored lines, so it is easy to note the
parts of the island celebrated for natural beauty. Bus
Eireann specializes in delighting visitors with the glories
of the landscape and provides day trips directly to the
most spectacular places.

How glorious is it? An American's response can be
quite subjective, sometimes depending on where he or
she lives. If from Chicago, New York or Des Moines,
Ireland's mountains, valleys and seascapes are more
likely to be declared magnificent. Visitors from states

well endowed with spectacular scenery, such as Colorado, Utah, California or Arizona, are not as likely to be impressed by Ireland's scenery. North America still has vast stretches of unexploited natural beauty which, if found in Ireland, would surely be furnished with romantic names, ancient legends and parking lots for tour buses.

Many visitors may have to guard against being let down at famous scenic sights. Over time such places have received considerable hype from diverse sources. Photographs in travel literature display only the very best views on lovely days. Moreover, the memories of Irish immigrants in America tend to be selective and romantic. After all, nearly everyone has heard the song about Ireland that begins: "A little bit of heaven fell from out the sky one day. . . ."

It can be argued that what makes Ireland's scenery truly special, memorable and unique are the reminders of centuries of effort expended in building civilization, reminders that still stud the landscape—castles, cathedrals, monastic settlements and historic towns, all of which have no counterparts in the United States.

Ireland's natural beauty is greatest around the rim of the island and not in the flat center, which is relatively dull. Ireland's mountains are along the rim where they meet the sea and sky, often in a gorgeous interplay. The west of Ireland has most of the famous scenic areas. The west is wetter, economically weaker, and more sparsely populated. In the west the more scenic areas often coincide with the *Ghaeltacht,* or places where the old Irish language is still spoken as the first language in the home. The accompanying map indicates distinct places noted for scenic highlights. Brief descriptions of each are in order to help the visitor who has a limited amount of time available and who must choose from among several Bus Eireann tours or who must plan an itinerary for a trip in a rented car. The more scenic areas have less populated roads, but they are likely to be narrow and curvaceous and require considerable time to traverse. Ambitious plans to drive through two or three scenic regions on one trip have been known to shrink to encompass only one region.

Donegal

Starting in the northwest and moving counterclockwise, County Donegal needs to be cited because its green hills and mountains have a unique, fresh, bright beauty that is particularly gentle. Sometimes visitors proceed up to the town bearing the same name as the county and proceed no further. They should, because the best Donegal scenery is to be found many miles to the northwest of the town, much of it along the irregular coastline. Western Donegal is still Irish speaking to some extent.

Connemara

The Connemara is a rocky, splendid region all the way across on the opposite side of the island from Dublin. It extends north and west from the city of Galway in the western part of county Galway. Clifden, picturesque and on the Atlantic, is the most important town in the Connemara and is close to Connemara National Park. Many expanses of bare grey mountainside make the region reminiscent of parts of the Rocky Mountains. But the Rockies do not have the sandy beaches, dramatic seascapes and numerous loughs (pronounced the same as the Scottish "loch" and sharing the same meaning, a large lake). There are also landscape patterns of small fields enclosed by stone walls. Donkeys are likely to stray into the roads. Beautiful and quaint as so much of the Connemara might be, it is obvious that it is not an easy place to wrest a living from nature, which explains why so many sons and daughters of County Galway have left as emigrants.

The Burren

The Burren is south of Galway in County Clare. It is another unique region, consisting of flat tableland of such stark barrenness that it has been described as a lunar landscape. One of Oliver Cromwell's generals complained that the Burren did not have enough earth to bury a man, not enough timber to hang him nor enough water to drown him in. Underground rivers and caves and exotic vegetation, which includes alpine flora, are found in this barren region.

Lisdoonvarna is a holiday resort town in the region celebrated for its spas and matchmaking for rural Irish vacationers. The picturesque small fishing village of Doolin is a short distance from Lisdoonvarna, and from there boats can be taken to Inisheer, one of the Aran Islands. Further down the coast are the truly spectacular, monumental Cliffs of Moher. On some days fog obscures their vistas.

The Aran Islands

The deep indentation of Galway Bay is between the Connemara and the Burren, and in this bay, just west of the Burren, lie the famous, romantic Aran Islands. Thatched cottages, monastic remains and small fields surrounded by stone walls add to their charm. The largest island, Inishmore, has what has been called the most impressive Iron Age structure in the world, the primitively massive fort of Dun Aengus. Its size is tremendous, featuring semi-circular stone walls, and its western edge is a sheer cliff overlooking a 200 ft. drop to the sea, a site where observers need to be very cautious and careful as they scramble about.

Unfortunately the proud, picturesque, Irish speaking inhabitants of the islands have been commercialized to an extent by tourism. For example, the pony cart rides on Inishmore are exorbitant, and alternative mini-buses cost almost the same. Tourists who are out for a day to see Dun Aengus must hire such transportation in order to return in time to the slow boat for Galway. It may be better to spend a night on Inishmore and hike or rent a bicycle. The question that needs to be considered by visitors with very limited time is whether or not they should invest so much of it seeing these islands.

Kerry

County Kerry, containing some of the most celebrated scenery in all of Ireland, is far to the south, below and west of Limerick. The Dingle peninsula jutting west of the town of Tralee is the special favorite spot of many visitors to Ireland. It is noted for Irish speaking areas surrounded by superb seascapes. The remote Gallarus Oratory is a striking example of 8th century stone-masonry. It is built in the shape of an upturned boat, and has walls over three feet thick that were carefully constructed without the use of mortar. There are other ancient structures elsewhere on the peninsula.

The Iveragh peninsula is just south of the Dingle peninsula, and it contains the famous "Ring of Kerry," a 100 mile circular drive past some of the best shoreline of the island. It is a long 100 miles because of the twists, turns and traffic. Perhaps following just part of the route will suffice for most visitors.

At the eastern end of the Ring of Kerry is what has been called the worst tourist trap in all of Ireland, Killarney. Despite the lovely lakes surrounding it, the town is somewhat unexceptional, but it concentrates zealously on the tourist business. Pony carts abound in order to ferry visitors to the lakes. Since traffic jams are likely in Killarney, it may be wise to plan a route through Kerry that detours around this town.

West Cork

County Cork is southeast of County Kerry. Like Kerry, Cork is large and contains exceptional scenery. Kerry's coast is western, and Cork's southern, and of the two coasts, the southern is regarded as less developed commercially. The most appealing part of the south coast is west of the large city of Cork. The bays and inlets of west Cork seem to have a warmer, moister atmosphere than anywhere in Ireland. The coast around Skibbereen, dotted with hills and brightly painted villages, is simply charming. Buildings in many

Irish towns are painted in bright colors, but the west Cork towns seem to have a higher concentration of bright hues.

Wicklow

County Wicklow, just south of Dublin, is a mountainous area close to the sea. Wicklow's mountains are higher than anywhere else in Ireland, although those familiar with the Rocky Mountains or certain scenic portions of the Appalachians may be inclined to make unfavorable comparisons about size, ruggedness and remoteness, but the places tucked away in the Wicklow Mountains, including moorlands, the Powerscourt Waterfall and some old habitations make the area incomparable. There is also a small but impressive, German maintained and somewhat disturbing cemetery for Nazi flyers who crashed in neutral Ireland during World War Two. Glendalough, a gem of an early monastic settlement, is the featured highlight of the Bus Eireann tour of this region. The "Wicklow Way" is a long hiking trail through the region. The Tourist Board has detailed information about it.

THINKING IN CATEGORIES: HISTORIC TOWNS

Ordinary guide books overwhelm readers by describing hundreds of places to see. The limited time most visitors have at their disposal demands that a few towns be singled out as top priority places to visit, places that are guaranteed not to be disappointing. Of course, other towns could be as rewarding to individuals, but many towns do not have as much to offer as those specially selected for this section. The three towns featured below are historic and strategically located, places where time can be spent effectively. In addition, a brief list of other towns well worth visiting is included.

Kilkenny

Kilkenny, 73 miles southwest of Dublin and in the county of the same name, is a unique, historic town. It is compact, containing several good sights within easy walking distance. It has winding streets that rise and fall and curve, giving Kilkenny more of the atmosphere of a Medieval European town. It is also a busy, lively modern place, whose inhabitants are friendly and kind towards visitors. The historical significance of the town is apparent. It started as a small, walled, fortified Norman trading town, and grew in importance in the Middle Ages to the extent that several Parliaments were held within its walls.

Among Kilkenny's many historic buildings, the Rothe House, Kilkenny Castle and St. Canice's Cathedral are outstanding. The Tourist Information Office is centrally located at the ancient Shee Alms House, and maps can be acquired showing the location of these and many other historic buildings worth seeing.

The Rothe House is exceptional because so few examples of Elizabethan architecture have survived in Ireland. It has been carefully restored in recent years, and detailed orientation is provided by a video presentation. The Rothe House has an impressive courtyard and an interesting museum.

St. Canice's Cathedral is one of the largest and most famous church buildings in Ireland. It was begun in the 13th century, ravaged by Cromwell's troops and substantially restored according to the imaginations of busy 19th-century Victorians. Important aspects, such as the squat tower, escaped their attention. It has some very impressive tombs, dating from the late 13th century onwards. Just outside is an old round tower, a delight for the energetic and healthy, because for a small fee it can be climbed. It offers a grand view of Kilkenny and the undulating landscape surrounding the town.

Kilkenny Castle is attractively situated above the Nore river. It is one of those castles which has been occupied up until recently. Therefore parts of it have been demolished and additions have been made over the centuries. Among the additions is a pseudo-Medieval banquet hall which could serve as a stage background for a Wagnerian opera. Even so, the spaciousness and character of the other rooms, enhanced by dark wood paneling, appropriate portraits, and accurate furnishings, all contribute to the rich atmosphere. What is more, the staff is extraordinarily helpful and gracious.

One of Kilkenny's unique attributes is the existence of slips, which are narrow covered passageways leading from one street to another. Look for them between High Street and St. Kieran Street. Kyteler's Inn is a large building on St. Kieran Street, said to be the oldest structure still standing in the town. It continues to function as an inn, but the redone interior does not match the impressive, historic exterior. Tall tales about witchcraft and ghosts are associated with it.

Galway

Galway is in a beautiful setting on the west coast, along the edge of a great bay with the same name. It has long been a tourist attraction for Irish people themselves, so that strip development of quaint and somewhat tawdry seaside hotels, shops and amusements extends westwards from Galway through the town of Salthill. It would be an understatement to say that the waters of the Atlantic along this coast are brisk and bracing, those English euphemisms for cold. Swimming here can become a heroic, numbing experience.

It is quite possible to visit Galway on a long day trip from Dublin because trains go directly across the island from one city to the other. Even so, Galway's strategic location makes it a good base of operations for the west. Several highly scenic Bus Eireann day trips depart from Galway, including one to the Connemara region and another to the Cliffs of Moher and the Burren region.

Galway has a nice, bustling atmosphere, as well as a charming ambience aided by the fresh sea breezes. Many of its crowded streets are narrow and winding and contain interesting shops and good seafood restaurants. Nearly all of Galway's buildings date from the last 250 years, but a few older treasures still grace the city. Lynch's Castle is a large 16th-century building on a busy shopping street. It was not really a castle but rather an opulent home of an aristocratic family. It is now a bank. St. Nicholas' Church dates from the 14th century and still has many original Medieval features. An old town gate remains, called the Spanish Arch, and it is now connected to the interesting Galway City Museum.

Galway looks to the sea and still has lively activity in its harbor. In previous centuries Galway had important trade with France and Spain, so that the influence of these Latin countries has been more pronounced in Galway than elsewhere in Ireland. It is also in the middle of a large part of the remaining *Ghaeltacht,* or Irish speaking area, and Irish can be heard more readily in Galway than in other large Irish cities.

Expect Galway to be a busy place in summer and winter. It is at once a university town, a market town for a large part of the hinterland and a place that has strong attraction for tourists of all nationalities.

Limerick

Limerick appears to be drabber and poorer than prosperous Galway, but it has its charms. Irish people grumble at what a traffic bottleneck Limerick presents, but this does denote its strategic location as an intersection for several main roads. Shannon Airport is close, and Bunratty Folk Park and Castle are on the road from Shannon to Limerick. The Craggaunowen Project for early Irish history is not far to the north and the notable Lough Gur prehistoric site is just over twelve miles south of the city.

One of the most impressive castles in Ireland is right in the middle of the city, sternly guarding the river Shannon. Set above roiling water, King John's Castle is an imposing sight, either from a distance or from the walls and towers, which are open to the public. The 12th-century castle was taken and retaken in the wars of the 17th century, but it actually suffered more damage in the 18th century from barracks building and in the 20th century from erecting public housing nearby. Ironically, these structures have weathered time less successfully than the medieval castle.

St. Mary's Cathedral is another of Limerick's highlights. Despite the name and ancient appearance, it belongs to the Church of Ireland, a Protestant denomination. During the tourist season, it hosts a sound and light show that is well worth seeing. Extremely pleasant people assist at the cathedral.

Limerick has many other attractions, including an 18th century square, a museum, an art gallery and portions of the old town wall. Brightly painted doors on Georgian buildings in some sections are reminiscent of Dublin. Three miles up the Shannon from Limerick, near Plassey, is the National Institute for Higher Education, which houses part of the excellent Hunt Collection of art from the earliest times to the 18th century.

Limerick is a busy, workaday place, thronged with shoppers drawn from a wide region. Some parts of the city are rundown and other parts are newly constructed. One of Limerick's pressing needs, something which can be said of many Irish cities, is a system of traffic bypasses to help unclog the city center.

Other Towns

Several other major towns in Ireland well worth visiting deserve special mention. Each is a significant center in its region, and each is very interesting in its own way.

Cork is the second largest city in Ireland, con-

taining over 130,000 people, which still puts it far behind Dublin in population. Nonetheless, it is an
important port, industrial and educational center. Cork
suffered violent destruction from wars as far back as the
12th century and as recent as 1920, so the city lacks old
sections, although some colorful 18th and 19th century
streets can be seen. Cork people are proud of their city
and they themselves have been called the "Prussians of
Ireland" because of their bustle and industry. Dubliners
tend to be wary of people from Cork because they are
believed to be too crafty. Much good natured banter
passes between the two cities.

Sligo is the largest city in the northwest. It can be
reached easily by a direct train from Dublin which ter-
minates in Sligo. Since the Nobel Prize–winning poet
William Butler Yeats lived in Sligo for some time and
incorporated the surrounding area in his works, he is
linked to Sligo's tourist operations. His brother, Jack B.
Yeats, was a noted artist who celebrated the Sligo region
in his paintings. Sligo is a pleasant, busy city that has
several old buildings of note, a County Museum and an
art gallery.

Waterford is a seaport town along the river Suir
famous for its crystal manufacturing which can be observed at the Waterford Glass Factory. Most of the significant industrial sights are on streets leading from the
quay, or dockside. A great hulking round tower,
Reginald's Tower, is on the quay, and well worth a visit.

Wexford, a short distance north of Waterford, is
another very old seaport town along the southeastern
corner of Ireland. It also has a quay and the streets
leading off of it have the town's oldest buildings. Wexford has a maritime museum housed in an old lightship.

THINKING IN CATEGORIES: EARLY MONASTIC SETTLEMENTS

Ireland is endowed with three outstanding early church settlements: Clonmacnoise, Monasterboice, and Glendalough. Each has its own uniqueness and different setting, but overall the similarities outweigh the differences. Each settlement features high crosses, an impressive round tower, and ancient church buildings and graves. Visitors with a limited amount of time available would be wise to select just one of them.

A visit to Ireland should definitely include one of these settlements, because each imparts a strong feeling for an important period of Irish history. The early church in Ireland was centered on these monastic settlements because Celtic Ireland did not develop town life the way other European areas did in the early Middle Ages. Therefore these settlements are uniquely Irish. They are photographed time and again for Irish tourist literature for this very good reason.

All three places can be reached by Bus Eireann tours. Monasterboice is the closest to Dublin and the easiest to reach, since it is only six miles northwest of Drogheda. Glendalough is south of Dublin, deep in the beautiful Wicklow Mountains. Clonmacnoise is out in the middle of Ireland on the banks of the Shannon. The Cross of the Scriptures is singled out as a special treasure of Clonmacnoise; Muireadach's Cross is the pride of Monasterboice; and Glendalough has its very special lakeside setting in the mountains. Glendalough also has a small museum and offers an audio-visual presentation.

THINKING IN CATEGORIES:
CATHEDRALS

Considering its small population, Ireland is richly endowed with cathedrals, but several generalizations about them need to be kept in mind. First of all, Ireland's cathedrals are generally smaller and less grand than Continental or British cathedrals. The medieval population of Ireland simply did not have the urban numbers nor the resources to build and use gigantic structures. In medieval France, Germany, Spain, Italy and England, great cities built and maintained great cathedrals.

Second, a minority of Protestants has controlled the ancient cathedrals from the 16th century to the present day. Their denomination is called the Church *of* Ireland and is not to be confused with the Roman Catholic designation for themselves as the Church *in* Ireland. Catholics hope to reclaim these buildings in the future, as the Protestant minority continues to dwindle into an insignificant number and as ecumenicism, or worldwide religious cooperation, continues as a dominant theme in modern Christianity. Therefore the Catholic seats of bishops have often been designated pro-cathedrals, or temporary cathedrals. Most of these buildings are usually quite new by European standards, dating back only to the 19th century.

Third, the long period of Protestant control has altered the old cathedrals considerably from their medieval appearance. In some cases this is from violent destruction on the part of Cromwell and his forces, and in others from a Protestant streamlining or stripping of the rich imagery and colorful interiors for which medieval Catholicism was noted. Moreover, these Church of Ireland cathedrals have been utilized to celebrate the lives, deaths, and accomplishments of what was the "establishment" in Ireland, the "Protestant Ascendancy." In many cathedrals, this takes the form of British regimental monuments and flags, tablets commemorating various British victories and defeats in the Empire's wars, and numerous patriotic inscriptions. The visitor who asks "What is this doing in Ireland?" needs to be referred to the history section of this volume. Clearly, these cathedrals offer evidence that for a long time Ireland was, at least in the minds of its establishment, an integral part of Britain.

Last, the energetic Victorians of the 19th century burdened many of these buildings with their "improvements." In religion, many of them tended to be romantic and therefore treasured the medieval heritage of the church, even though the Anglo-Irish Victorians were Protestants, generally, and the medieval church existed before Protestantism appeared. Be that as it may, busy Victorians sought to "improve" medieval churches with their 19th-century conceptions of what old churches of the Middle Ages should look like. When commissioned to build new churches, they often erected massive "Victorian Gothic" buildings which sometimes fool tourists into thinking that they date from over 400 years ago.

All the major cities of Ireland have rival Catholic and Protestant cathedrals. Catholic cathedrals tend to be large, grey and built in the 19th century. The Protestant cathedrals tend to be the most historic buildings. Among the many to choose from, St. Patrick's and Christ Church in Dublin, St. Mary's in Limerick and St.

Nicholas' in Galway and St. Canice's in Kilkenny are noteworthy. All five are not Roman Catholic, but Catholics are inclined to add the word "yet" to this statement.

ONE OF A KIND PLACES

Several special places in Ireland defy categorization. Each is worth a visit.

Cashel

The great Rock of Cashel, crowned with ruined buildings, juts up from the land surface of County Tipperary dramatically. Pictures of the Rock of Cashel are ubiquitous in tourist literature, and justifiably, because this is one of the most impressive historic sites in all of Ireland.

For a long time Cashel was the seat of Christian kings. In the early 12th century it was donated to the church. Now the ruins of a 13th century cathedral dominate the crest. One older part, Cormac's Chapel, built between 1127 and 1134, is a gem of architectural history because it is in the early medieval, or Romanesque, style. English and Continental influences are pronounced. There is also a very well preserved round tower.

Cashel is an exciting place for several reasons. The views, both of the rock itself and of the green countryside seen from it, are spectacular. Cashel is also associated with dramatic figures and events in Irish history. St. Patrick was supposed to have preached there, and Brian Boru, a legendary Celtic hero king, is said to have been crowned there. Cashel is also exciting because so

much archaeological and artistic restoration work is
going on.

Bunratty Folk Park

Bunratty Folk Park, an open air museum between
Limerick and Shannon, is a carefully constructed, historically accurate collection of over two dozen 19th century buildings brought here from various places in
western Ireland, all well appointed and well situated.
The Folk Park offers something of a contrast with
Bunratty Castle which adjoins it, because history tends
to be romanticized during the castle's much advertised
medieval banquets.

Visitors can stroll into the buildings of the Folk Park
and feel that they have gone a hundred years into the
past. Details are given careful attention, and turf fires in
some buildings add to the atmosphere. The variety of
old buildings includes a minor gentleman's house, the
humble dwelling of a common laborer, a mountain
farmhouse, an artisan's house, an old rural house designed for humans who cohabit with their cows, and a
fisherman's house. Several of the buildings are clustered
in a village, where visitors can walk into shops, some of
which sell items, a post office and a pub. Walking about
in this large folk park is a treat for people of all ages and
it is a delight for those concerned about historical accuracy.

Craggaunowen

The Craggaunowen Project is not far from Shannon Airport, just north of Limerick, close to the village

of Quinn. Sometimes it is not well marked on maps. Craggaunowen Castle is part of the project and contains a small but interesting collection of medieval art. The castle grounds contain several reconstructions from the prehistoric period. A fortified lake dwelling, called a crannog, and a ring fort containing four buildings with underground rooms, called sutterains, are highlights of the exhibit.

Irish Americans are likely to be very interested in the *Brendan,* a reconstruction of a leather hide-covered boat in which a group of adventurers sailed the Atlantic in 1976 and 1977, events singled out for attention by the National Geographic Society. The point of the exercise was to demonstrate whether or not St. Brendan the Navigator could have discovered America in the 6th century.

A visit to the Craggaunowen Project is particularly enjoyable for younger visitors because energy has to be expended to hike about and scramble into buildings and underground rooms. The experience is enhanced when the guides are eager, energetic, knowledgeable and patient. Sad to say, this is not always the case.

THINKING IN CATEGORIES:
CASTLES

All of Ireland is sprinkled with castles. They can pop up on the horizon any time along Irish roads. They vary considerably: Some are in ruins and some are restored; most are small but a few are gigantic.

Many of the buildings called castles were really fortified tower houses, built just after the end of the

Middle Ages, when castle building elsewhere in Europe
had come to an end because of the power of kings and
their cannons. Ireland lagged behind. Powerful Anglo-
Irish and Gaelic lords still found comfort behind thick
stone walls which acted as insulation against the tumults
of Irish politics.

The truly great castles in Ireland are the earlier
ones, put up by those most energetic builders and
rulers, the Normans, around the 13th century. They
resemble the great castles of England built by the same
ruling elite. Even in this century of ours which builds so
massively, the size of the great Norman castles remains
very impressive.

King John's Castle in Limerick is one of the best to
see in Ireland. (See the section on Limerick for details.)
So is Cahir Castle, where romantic films about the
medieval period have been shot. It is in a small town of
the same name just south of the Rock of Cashel. The
castle was built from the 12th to the 15th centuries. Parts
have been restored recently, and a museum has been
added. Visitors can walk around the grounds, along the
walls, and up the towers. Cahir gives a good impression
of how a medieval castle looked centuries ago, a great
grim hulk guarding a strategic waterway.

Some people prefer castle ruins to restored castles.
For them, the ruins of the gigantic castle in the town of
Trim can be recommended. It was the largest Anglo-
Norman castle in all of Ireland, covering a grand total of
three acres. Visitors can climb around parts of Trim
Castle today, but there are warning signs to discourage
exploration of some parts. Trim is just northwest of
Dublin, along the Boyne River, a pleasant town that can
be reached easily from Dublin, either by car or on a day

trip via the ordinary public bus. Trim has several historical landmarks of interest, including the Yellow Steeple
across from the castle.

TRAVEL IN NORTHERN IRELAND

Many Americans will not want to travel in Northern
Ireland because of the reports of violence that have been
featured in the media for decades. Others will not want
to go because they have no regard for the civil authority
in Northern Ireland and do not want to go where the
British flag flies over Irish soil. Others will want to go
out of a spirit of adventure or a desire to observe a
troubled situation for themselves. While this book is for
American visitors of the Republic, the following general
observations are included for those who may con-
template a brief sojourn in the north.

Those who do go will be surprised by the peace-
fulness that they will almost invariably encounter.
American cities are far more violent in terms of homicides, rapes, and muggings than any city in the north.
When a bombing or a shooting does take place, it is
usually in a strife torn area, and the camera crews are
among the first to arrive so that the blood or wreckage
can be seen worldwide. Meanwhile, for the rest of
Northern Ireland, life goes on as usual, unreported in
the media.

The apparatus in place to prevent violence may
daunt some American visitors and excite others. Border
checks are thorough; the army may stop and question
visitors, particularly if they are young; police barracks

are heavily sandbagged and barricaded; some areas can have no parked cars in them; in other areas parked cars must have a person sitting in them or they will be blown up by the authorities; shoppers must go through metal detectors or have their packages inspected; military helicopters hover overhead; armored army vehicles with soldiers pointing guns menacingly out of them whiz about. All this is part of the costly and thorough security imposed by the British army and the Northern Ireland police.

It is difficult to avoid the uneasy feeling that out there in the grim neighborhoods and remote rural areas there are forces ready and willing to attack if they have the opportunity, not only the Irish Republican Army and the factions derived from it, but also the armed Ulster Protestant vigilante groups. More tangible are the clear indications of deep hostility in opposing neighborhoods: colorful graffiti, murals and street decorations evoke episodes and events in Irish history and reveal deep loyalty to the Republic on the one side and to Britain or to the Protestant cause on the other.

Many people regard these indications of smoldering civil war as too unpleasant for a vacation and avoid Northern Ireland altogether. Yet outside of Belfast and Londonderry, or simply Derry as Catholics strongly prefer to call the city, Northern Ireland can be quite beautiful and peaceful. Among the exceptional sights are the Giant's Causeway, a surprising natural rock formation along the northern coast; Dunluce Castle, which consists of ruins in a wild seascape; and in Belfast, the Ulster Museum which depicts the achievements of Ulster people through the centuries.

It is good advice for Americans to observe the tragic political situation without much comment. Above all, do not volunteer explanations or opinions freely and do not become a champion of one side or another. By being quiet observers, Americans will discover that Northerners, be they Protestant or Catholic, are warm, friendly, proud of their region and eager to point out its beauties.

CHAPTER TWO

Old Romantic Images Versus Contemporary Irish Realities

WHAT THE IRISH MAY THINK OF AMERICANS

What do Irish people really think of Americans? Is it hard to tell, despite all of the millions of exchanges that take place as Americans arrive every year by the planeload?

There are some good reasons why Irish people are

likely to be guarded about how they really feel about Americans. First of all, Ireland depends on a flow of dollar laden tourists that must continue. Since tourism is a vital industry, Americans must be kept happy in Ireland so that they will come back again and urge their friends to visit Ireland. Second, most Irish people have a basic politeness and reserve that usually brasher Americans are not tuned into, and the same can be said about the subtlety of furtive wit and gentle sarcasm that Irish people practice so very skillfully. Third, it should never be forgotten that rich and powerful English people came to Ireland for centuries, not only as tourists but also as landlords and rulers. The wily Irish learned how to please and charm them while hiding their true and more bitter feelings. Sometimes Americans who are loud, rich and arrogant get the same treatment.

One guess about Irish feelings towards Americans is that it is some sort of mixture of admiration and contempt, with one or the other feeling predominating, depending upon the circumstances or the individual. Another guess, actually a cliché, is "derisive affection." Just what do the Irish seem to be contemptuous and derisive about, specifically?

Americans tend to be loud. Ireland itself is not a quiet country, compared to the states of northern Europe anyway, but in Ireland and everywhere else in the region, Americans stand out because of their volume. To be sure, there are many quiet American visitors who may never be noticed, but those who yell, shout and gesticulate to one another make up for them easily. Naturally, tourists are likely to have high spirits because they are on vacation, but a case can be made that too many Americans let themselves go too far. Shouting to one another over considerable distances in crowded, public places is an American hallmark.

Not only voices are loud. So is the clothing that many tourists wear, which is also sometimes ill-fitting and ill-cut. Naturally, the very Americans who wear staid business suits or dresses at work go on vacations in an array of bright colors, sporty shorts and skirts and silly hats. Yet what might look normal at Disneyland might look out of place in an Irish cathedral, graveyard or museum. Americans can usually be spotted in such places wearing startlingly brightly colored golfing shirts or windbreakers or shorts.

Flaunting wealth the way some Americans do in Ireland is also not appreciated. Some conspicuous spenders throw their money around, while other Americans are what Irish people call "mean" because they are so stingy. Irish people wonder why tourists who boast of how well off they are in the American land of milk and honey leave such meager tips and are so worried and distrusting about small expenses.

Many Americans obsessed with size point out repetitiously how small everything Irish is, including the country. Such invidious comparisons of size are made about all sorts of things, including cars, refrigerators, houses, kitchens, and television sets. Their message that large is better than small comes through unmistakably.

Another American characteristic that Irish people find annoying is the penchant to tell people how to do things better than their accustomed ways. Frequently, American methods are touted as infinitely superior on the grounds of speed or efficiency. "We do things better in our country" is something the Irish have heard for hundreds of years from the English, so they hardly relish hearing the same from Americans. Sadly, in some situations the Irish are inwardly convinced that their methods are indeed backward and inferior. When visitors chide, it merely rubs it in.

Sometimes Irish people are mildly annoyed or somewhat amused at the tendency of Americans to take up clichés and fads. "Have a nice day" might sound rather silly to people not used to the expression. "I am a very caring person" sounds like absurd self-advertisement to Irish ears. The Irish person who does not fit this description is exceptional!

Food resources are not as abundant in Ireland today as in America, particularly for countless ordinary and poor families who must be very careful and improvise in order to make their food budget cover needs. Also, Ireland is a country that knew mass starvation in the last century. For these reasons, it is disturbing to see American tourists gorging themselves and leaving food on their plates to go to waste. It is wise for Americans in Ireland to follow the rule of the depression era and leave empty plates. When breakfast is included with the price of a room, the usual case in Ireland, it is gauche to gorge in order to cut down on the anticipated costs of lunch. Such behavior would definitely be interpreted by the hosts as an example of American "meanness."

Irish people are convinced that Americans have too much of everything. Obese and overweight tourists confirm the Irish view that Americans consume too much food. The Irish population seems to have a much smaller proportion of overweight individuals. Americans are also accused of consuming too much in material goods of all kinds, of living with unnecessary extravagance and of wasting resources. What Irish people do not see are the poor and homeless in American society. Of course, well educated Irish people are aware of these inequities, but the stereotype of an American which is projected to ordinary Irish people by many tourists is that of an overweight, materialistic, well-to-do white person.

The whims and shortcomings of American tourists are well known and fully anticipated in Ireland. Unlike the readers of this book, many Americans who arrive really know little about Ireland. "Here I am so show me a good time," is an ordinary attitude. In any dealings with hotel proprietors or others in the tourist industry, most visiting Americans have the disadvantage of unfamiliarity while their hosts enjoy the advantage of years of experience with tourists from the United States. In some cases, Irish people have relatives or close friends working in the United States or they have been there themselves.

Even with such experience, and beyond a certain low level of interaction, Americans and life in America are terribly confusing to the Irish, as well as to much of the rest of the world. So much of American life is a set of contrasts: riches and poverty; greed and altruism; peaceful domesticity and alarming violence; appalling ignorance and amazing knowledge. The essential point about the United States that so many people in Ireland and in the world fail to grasp is that America is so large and so complex that it can be compared to a continent. Divisions of religion, ethnicity, class, religion, education and politics are profound. It is very hard to explain to Irish people the cross currents, contradictions and opposing interests at work in our huge nation. It is difficult enough to comprehend them ourselves.

Compared to America, Ireland is a very small, very homogeneous country, composed almost entirely of people who have the same cultural background, including religion, and the same historic past. They are bound together by close knit human ties of family. Ireland is not a pluralistic nor diverse society. America, on the other hand, may be the most pluralistic, and most diverse, and most exciting nation known to history.

While the Irish might be used to the predictable quirks of Americans who come over to visit, Irish people can become overwhelmed and confused by the America they read about or see on television, or by diversity in the behavior of Americans in Ireland. For example, when two noted American college football teams played in Ireland recently, resident Americans were expected to attend and support the spectacle. Protests by some that they never watched football games at home so why should they do so now were met with incredulity. Attending was regarded as an American thing to do, just as Ireland's culturally homogeneous citizens would get behind an Irish entertainment or cause.

Many Irish people, particularly younger ones, are displeased with the American role in the Third World, especially in Central America. Irish political activists are likely to champion left wing causes in that part of the world and deride American support for what they perceive as oppressive regimes. They are also annoyed that so many Americans are not very well informed about current events.

Sometimes a loud and earnest zealot will blame nearly all of the woes of the world upon the United States, a viewpoint not all that dissimilar from that of certain leaders in the Persian Gulf region. All sorts of evil schemes and machinations are attributed to the State Department or the C.I.A. and are offered as a simple explanation for what is going wrong in the world. Individuals espousing such a demonology, when fanatical, are exhausting and best avoided. Fortunately they are rare in Ireland.

Besides such individuals, and a larger number of informed Irish persons concerned about Third World issues or economic injustice in America, quite a reservoir of pro-American sentiment still exists in Ireland, and not just because tourists bring in dollars. Current debate about this or that issue aside, the bottom line on Irish-American relations is that America is regarded as the big, open, generous country that has offered a home and a brighter future to millions of Irish people over the centuries. Most of the immigrants prospered and some of them went on to do great things in the United States. That is the real reason why the general welcome for Americans is still warm in Ireland, and why American flags sprout so readily in that country.

AMERICANS WHO SAY "I'M IRISH" AND THE IRISH NATIONALITY ITSELF

It is particularly annoying for Irish people to hear visiting Americans declare: "I'm Irish." This statement often provokes gentle scarcasm: "And where in Ireland were you born?" The fact is that a person born in Boston with the name Erin O'Clancy is clearly regarded as nothing else but American in Ireland. It is curious that millions of Americans claim to be something other than American. Some say they are Italian or Polish or German. Millions of others state that they are just "plain American," which usually denotes descent from Britain, or from a tangled mix of nationalities, or from austere American Colonial ancestors.

Irish Americans actually may have much more tenuous roots across the Atlantic than Americans of many other origins. The reason for this is that most Irish Americans descend from waves of mid- and late-19th-century immigration. Over more than 100 years, Irish Americans generally have achieved prosperity and success in the United States, but not without a long struggle. Prejudice against their Catholicism, which was rampant as late as the 1920's, has all but disappeared. Affluent Irish Americans in the suburbs are hardly different from those "plain American" neighbors who maintain that their ancestors contributed to what must have been an overload on the *Mayflower*. Of course, they celebrate St. Patrick's Day, sometimes complete with green beer, and share some stories of the old country that have been handed down, and tease about Irish charm or Irish temper in some family members. Yet all of these allusions to the old country do not counteract the hard fact that these Americans have come so far from their Irish roots that their Irishness is more of romantic sentiment than reality. The very best way to prove this is to have Irish Americans go to Ireland, where, in the midst of Irish society, they will discover how different and how American they really are. In fact, scores of Irish Americans travel to Ireland or take

Irish studies classes or look up ancestors in Ireland to find and revitalize roots that have become so distant and so tenuous.

When they return to Ireland, some Irish Americans are perceived as out-of-touch sentimentalists who are rapturous over Ireland. At worst, some of them sport a naive Irish nationalism that demands a united Ireland now. Irish people in general do not appreciate a winking, nudging expression of support for the outlawed Irish Republican Army. These Americans have an image of the I.R.A. in their minds harking back to the guerilla struggle against Britain in the period right after World War One, 1919 to 1922, which enabled an independent Irish Free State to come into existence. These Americans do not associate the I.R.A. and its offshoots with the delinquents, thugs, bankrobbers, incompetent bombers, Marxists, nihilists and clients of Libya who presently try to lay claims on the mantle of the nationalist organization of the 1920's. The Dublin government is unhappy that some Irish American groups are too pro-I.R.A. and regrets that some American financial aid flows into the pockets of militant groups.

Irish Americans are extremely numerous. According to the United States census of 1980, 40 million people claim some Irish ancestry. One quarter of this group, 10 million, claim to be entirely of Irish descent on both sides. Considering that five million Irish emigrated to North America at most, their reproductive achievement in the New World has been heroic. It means that for every person on the island of Ireland there are eight relatives or descendants living in the United States.

Origins of the Irish Nationality

Even those Irish Americans claiming to be "all Irish" in ancestry may be surprised at how the Irish genetic inheritance is highly varied. Irish people are usually assumed to be descendants of the Celts, just as English people are assumed to be descendants of Anglo-Saxons. Celts are likely to be but one of a number of contributors to the biological background of contemporary Irish people. Relatively little known pre-Celtic people from central or southern Europe blended with the invading Celts. After that, vigorous Scandinavians raided, looted, settled and merged into the population. The Normans added another strain, and they themselves were a blend of Scandinavians and French, and many of those who came to Ireland had blended with the Welsh as well. From the Middle Ages onward, the English came to Ireland in relatively small numbers, they themselves a blend of Norman and Anglo-Saxon stock. The early English settlers became the "Old English" who largely remained Roman Catholic and interbred with Irish families to the extent that they became almost indistinguishable from the rest of the population. After England became Protestant, English Protestant monarchs initiated new waves of conquest and settlement. Protestant settlers from England blended more slowly, and Scots Presbyterians who came in large numbers to Ulster tended not to blend at all. Even so, most of the so-called Anglo-Irish families have mixed in with the general population to some extent, and many individuals descended from this group became champions of Irish nationalism.

All of this mixing and blending means that the

ordinary Irish person of today may descend from prehistoric central and southern Europeans, Celts, Scandinavians, Normans and English. To recognize this does
not detract from the concept of Irish nationality. All
European nationalities, such as the French, the German,
the English and the Italian, are blends from the ebb and
flow of conquest and mixing over the centuries.

In the 20th century superpatriotic nationalists in
Europe have described the "race" or the "blood" of a
given nationality as the reason for certain attributes,
behaviors, or achievements or lack of them. The use of
the term "race" for a nationality is intellectually absurd.
Biologists may use the term "race" for a species of plant
or animal that may have evolved in isolation, such as a
race of wheat, but human groups have not evolved in
isolation. There have always been contacts and mixing at
the fringes of societies if not at the centers of them.
Therefore, it is best not to use the term "the Irish race,"
but it is fine to speak of the Irish nationality.

LOOKING FOR ANCESTORS

Many Irish Americans who realize that their roots
are dim and distant come to Ireland to revitalize them
by hunting for their ancestors. The project always looks
much easier to accomplish when contemplated in America than when put into action in Ireland. Americans
need to arrive with solid information in order to have
any hope at all of tracing immigrant kin who have fallen
from living memory. Information for a successful search
includes the names of the county and village of origin,

the month and year of arrival in America, and the name of the ship that brought them.

Unsure of such basic facts, the task of finding Irish ancestors can be almost hopeless since records in Ireland are scattered and scanty. There are several reasons for this, one of which is that most of the people who emigrated were in poverty or close to it, especially when millions fled Ireland in desperation during years of famine. Bureaucrats and clerks working in such times of social chaos did not keep accurate records. Also, civil war in the 20th century destroyed many of the records which had survived up until then. Church records vary greatly in quality and completeness from parish to parish and in the earlier times of persecution the Catholic Church was underground and kept relatively few records. Difficulties are compounded by the astounding number of people bearing identical surnames. Irish Americans who are convinced that they have a rare or unusual surname find that in Ireland there may have been hundreds or even thousands of people who bore that same name in a given locality.

Despite all of these difficulties, the Irish make great efforts to give those searching for ancestors what they want. Various commercial firms will trace ancestors, for a good fee, of course. If blind alleys are encountered, the imagination will fill in the gaps. Some great and noble family will be found somewhere bearing the same surname, and on the slim possibility that someone from the Irish American's family might have been in the locale at some time in the past, a great leap of faith is undertaken and the ancestor is pronounced to have been a member of the noble family and, naturally, worthy to bear the appropriate coat-of-arms. Sometimes another fee will produce a replica of the coat-of-arms and a fancy certificate. Such firms omit mentioning that there was an analogy between the Irish who took the names of families for whom they worked and the slaves of the American South who took the names of the master in the big house. Over time, those who were bound to work in the fields or kitchens of a great Irish family were likely to have that family's surname.

If the ancestor is fairly recent, say a grandfather, and the Irish American knows the village or town the grandfather came from, a pilgrimage there may bring forth another kind of subterfuge. Elderly locals in the village pub may rack their memories and, lubricated by a pint or two, they may oblige with colorful stories about the departed grandfather. The Irish American will never quite know just what is being invented on the spot to serve as a sport for the locals or how many times they have told the same stories for other Irish Americans on similar quests.

Ordinary Irish people do not seem to take the Irish Americans' intense search for ancestors very seriously. "Why do you want to know about them?" is an ordinary attitude. After all, the Irish American is a more important person than the ancestors, because he or she has obviously done well enough in the New World to afford trips back to Ireland. The ancestors were poor, obscure people who could not make a go of it in Ireland and had to sail away.

Despite all of the obstacles, some Irish Americans will still regard the quest for ancestry as fun, or as something to give greater structure and purpose to a vacation in Ireland. Once having gathered every detail and scrap of information available in America first, the

best way to continue the formidable task in Ireland is go
to local librarians and clerks and lay the problem before
them. They should be able to either steer the searcher in
the right direction or make the hopelessness of the task
more readily apparent. Either way, they will most likely
be very kind, helpful and interesting Irish people, well
worth meeting.

LOOKING FOR THE ROMANTIC IRELAND OF ANCESTORS' MEMORIES

Romantic sentiments about Ireland keep the tourist
trade brisk, even if the Irish often get annoyed at the
starry-eyed images Americans hold about the country.
In many cases, these images were imparted by the
fondly remembered visions of immigrant grandparents
or great-grandparents, or what was passed down in a
family from even earlier arrivals in the United States.
The selective memories of immigrants often conjure an
old home country of sweet gentleness, leaving out the
harshness of economic privations. This image of Ireland
features thatched cottages in an unspoiled countryside,
saintly old ladies knitting by the fire, wise, charming and
clever locals at the cozy neighborhood pub, and fresh
and innocent children who are kept so by dedicated
priests and nuns. Pigs and chickens are everywhere in
this image, sometimes sharing rural homes with the
homespun people who will eat them. In its most extreme
form, sentimental romanticism draws upon the lore of
fairies and spirits, leprechauns and banshees.

For Americans steeped in such romanticism, the modern realities of Ireland can come as a terrible shock. Ireland has become a society dedicated to acquiring wealth and joining the rest of Europe in post-industrial abundance. It is a society where the amount of throw away waste and the number of crimes grow at an alarming rate, where droves of young people stay away from Mass, and where the energetic flee life in rural areas for the bright lights of Dublin, London or New York. Dublin itself is noisy, dirty and congested, and beset with interconnected problems of drug use, prostitution and AIDS.

Sweeping changes have occurred in Ireland, accelerating swiftly in the 1960s. Along with a surge of material prosperity, marital breakdowns and alcohol abuse have soared. The old style families dominated by strong fathers are being replaced in urban areas with families that negotiate, fathers who help in housework, mothers who work outside the home, and couples who act as partners in everything. Male and female roles are beginning to blur.

Rural Ireland has not escaped the impact of the 20th century. High tech industry sprouts here and there. Development for the sake of tourism has made its mark on every scenic area. Fewer people farm and the drift to the towns and cities is steady. In rural homes electricity has replaced the fireside storyteller with American and British television shows, many of them presenting material that would be rated "R" in American theaters. So-called progress can be noted in the disappearance of prehistoric mounds in the countryside. Rural folk had treated them with superstitious respect, calling them "fairy forts." Most were probably raths, or enclosed prehistoric farmsteads. Today they are being flattened by bulldozers.

Irish people who have returned recently after long stays in America can be upset by changes in their homeland. Some are annoyed at finding some of the least desirable features of late 20th century life, such as blaring portable radios, transplanted to Ireland. Some who come back to the mother country with intentions to retire there have enough of the new Ireland after a few months and return to their adopted land for their sunset years.

GIVE THE TOURISTS WHAT THEY WANT: ROMANTICISM FROM GIFT SHOPS TO MEDIEVAL BANQUETS

The tourist industry has leapt into the gap between Americans' romantic expectations and the harsher realities of contemporary Ireland with gusto. For example, tour buses are sure to go out of their way in order to drive by the few remaining thatched cottages in the region. The drivers will be sure to regale the passengers from a fund of charming tales and clever old Irish sayings all delivered in the thickest brogue that can be summoned. Some older Americans love to "coo" over quaint reminders of romantic Ireland, and people in the tourism industry make it their job to conjure up as many reminders as possible.

"Give the tourists what they want" is the motto and hard currency is the reward. Ubiquitous official souvenir shops sell all kinds of sentimental items inspired by the agrarian Ireland of half a century or more ago. The shops present aspects of Irish culture as if they were contemporary instead of anachronisms. All sorts of bric-a-brac fill the shelves, including little green leprechauns and linens bearing wise old sayings.

Giving the tourists what they want also involves cooking up Irish history into Disney-style concoctions. Medieval banquets are the prime examples of this. Of course, people should go to one Irish medieval banquet and have a good time, but if tickets were awarded as prizes, first prize would be a free ticket and second prize would be free tickets to two medieval banquets. The sweet, stylized, sanitized, mass produced meals and songs lose much of their lustre the second time around.

The real environment of medieval Ireland was far less pleasant. It was a time of hardship, suffering and exploitation for well over nine out of ten Irish people, who had to be subservient and grovel before a violent, quarrelsome aristocracy that enjoyed the thrills of war and demanded obedience. In these bloody, vicious times the aristocracy, which was mostly English or descended from English conquerors, lived far better than the masses, but even they had to endure filth and disease. Their banqueting halls were covered with vile straw that housed vermin and evil stenches. No real medieval banquet was complete without flea-bitten dogs and flea-bitten aristocrats.

Bright eyed and often inebriated American tourists have replaced the old barons and their guests today. Many of them react strongly to the potent brew of mead, a fermented honey drink, which is served at the entrance. The banquet hall is clean, free of straw and animals, and servants appear to be pretty, young and happy, and they wear neat, colorful costumes and show no signs of medieval bondage. Entertainment is the keynote. Servants double as singers, accompanied by harps and other traditional instruments. All is very light, charming and sweet, too sweet for some.

Audience participation is induced by such ploys as selecting a king and queen as well as by threatening one hapless tourist with time in the dungeon on account of trumped-up indiscretions towards a local damsel. All of this is carried out with the heavy, fulsome quaintness of stage pseudo-medievalism. Most tourists are delighted, but it is the same predictable show all season, season after season.

The meal arrives between the drinking and the entertainment. Like the rest, it is produced for the masses, and usually consists of chicken and ribs. The great medieval roasts of wild animals, cattle and sheep are not replicated. Nevertheless, the food is a step upward from most airlines. A few medieval touches, such as wearing bibs, using the hands and copies of some medieval utensils dress up the rather ordinary fare. Wine decanters and plates of fruit are generally available also, including the inexplicable medieval bananas.

This is all show business, of course, a fact clearly revealed by the staff in moments of repose. Charming servant girls in medieval attire will stand behind diners for photographs. Their faces change from on camera to off camera as they go from group to group. Instant pleasant, plastic smiles appear and disappear with regularity. Such banquets are incomplete without a steward to bellow medievally at the tourists in order to herd them from one hall to another. He is also charged with such tasks as imposing silence during the singing and ensuring that all guests are turned towards the entertainers, thereby discouraging talk. While singing, this fierce disciplinarian becomes the very picture of angelic Irishness, posing as a charming old rogue.

THE DOWNSIDE OF VISITING IRELAND

All places in this world, no matter how wonderful, have a downside, or unfortunate aspects. Ireland is no exception, but Irish people are very sensitive about negative criticism from outsiders. They have a tendency to solicit favorable reassurances from visitors. Such sensitivity to criticism was clearly revealed a few years ago when a private letter from an American diplomat stationed in Ireland was leaked to the press and caused an uproar. The diplomat described Ireland as an "isolated and provincial country" with "dull" food, charming but "enigmatic and unpredictable people." He found the "long, dark, damp winters" and "dreary urbanscapes" depressing. He had a point, although the tourists' Ireland during a few weeks in the relatively warmest and driest season, the summer, gives a different impression than that held by those who have to slog through a longer, drearier stay. Even so, it is necessary to bring up the worst that Ireland has to offer, despite Irish sensitivity, because it is better to be forewarned than to discover these things more painfully through experience on the spot.

Begging

It is sad to see little children, besmudged and dressed in ragged, stained clothes, piously holding forth beggars' cups. If ignored, some will thrust the cups at passersby energetically, or grasp an arm or an elbow, importuning vigorously. Given a chance, some will slip a hand into a pocket or purse. Disheveled mothers with unclean infants and small children actually stake out locations on the sidewalks where they appear day after day, clutching one another, their hands extended in pitiful supplication. For most of them, it is a business that works most of the time.

In some social subgroupings, little children beg as a duty towards their family just as suburban children mow lawns or clean up their rooms. Their parents are likely to live on the edge of town in an Irish equivalent of a trailer community or in a rundown slum. Parents live on the proceeds from begging, government assistance, odd jobs, collecting junk and, perhaps, thievery. Begging is a great annoyance for visitors. Those who feel guilty about brushing beggars off may wish to make a lump sum donation to Irish Catholic charities while in the country. This would be a much more efficient way of helping Ireland's poor.

Theft

Pickpockets hover around places frequented by large numbers of tourists, such as the American Express Office or O'Connell Street near the Liffey. Some of them are amazingly slick and others are crude bumblers. Beware of leaving property unattended in public places, even for the shortest time. It can disappear in a wink.

Mugging occurs much more rarely than in American cities. In fact, crimes against persons are far fewer in Ireland, even in the capital. A person has to be in a bad, dark neighborhood and intoxicated to become a likely target for muggers in Dublin in nearly all instances. It is wise to stay away from the western part of the inner city along the Liffey at night. The same can be said for the area near Conolly Station, either behind the station or on Sheriff Street or Foley Street.

Drunks

An old saying about Dublin is that the pubs in the city outnumber the priests. So must the drunks. The downside of having so many bright, cheerful, gregarious, colorful, interesting pubs is having so many loud, raucous or disgusting drunks. Just how much of the nation's consumer income is spent on alcohol is a matter of hot debate, but many believe that the percentage is the highest in Europe. Even so, and in many cases because of it, up to a quarter of Ireland's adult population is said to abstain from alcohol entirely. The other three quarters contain a high number of chronic alcoholics, suffering from a disease which has claimed many more lives than statistics indicate because deaths from alcoholicsm are traditionally cloaked as deaths from other causes, such as liver failure. If the suffering of relatives is taken into account, alcoholism touches the lives of all too many Irish people. It has long been a well known national malaise. Nevertheless, all too many Irish people continue to laugh it off or deny it. What is worse, many condone excessive drinking admiringly, describing it as "a good man's failing."

Visitors may be accosted on the street by a singing or madly shouting drunk. While an abberant public

performance might not startle someone from New York
City, it may disconcert someone from a more sheltered
environment in the United States. Drunks who sidle up
to visitors and insist on engaging in incoherent, one-
sided conversations are also a problem. Those who get
sick from alcohol decorate sundry streets of Dublin with
clumps of vomit. Worse are the cases of vomiting in
pubs. Some places have buckets of sand handy, so that
the evidence of overindulgence can be smothered
quickly. Another problem is that heavy imbibers often
lack discretion in choosing locations to urinate once they
are outside of the pubs. The overall result of Dublin's
notoriety as "the drinking man's capital of the world" is a
faint reek of beer and urine here and there in the city.

Air Pollution

Smoking is much more likely to accompany drinking in Ireland than in the United States. Some pubs and
other public places can only be seen through a heavy
haze of tobacco smoke. Since cigarettes are heavily taxed
in Ireland, smokers tend to puff them down to the very
end. Yellowing fingers and teeth are commonplace. The
great American attack on smoking in public and work
places has barely begun in Ireland. Therefore Americans sensitive to cigarette smoke can anticipate difficult
times in Ireland.

Dublin's air is bad inside from tobacco and bad
outside from engine exhaust. Restrictions on emissions
of all kinds have not been applied as vigorously in
Ireland as they have been in the United States. For
example, lead free gasoline is rare. Models of cars which
use lead free gasoline exclusively in the United States
take leaded gas in Ireland. The dense congestion of

traffic in Dublin guarantees that the acrid stench of exhaust will assault the nostrils continuously. To make matters worse, many Irish people still burn trash in their backyards.

Noise pollution is another problem. Motorcycles careen along, screeching and roaring and leaving purple trails of exhaust behind them. Rattling old trucks and cars without mufflers add to the cacophony. On many streets traffic is bumper to bumper most of the time.

On cold days without much wind, a dense, dark, deadly, choking smog is likely to engulf the city. It is as bad as anything Los Angeles suffers through. The pall is so bad that it looks as if it is evening at mid-day, and viewed from hillsides miles away, only a few tall chimneys and spires indicate where the city lies beneath the dense cloud. Fortunately on most days winds blow the bad air away, but on cold, windstill, winter days the ugly brown cloud can intensify by the hour. Authorities have indicated that coal burning is the major cause of it. Efforts are underway to substitute types of coal and peat that do not pollute as much, and the very worst districts have had intermittent coal burning bans placed on them. Years ago, London suffered from killer smogs called "pea-soupers" until coal burning was banned altogether. Here is a specific example of Ireland's need to catch up with the rest of Europe.

IRISH AMBIGUITIES

Smog, alcoholism, begging and tobacco smoke are clearly negative features in contemporary Ireland. Many other features are clearly positive, such as the warmth, friendliness, hospitality, wit and gregariousness of Irish people. When asked about most places in the world, Americans like to tick off such lists of desirable and undesirable aspects. Irish life simply does not lend itself well to a rational analysis of positive and negative features. Many characteristics of Irish life can seem both desirable and undesirable at the same time. Americans will find themselves liking and disliking some aspects of Ireland simultaneously. The Republic of Ireland is too mellow and mild a place for these feelings to be taken to the extremes of love-hate responses, but Americans who are not used to equivocal circumstances may be confused by their feelings of both bemusement and annoyance. Such aspects can be called Irish ambiguities.

Talk

Talk is a prime example. All social interaction in Ireland involves a considerable amount of it. Even such mundane activities as buying a newspaper requires conversation. Wit, cleverness and originality in the use of words is always highly appreciated by all classes of society. People stop each other on the busiest of streets to engage in rich dialogue. Pub conversations can become magnificent flights of discourse at the thunk of an empty glass on the counter. They can build up very quickly to what can be called baroque proportions, studded with sayings and quotations and containing arguments that are strung out and elaborated.

In Ireland there is no such thing as a simple question and a simple answer. American conversations often build on the basis of a short question followed by a short answer which is followed by another short question, and so on. In an Irish conversation, an answer proceeds through a labyrinth of thoughts, reflections and digressions. Where an American will tend to answer a question in one sentence, an Irish person will answer the same question richly, fully, and delightfully in the course of a twenty-minute monologue.

Talk takes time and can become a substitute for action. If every little interaction requires talk, then more significant matters require much more of it, sometimes to the point of talking a topic to death. By the time the plans and schemes and pros and cons of doing a task are weighed and reweighed in conversation, the very time to get it done slips away. Ireland's severest critics, most of them Irish, proclaim that all the Irish want to do is drink and talk because it is so much easier than getting things done.

Visitors soon learn how easy it is to talk away the hours of the day, no matter how fine the conversations are in contrast to the abrupt businesslike communications that tend to prevail in America. Many accomplished Irish people, including several famous writers, have declared that they had to leave Ireland to do anything of significance. If they had stayed, their energies would have been continually drained away by rich and wonderful talk.

Irish Weather

Feelings about Irish weather can easily become ambiguous. Visitors quickly observe that it rains too frequently and that dark, low hanging clouds shroud the country too often. Grey is the color most usually associated with Irish weather. Mist, drizzle and puddles can be expected as the norm.

On the other hand, on many days a very gentle rain appears that is almost imperceptible from fog and mist. These are called "soft" days in Ireland and they occur when the calendar indicates that blizzards can be expected in parts of North America and snow in parts of Continental Europe. Instead of ferocious weather, Ireland has an invigorating coolness, a dampness conducive to growing plants in great green profusion. The chill does not permit many insect pests that bother Americans. Note that Irish windows do not have screens.

Ireland's predictable seaborne mildness in winter and coolness in summer has led to the saying that the seasons cannot be told apart, something that older Irish people regard as a relatively recent phenomenon. Visitors can count on cool, wet, gentle weather nearly all of the time. Some days of bitter, nasty rain occur in all seasons, and in winter only a very few days of harsh sleet, ice or snow can be expected. These rare days of bitter weather are counterbalanced by the equally rare glorious sunny days of clear, bright, blue skies and gentle warmth. Irish people will grumble about the weather masochistically and dream of vacations on sunny Spanish islands while American visitors may find that they like and dislike ordinary Irish weather at the same time.

Punctuality

Lack of punctuality is another feature of Irish life that Americans may come to feel very ambiguous about. "Irish time" is very flexible, unlike American time. People invited for the evening may show up hours late and then stay far into the early hours of the morning. Business schedules are only rough, optimistic approximations. Dublin bus schedules are almost worthless. There is a classic story about an Irish policeman who was asked the exact time and replied that it was "exactly between three and four." To make matters worse, it seems that most of the clocks in Ireland tend to be wrong.

Irish people give marvelous excuses for being late. "Having no sense of time" is a popular explanation, or "when God made time he made a lot of it." At first, keeping Irish time can seem amusing or frustrating to Americans, or both. After a while, they may begin to wonder if they are too exacting, too demanding in terms of the clock. They may ask, is it better to be more casual about appointments and schedules, or is it simply maddening and inefficient to live and work without punctuality?

Flexibility

Flexibility about time is just one aspect of a general Irish flexibility toward life in general. Whatever rules may be imposed, there are always exceptions, always ways around them. Skill and cleverness come to the fore to bend and slide around regulations, provisions and laws. The emphasis is usually upon the immediate circumstances and the personal interchange rather than upon duty towards distant upholders of dry regulations. With a wink and a nod, evasion can be accomplished.

Intellectuals have long attributed this remarkable flexibility to the long period of colonial domination when it was essential for Irish Catholics to get around the often unfair rules and regulations of the dry, formal, legalistic British who were in charge. Another explanation that has been offered is that the Celtic nature of doing business has much more of an *ad hoc* and outwardly chaotic style of Mediterranean or Latin countries rather than the cold, regular precision characteristic of northern European countries. Whatever the explanation, flexibility permeates Irish life, and for the American visitor its results can range from being infuriating to pleasantly accommodating. It often depends on rapport with the person in charge, who can either play the situation "by the book" in British style, or make an on the spot "arrangement" in Irish style.

For one example, consider the author's plight when seeking to pay £100 for a rented car with an Irish bank checkbook. The young lady in charge said that a check would not do because the daily bank guarantee only covered a check up to £50. When the author lamented that he had no other means on hand, there was a short pause before a revelation of Irish flexibility at its best: "Write two checks for £50," the young lady sighed. "Make one out for yesterday and make the other out for today."

The truth is bent in Ireland not just to smooth out difficulties but also to attempt to convey bad news as if it were good news. When there is no way to mollify bad news, "It could have been worse," is likely to be added. The truth is also bent to help people save face and avoid embarrassment. The author was aboard a chartered bus that almost rammed the rear end of a car that had stopped for a red light. After the bus had swerved and screeched to a stop, an Irish acquaintance of the driver who was also a friend of the author shouted in the direction of the car: "The stupid bastard! He just doesn't know how to drive." I mentioned in a whisper that the bus driver had not seen the red light because he had been fiddling with the radio. "I know," my Irish friend replied in a whisper accompanied by a wink. Later he explained that his outburst was just to ease the driver's embarrassment.

Getting Directions

Even such a simple matter as asking directions can bring on ambiguous feelings in Ireland. Irish people are very keen on giving elaborate directions, and feel disappointment if they cannot comply. When vagueness exists about a place or a street in their own minds, many will invent or contrive directions just to be obliging. No matter how unsure they may be of a given destination, they will conclude their advice with a hearty: "You can't miss it." Often it can be missed quite easily. Only very rarely does the visitor hear, "I don't know." At the very minimum a response is something like, "Go this way and that and when you get down there ask somebody else."

Certainly the warm and earnest manner of giving directions in Ireland stands in favorable contrast to the stoic shrugs of Parisians. But there is a strong tendency to overdo it in Ireland, where no simple question begets a simple answer. If one asks for directions out of a car window, the person asked might open the car door, sit down and commence a detailed description and discuss several other topics as well.

For travel around Dublin it is often more convenient to carry a large, detailed map of the city, the kind that can be purchased from the Tourist Information

Office. It is frequently much more efficient to take bearings from such a map than to ask the zealously helpful Irish. On long walks around the city, sometimes wearing clothes bought in Ireland, the author was now and then asked directions by Irish people who mistook him for a Dubliner. In such circumstances any response in an American accent invariably brings a smile and an apology. Yet armed with a detailed Dublin map, it is possible to whip it open, take a bearing on two streets, say, "You are here," and, aided by the street index, say, "You want to go here, so I'd take this way . . ." and point out the route on the map. The dead accuracy of such a procedure can astound Irish folk who undoubtedly expect a long digression that may contain questionable information. It is difficult to refrain from adding, "You can't miss it."

The Irish Work Ethic

The Irish work ethic is a topic that infuriates many people, including Irish people, and it amuses many others. Depending on the circumstances, the American visitor can be frustrated or entertained by the way the Irish work, or both.

Perhaps the people who suffer the most from the Irish work ethic are those few Japanese left behind to supervise Japanese owned factories in Ireland. A sharp contrast can be drawn between the Japanese and the Irish way of working. Unlike the Japanese, the Irish do not stress loyalty to the company, willingness to work on a task until it is done, and exhaustive application of effort to even the tiniest detail. Most Irish workers do not tackle work with Puritan relish. They like to scout it and consider it first, and defer it for a while. If it just has to be done, eventually, it can be accomplished with surprising grace. For most Irish workers, holidays, time off and time to quit are paramount considerations. Individual initiative to work harder than one's fellows is often not appreciated. An old saying declares: "He who tries and does his best goes down the road like all the rest." For most, work is simply a necessary evil, something that interferes with the pleasantries of life. To use an American phrase, when it comes to work, the Irish definitely tend to be "laid back."

Americans can be both charmed and frustrated over the manner in which the Irish do business. Business in Ireland invariably involves a great deal of talk and speculation, dreams and digressions, and it usually takes place in informal settings, over lunch or dinner or a few pints in a pub. A handshake and a thump on the back can conclude a deal. The more orderly procedures of memoranda and contracts are mere afterthoughts, and are usually kept to a minimum, since it is so much more pleasant to talk rather than to write or dictate. Besides, written communications are so cold, formal and impersonal. A problem that often arises, though, is that the participants in a deal may have quite different views of just what actually transpired. Oh well, that calls for another lunch or another trip to the pub to set it right.

Highly stressed Americans who come from environments where frantic workaholics abound may find Ireland's pace of work a delightful change, at least until they need service or repairs. Then they will encounter the litany over "the man who comes around." When the plumbing backs up or a window breaks or if the stove refuses to turn on, the American is likely to be told that, "We'll have the man come around and have a look at it."

It can take time to get a call through to him, of course, and even if he promises to show up on a given day he may not arrive. Ireland's habitations have countless broken bits and pieces waiting for the look of the man who comes around. Public facilities also bear chronic signs of disrepair. For example, a high percentage of phones do not work; traffic lights knocked out by bad weather are likely to stay in that condition for quite some time. Despite their charming manners, many people are unreliable in Ireland, and it is in this regard that the country can sometimes resemble Third World countries which have not mastered some of the disciplines of modern, urban, industrialized society.

Perhaps the worst example of the failings of the Irish work ethic is displayed by those glum men who drive Dublin's buses late at night, close to quitting time. The buses go into formation, following each other bumper to bumper, in a convoy of three, four or five buses. The first bus is likely to be filled up with passengers picked up far down the route, and cannot stop for any new fares. The buses huddled behind the full leader are starkly empty. The whole convoy hurtles past long lines of would-be passengers who are waiting for the last bus of the evening and who may have been standing in rain for over an hour. As the buses zoom into the garage, the people who had waited for them have to find some other way home.

THE UPSIDE OF VISITING IRELAND

Everyone who goes to Ireland will return with happy memories of good times and pleasant experi-

ences, regardless of the negative and ambiguous features of contemporary Ireland that have been described
in this chapter. At the root of the good experiences are
the warm human contacts to be found everywhere in
Ireland as well as the sprightly wit that keeps laughter
perpetually alive. It is appropriate to conclude this
sometimes critical chapter with a look at a few outstanding positive features of Irish life.

Human Connections and the Family

Human connections are of paramount importance
in Ireland. Even in fast moving Dublin, neighbors know
one another, pass the time of day, freely go in and out of
one another's habitations, visit, and keep an eye out for
one another, their children and their property. A network of human contact and interaction seems to absorb
nearly everyone. It does not take long for foreigners in
Ireland to become aware of these thick webs holding
people together. Unlike all too many Americans, Irish
people do not float about as anonymous, restless atoms.
Almost invariably, each Irish person is known, watched,
and belongs to a certain location and to a group of
people by ties of blood. By contrast, American society is
much more geared towards autonomy, mobility, and
individual existence. As many people know, there are
Americans who live devoid of serious human connections or even contact, and in the worst cases this can lead
to violent, tragic consequences.

Many Irish people are convinced that America is a
cold and lonely place compared to their homeland. This
view is often strongly reinforced by recent Irish immigrants who send reports from New York and other large

American cities about the loneliness of life in the United States. American shopping malls typify this condition, according to some Irish people, who perceive cold, lonely, materialistic throngs patronizing them.

Family comes first in Ireland, ahead of careers. The Irish family remains a stronger unit than the typical European or American family, and in special recognition of the fundamental importance of families in Ireland, specific provisions of the Irish constitution seek to protect them. Most Irish families continue to be extended, so that distant cousins tend to be not very distant. Ordinarily, family history and family connections are constant social preoccupations, often leading to detailed conversations about such things as who is married to whom, what their children do, or whose aunt is somebody's brother's cousin. Although some individuals feel smothering effects from these webs of family connections, most find them very supportive, fostering the security of the individuals involved.

Americans who plan to interact with Irish families need to be aware of one or two prevalent characteristics that come into play. Despite the warm greetings and generous hospitality of Irish people in general, they do have an inner wall of tact and reserve. Certain topics are not brought up and certain personal questions are not asked. By contrast, Americans are rather breezy, even about deeply felt matters. All most Americans need to launch their life histories is a chair and a drink and ten minutes. At times Irish people are uncomfortable facing blunt American assertiveness. In Ireland as elsewhere in the world, many Americans need to go more slowly in interpersonal situations.

A good example of Irish reserve involves the ritual

of politely refusing food or favors several times before conceding reluctantly to the insistent urgings of the host. This ritual is shared by several European peoples, but not by many Americans who, instead of making such statements as, "Oh, no, I could not possibly take another slice of gateau," might simply say, "Sure, thanks," and thereby abort the elaborate ritual of begging and refusing between host and guest. Irish people who know Americans well note that Americans are apt to say what they mean in social situations in contrast to Irish people who tend to be politely indirect.

Irish Humor

Irish humor is irrepressible, ever present and varied. It can range from long, elaborate stories to pithy expressions, such as: "If you want praise, die; if you want blame, marry." Even death is a topic of humor. A famous Irish marriage proposal consisted of only one question: "How would you like to be buried with my people?" When one newspaper gave an account about a funeral where a relative stumbled over a grave and broke his leg, this celebrated remark was included: "This unfortunate occurrence cast a gloom over the whole proceedings."

Irish humor can flash like quicksilver when it erupts spontaneously because of an odd situation. Nearly everyone who has been to Ireland has at least one or two favorite stories in which the visitor plays the straight man or woman and the punch line or lines are delivered by the Irish. For example, the author remembers his attempt to find the exit in a crowded, noisy Dublin restaurant, the kind of place where customers and waitresses ordinarily engage in lively banter. Unfortunately, I mistook the door to the kitchen for the exit door, and as I approached a middle-aged waitress was backing up in the same direction from her tables, laden with trays. We collided, and as the waitress fell off balance I caught her around the waist. We ended up with the waitress bent backwards and me bent forwards, and, except for the trays which she miraculously continued to balance, it looked like a pose for an old black and white movie poster. "I'm sorry," I said, "I was just looking for the exit and went to the wrong door." "Ah," she wailed, to the delight of her onlooking customers, "and I thought me luck had changed!"

Another favorite recollection is that of a breakfast at a religious house outside of Limerick. I sat with a number of American school teachers, most of them female, whom I had brought to Ireland on a tour. At an adjacent table sat a group of former priests and nuns who were on a retreat. As breakfast progressed, I noticed that many at my table were pushing their short, brown sausages to the sides of their plates where they would remain uneaten. These sausages are called "bangers" in Britain. Not wishing to see the food go to waste, particularly in Ireland, I walked over to the table of former priests and nuns and said: "We have a slight problem over at our table. We have a surplus of bangers. Do you want them?" There was a brief pause of utter silence, and then a high pitched male voice with a strong Irish accent declared: "Is that a nice thing, now, to call those ladies?"

CHAPTER THREE

Language and Its Uses

HIGHLIGHTS OF THE IRISH CONTRIBUTION TO LITERATURE

The most famous Irish achievements have involved the use of words. Plays, short stories, poems and novels by Irish people are known and admired worldwide. Almost all of this great Irish contribution to world literature has been written in the English language. To distinguish these works from Irish literature that is written in Irish or English literature that is written by British people, the term Anglo-Irish literature is used ordinarily.

Sometimes it is difficult to tell the Irishness of some

of the noteworthy contributions by 18th century Irish people who wrote for the elegant world of London. Oliver Goldsmith and Richard Sheridan would be in this category. Johnathan Swift was not. Appointed Dean of St. Patrick's Cathedral in 1714, Swift became passionately involved in Irish politics. His *Gulliver's Travels* and *A Modest Proposal on Populousness* reveal a scathing, cynical wit immersed in Irish concerns.

A remarkable outpouring of Irish creativity occurred during a literary renaissance starting in the 1890s and continuing until the early 20th century. In a thirty year period, Ireland produced four of the world's greatest playwrights: Oscar Wilde, George Bernard Shaw, John Millington Synge and Sean O'Casey; a revolutionary writer, James Joyce; and a great poet, William Butler Yeats. Much of the excitement centered around the Abbey Theatre in Dublin, which opened in 1904 and is still in existence as a state operated enterprise in a new and cold modern shell. Shaw and Wilde divided the London stage between them, while Synge's *avant garde* plays, especially *Playboy of the Western World,* caused an uproar at home. O'Casey's plays came later, in the 1920's. Three of his masterpieces are still produced throughout the English speaking world: *The Shadow of a Gunman, The Plow and the Stars.* and *Juno and the Paycock.*

James Joyce has been hailed as a literary giant and genius, particularly for *Ulysses,* a revolutionary novel revealing the flow of human consciousness on one June day in 1904, subsequently immortalized as "Bloomsday." Joyce admirers flock to Dublin to visit sights in the novel. Organized walks to these places in downtown Dublin are regularly held in the summer, and Joyce is the focal point of international literary conferences held in Dublin from time to time. Those who find *Ulysses* too daunting, either because of length or complexity, are likely to find his collection of short stories, *Dubliners,* delightful. Reading *Dubliners* can be an excellent means of grasping the ambience of turn of the century Dublin prior to a visit to the older parts of the city.

Admirers of William Butler Yeats flock to the area around Sligo. Yeats was a dominant poet for a significant time. His most famous lines of all celebrate the hopeless sacrifice of the 1916 rising:

> All changed, changed utterly:
> A terrible beauty is born.

Ireland has continued to produce numerous poets down to the present day, some fairly well known and others little known, most writing in English and some writing in Irish. In general, the love and celebration of poetry is much more prevalent in Ireland than in America. To some extent, the same can be said for short stories and plays, two types of composition that have flourished in Ireland. Novels have not made their mark to the extent that these other literary forms have.

Ireland's most towering dramatist and writer of the contemporary era has been Samuel Beckett, whose works grapple with the absurd in life. *Waiting for Godot* is one of his more famous plays. Beckett himself illustrates an important characteristic of many of the more famous contributors to Anglo-Irish literature: They do their best work away from Ireland. Beckett and Joyce were voluntary exiles on the Continent and Wilde and Shaw were inseparable from London. Joyce's *Ulysses* can serve as an interesting case in point. It was written hundreds of miles from Dublin, even though its richly detailed scenes take place in the city. When it was published and hailed elsewhere, it was banned in Ireland and condemned as pornography.

Various explanations of why some Irish authors work so productively in self-imposed exile have been offered. The censorship of the Catholic Church has been cited as a factor. Although quite relaxed nowadays, in the past Church censorship banned tens of thousands of books, mostly because of sexual content. Cynics have remarked that the list of banned books made an excellent guide to worthwhile literature. Another reason put forth is that the verbal intensity of Dublin life is such that authors are prone to spew forth their artistic energies in pubs over too many pints. A less gregarious existence abroad is seen as much more conducive to putting pen to paper. Another argument is that Irish religious or nationalistic zealots are so intrusive that writers feel more comfortable away from them. Last, some regard London as the inevitable great magnet that attracts many worthy writers in English, be they Irish or not.

HIGHLIGHTS OF IRISH CONTRIBUTIONS TO OTHER ARTS

Before considering specific uses of language in Ireland, the great achievement in literature needs to be contrasted with Irish achievements in other arts. Claims of worldwide recognition and admiration cannot be made for Irish painting and sculpture. For a long time the patrons of Irish art were members of the Protestant

Ascendancy whose world is clearly depicted on hundreds of canvases in the National Gallery. In the 19th and 20th centuries, painters feeling strong nationalistic enthusiasm tried to revive Celtic colors, forms and designs from the distant, pre-English past, but such art had to be contrived to a degree because it did not grow out of a continuous indigenous tradition. One painter, however, is singled out as an important Irish artist of the early 20th century. He is Jack B. Yeats, the brother of the famous poet.

Two forms of art, film and music, regularly capture the attention of huge numbers of people in the late 20th century. These two forms also build bridges between people working in the arts and those working in the sciences and in technical fields. In film, Ireland has been the location for several celebrated international productions, including *Ryan's Daughter* and *The Lion in Winter.* But little has originated in this field from Irish producers based in Ireland. This cannot be said for contemporary popular music. The number of composers and bands in rock music exists out of all proportion to the population. In recent years "U-2" and several other groups have gained international fame and inspired dozens of imitators, thereby making rock concerts an important feature of Dublin's creative entertainment.

There has also been a resurgence of interest in "traditional" Irish music, which has come to include old English and Scottish ballads imported to Ireland centuries ago. Traditional music festivals take place regularly in various locations and there are countless informal gatherings to play traditional music. Groups use some combination of *uilleann* (elbow) pipes, *bodkran* drum of stretched skin, tin whistle, fiddle, accordian, piano and flute. Many American visitors are very eager to hear it, and summer entertainments throughout Ireland have tended to feature traditional music. Irish people themselves enjoy all kinds of music. Many have a curious fondness for American country-western ballads, particularly in rural Ireland. Perhaps this American music serves as the counterpart to those sad and sprightly Irish rural ballads from the dim and distant past.

It must be noted that despite the vast popularity of rock and traditional music and the huge attendance they draw in concert, the most famous episode in the history of music in Ireland was the composition and premier performance of Handel's *Messiah* in Dublin in the 18th century.

FOLKLORE

The stories and traditions from Irish folklore have long served as inspiration for literature and as an element of a common cultural heritage. Today academic efforts must be made to preserve aspects of folklore that are rapidly vanishing. The Department of Irish Folklore at University College, Dublin, is at the forefront in this work.

Some elements of folklore still appear in the form of popular superstitions. For example, a pregnant woman is not supposed to associate with the dead in any way, meaning that she must avoid graveyards and funerals. On the other hand, if a pregnant woman visits a workshop, she is supposed to give good fortune to the workers. Also, to protect barns, crosses of straw are hung in them. Should milk be given to a neighbor, salt should be put into it. The list of popular superstitions is lengthy, although rural people are more likely to pay attention to them today.

Part of the heritage which is becoming extremely rare are the traditional folk celebrations of the rites of passage: birth, marriage and death. The wake for the dead, although normally a way to express sadness and grief, became famous for breaking out into revelry and rowdiness after bouts of heavy drinking. Rural weddings often involved the whole community, which would walk in procession to the church and then back to the bride's home. Another old rural custom was the *ceili*, or gathering of all the neighbors in one family's house to spend a night talking, storytelling, dancing and singing.

Another part of the heritage is derived from the calendar of rural life. Its traditions are really adaptations of annual ancient pagan celebrations. For example, St. Bridgid's Day, February 1, marks the beginning of the ploughing season. It used to be the old spring festival of Imbolic, marked by the onset of the lactation of sheep. One rural fair in County Kerry has been noted as a carryover from an ancient pagan spring fertility celebration because a male goat was exalted before the crowds. May Day has been celebrated as the time to put the cows out to summer pasture and Lammas Day, August 1, marks the first day of harvest reaping. November Day denotes preparations for winter.

Another attribute of the folk heritage is that it casts some light into the dark recesses of the prehistoric past. For example, Irish folklore provides a myth to describe waves of prehistoric invasions of the island. Ireland itself was associated with a goddess who actually came to bear several names. According to the myth, the primal goddess led the first invasion of Ireland herself and was then ravished by several waves of male invaders. A milder variation of the tale explains that subsequent newcomers became playthings and consorts of the goddess just for a night.

There are other stories which probably helped later settlers to come to terms with conquest and ancient pagan beliefs. Stories about the "little people" may have originated as stories about earlier inhabitants who were conquered and assimilated by the Celts. Stories about "fairies" are often likely to be tales about pre-Christian animist gods who inhabited certain specific places over which they cast spells. They are supposed to be elf-like creatures who live unseen by most mortals most of the time in the countryside, especially around burial mounds.

There is nothing very ferocious or frightening about tales from Irish folklore compared to tales from many other places. Evil is not concentrated upon as it is in other folk traditions. Conspicuously absent are devil figures, werewolves, bloodsucking ghouls, and other types that have served to inspire horror movies. They are simply not Irish.

Traditional storytellers, the masters among whom were called bards, preserved the sagas and epics of Celtic Ireland and enabled many of them to be passed down to the present day. Each storyteller had a repertoire of hundreds of tales stored away in his agile memory. Societies without writing are likely to put great emphasis on embedding knowledge in the memories of the next generation through patient drilling.

The old traditional stories are heroic tales of

mighty, bloody ancestral deeds designed to entertain royal and aristocratic audiences. The main characters themselves are aristocratic, living in a simple world on plundered cattle. Many of these tales center on a band of warriors, the *fianna*. In general, the early Irish epics can be compared to the heroic epics of Homer and the Scandinavians.

A few of the oldest and most famous subjects of folklore had a way of reappearing later on in a different form. Many of the miraculous attributes of St. Patrick once belonged to the legendary Celtic god named Lug. The ancient primal goddess was transformed into Kathleen ni Houlihan, the daughter of a legendary Celtic chieftan. More recently she has been transformed again into the personification of Ireland or as the muse for writers and artists. She is usually shown with a harp, and sometimes appears as a weeping beauty with a stringless harp. Often a wolfhound is at her feet and a round tower is behind her. Another subject of folklore, the *Fianna Fáil,* or band of legendary warriors, has lent a name to one or Ireland's major political parties.

Undoubtedly the preservation of this ancient heritage of folklore has contributed considerably to the vitality of modern Irish playwrights, poets and story-tellers. It undoubtedly nurtured them from childhood, just as Americans are nurtured by violent tales of frontier days.

THE IRISH LANGUAGE

Ireland, Canada, South Africa and Belgium are among the nations of the world that have two official languages. Ireland is unique among them, however, because one of the official languages, English, is spoken by nearly everyone, while the other, Irish, barely survives as a living modern language. This cannot be said for Flemish in Belgium, French in Canada, at least in Quebec, and Afrikaans in South Africa. The number of people in Ireland who use the Irish language as their primary and regular means of communication varies from source to source, but the numbers cited are all small compared to the over three and a half million persons living in Ireland. Common estimates range from 30,000 to 58,000, which puts the higher figures at fewer than 2% of the population. Nevertheless, nearly all of the rest of the population has some degree of familiarity with it, and some who use English at work are fluent in Irish also.

Irish belongs to the Celtic family of languages and is a member of that greater family of languages called Indo-European. It is related most closely to Welsh, which is widely spoken in Wales today; Manx, spoken on the Isle of Man; Scots Gaelic, spoken just on the very fringes of Scotland; Cornish, now a very rare language in Cornwall; and Breton, spoken locally in Brittany, France. (See language map). Irish does not belong to the Germanic languages nor to the Latin derived "romance" languages.

Irish was the language spoken by a majority of the people living in Ireland for over 2,000 years and it has been a written language for fourteen centuries. English, actually Norman French at first, was the language of the conquerors. Over the centuries the use of English spread to more and more of Ireland as the Celtic chieftains lost control of territory. Irish remained the language of the peasants in most conquered areas, but gradually English made its inroads even among them. Eventually it seemed that the Irish language might disappear altogether. By the turn of the 20th century, with only a few exceptions, Irish as a first language in the home, that is, the language taught to babies day by day, survived only on the fringes, in the most remote, most rural and most economically backward parts of the country. The Celtic revival that began in the 1890s changed this situation dramatically. Speaking Irish became a patriotic duty, a way of stating that the ancient culture had survived and that Ireland was really Irish and not British. Use of the language became so deeply involved with modern Irish nationalism that many educated and sophisticated Dubliners joined the fishermen of the west coast in enunciating Irish as tens of thousands went to classes all over the country to study the language. No longer was it associated just with backward provincials. Now it was the key to the golden age of Ireland's independent past, and another justification for an independent future. Many poets, story writers and playwrights gave up English for Irish, at least temporarily.

After the bloody break from Britain in the 1920s, everything Irish was emphasized, especially the language, in order to underline how different Ireland was from Britain. The Irish language became a compulsory subject in the schools, and a required language for entrance to the National University. Members of the police, army, and civil service had to be able to use it. Bilingual signs appeared everywhere, and some government bodies had only Irish names, which were soon to be used almost universally as abbreviations only, such as

C.I.E. and R.T.E. Those shrinking fringes in the west still speaking Irish as the primary language were designated the *Ghaeltacht,* and efforts were made to preserve them. Even today a special Department of the Ghaeltacht exists to promote the Irish language and assist the social and economic development of Irish speaking areas.

The high tide of the return to Irish seems to have subsided to a considerable extent. Many deeply emotional and bitter arguments about the use of the language have taken place over the years, sometimes filling the columns of letters to the editor in newspapers. For many critics, the Irish language was something that belonged in the past as a national language, but not in the present. To try to make a dying language into the living language of a modern nation was, in their view, hopeless. The time and effort spent by all students learning Irish should be spent learning French, German or Spanish to facilitate Ireland's participation in the European Economic Community. Critics maintain that too many students find learning Irish a pointless chore because it is not spoken in their environments. They argue that forced learning of Irish actually leads to a cooling of national ardor, so it should be made into an elective subject. Yet, despite these criticisms, some prosperous, well educated, middle class parents continue to support high quality schools where Irish is the language of instruction.

The decline in the momentum for reviving Irish is reflected in language requirement modifications of the early 1970s for the police, the army, the civil service and the National University. Demands for proficiency in Irish have been relaxed and there are now loopholes for some candidates. The decline in enthusiasm for Irish may have been helped along by the frequent arguments over pronunciation, spelling and grammar among users. Some desire a return to classical Irish and some want to follow contemporary popular speech. Many petty squabbles continue. Since it is not a phonetic language, standards of pronunciation have varied among even the most proficient. Phonetic languages, such as Spanish or German, have specific pronunciations for each letter. Irish does not, therefore it is particularly difficult for outsiders to pronounce Irish words. Mistakes are so easy to make that it is wise to avoid even trying.

In the *Ghaeltacht,* a flow of English speakers into the area continues, while many old families in the region are switching to English for practical reasons. Most native Irish speakers can speak fluent English as a second language, so for them the changeover is smooth. Consequently, it seems that more and more English and less and less Irish is heard on the playgrounds of the *Ghaeltacht.*

Use of the Irish language does not cause inconveniences for Americans in Ireland because it is so minimal. When written it is almost invariably accompanied by an English version. Also, Irish people are ordinarily too polite to lapse into Irish in the presence of visitors in order to cut them out of conversations the way many other national groups speaking their own local languages often do. Of course, tourists will be exposed deliberately to a few mandatory words of greeting and farewell in official operations, but this is a very brief patriotic gesture. A few songs, poems and sayings will be all in Irish, but local people will usually be more than happy to translate. Now and then a television talk program will switch from English to Irish, which is annoying, and some will be completely in Irish and therefore almost totally incomprehensible to non-Irish speakers. In many places signs for restrooms are only in Irish, but fortunately the two universal figures, one in trousers and one in a skirt, accompany the Irish designations.

Perhaps without knowing it, all Americans speak a few words of Irish that have been incorporated into English. The most used words from Irish are: colleen, donnybrook, hooligan, boycott, tantrum, smithereen, banshee, galore and bother. For many of the Irish themselves, the old Celtic language continues to influence the way they speak English. Inversions are indicative of this: "It is on his way home he was." As in Irish, the word "after" is used to denote the past tense: "I am after my prayers," or "I am after forgetting my purse." Yet as British English continues to permeate Irish life, thanks in large measure to British television, echoes of the ancient tongue become fainter.

IRISH ENGLISH

Irish English is a variety of English that is very close to British English in spelling, pronunciations and vocabulary, and differs from American English to a similar degree as British English does. Therefore an American cereal box may advertise with the exclamation: "Hey kids!", while an Irish or British cereal box will declare: "Look children!" To most American ears, the way English is spoken in Ireland seems more similar than different from the way English is spoken in Britain. There is an Irish accent, of course, which is most strongly pronounced by rural folk and the less educated. On the other hand, linguists affirm that educated Dublin upper middle class English has only a very few phonetic features to distinguish it from proper British English. Dublin news broadcasters confirm this point nicely. Often Irish English tends to drag many words out longer than in British or American English. For example, a loud and distinct "m" is put on the word "film," to make the pronunciation "fillem." Another quirk is the phonetic pronunciation of all letters in borrowed French words. For example, "fillet" has a hard and distinct "t" at the end, as does "debut."

VOCABULARY

What follows is a list of words from English as they are used in Ireland, along with some Irish words. The latter are underlined. There are also a few words from Dublin slang. Familiarity with these terms can help visiting Americans avoid some confusion and promote mutual understanding in Ireland, in everything from dealing with a landlord to reading a newspaper article. Readers may wish to use this section in Ireland as a short Irish English to American English dictionary.

Advert — It is the abbreviation for advertisement. "Ad" is used in America.

An Lar — This Irish phrase means city center. It is sometimes seen on bus signs.

Articulated Lorry — This is used for tractor trailer truck.

Athlete — This term usually refers to someone in track and field. The word athletics usually refers to track and field sports.

Aubergine — This is the word for eggplant.

Backbencher — The ordinary members of a political party, of the rank and file, sit on the back benches in the legislature.

Back garden — This is used instead of the American "back yard."

Balaclava — This is a knitted hat which is put over the face.

Bank Holiday — This is a day when the banks are closed, along with almost everything else. They occur on certain days and around other holidays.

Barrister — A barrister is a lawyer who pleads cases in higher courts. Ordinary legal paperwork and minor business is handled by a solicitor in Ireland.

Bathe — as a verb, this means to go for a swim, not to have a bath.

Bathroom — Literally, a room where people bathe. Americans curiously use it as a euphemism for toilet, because we usually have toilets in our bathrooms. Americans are cautioned not to ask for the bathroom, because the question may elicit this tired Irish joke: "Why, do you want to bathe?" European homes and hotels have tended not to have toilets in the bathrooms in the past, but this is changing.

Bed Sitter or *Bed Sit* — This is a room that serves as a living room and a sleeping room. Bed sits are advertised and refer to the smallest kind of apartment rental.

Bill — This noun is used instead of our word "check" in places such as restaurants.

Billion — A billion is a million million in Ireland and Britain. The American billion is expressed as a "thousand million."

Biscuit — is the word often used in Ireland for the American words 'cookie' or 'cracker.'

Bloody — This is a term of exasperation or annoyance, imported from Britain. Its origin was in a curse, "God's blood."

Bonnet — This is the term for the hood of the car.

Book — To book means to reserve. One books tickets for the theatre, or seats on a tour.

Boot — This is the term for what Americans call the trunk of a car.

Bord Failte — This is the Irish name of the Irish Tourist Board, literally, the "Board of the Welcomes."

Boyo — This is a slang term that is used either positively or negatively, as in "He is quite a boyo." It might mean a daredevil or sport, or it might mean something much worse, such as 'violent roughneck.'

Braces — This is the Irish and British word for suspenders, that which holds pants up. Suspenders in Ireland and Britain mean garters, that which holds socks up, or used to before modern fabrics.

Brit — This is a slang abbreviation for British.

Britain — This is the island which includes England, Scotland and Wales.

British — Any person or phenomenon from England, Scotland or Wales can properly be called British. A person can be, for example, Scottish and British, but never Scottish and English. Debate is strong over whether the Protestant majority in Northern Ireland can be called British rather than Irish.

Bum — This word does not mean hobo or lazy type as it does in America. It refers to the buttocks, euphemistically called the "behind" and other terms in America.

Busker — Buskers are street performers, singers, musicians of various kinds, and dancers who solicit voluntary contributions from people passing by.

Camp Bed — This is what Americans call a cot.

Campus — This word is not used as often in Ireland as in America. It is an American import. The word 'grounds' is used more often in Ireland.

Caravan — This word is used for a trailer or recreational vehicle. Ireland's traditional migrants, the traveling people, live in caravans. In America, it means a procession of vehicles or objects.

Car Park — This is the very literal phrase used in Ireland for parking lot.

Carriage — This word means railway car.

Celsius — This term is used for the temperature. The Celsius scale differs from the Fahrenheit scale used in the United States ordinarily. 0° Celsius is the same as 32° Fahrenheit; 100° Celsius is the same as 212° Fahrenheit, the boiling point of water.

Chapel — This noun refers to a religious meetinghouse or church of various Protestant denominations, excluding the Church of Ireland.

Check — Our use of this word for bill in such places as restaurants is not followed in Ireland. They say 'bill.'

Cheerio — This is a light way of saying goodbye.

Chemist — A chemist is a druggist in Ireland.

Chemist's Shop — This means drugstore, but drugstores in Ireland sell a narrower range of products than the American drugstore.

Chips — are potatoes that Americans call French fries. They are sometimes just 'fries' in Ireland.

Church of Ireland — This is the equivalent of the Episcopal Church in America and the Church of England in England. All are members of a worldwide Anglican group.

C.I.E. — These are the initials for the public transportation service in Ireland, the <u>*Coras Iompair Eireann.*</u> Everyone says C.I.E. for it.

Cold — This usually does not mean ice cold as it does in America. Americans would use the word cool to describe what is called cold in Ireland.

College — A college in Ireland is most usually a special secondary school. It usually does not refer to 'third level' or university level education.

Common — This word does not mean ordinary. It means lower class, usually pejoratively. The word is used without prejudice in America, where the 'common' man or woman is held in high esteem. Yet in Ireland, common can mean low, cheap or worthless. Ordinary, usual or ubiquitous can be used as substitutes for the American meaning.

Continent — Irish and British people use this term to describe Europe without their islands.

Convenience — This is a polite term for toilet. A public convenience means a public toilet.

Corn — is a word for all grains. The American word corn is translated as maize or Indian corn. It does not grow well in Ireland, and would be used as an animal food when available.

Cornet — This means cone, as in ice cream cone.

Corporation — This term means municipal government, what is called local government in many parts of the United States. The American word 'corporation' means Public Liability Company in Ireland, abbreviated P.L.C.

Corporation flat (or home) — This refers to subsidized public housing, what would be called a Council House in Britain.

Cot — A cot is a bed for a small child, what Americans call a crib. The American cot is a camp bed in Ireland.

Courgettes — are zucchini.

Crack — This is a very widely used term in Ireland to denote having a good time, usually a combination of good chat, drink and much laughter. It has nothing at all to do with the vicious drug that goes by that name in the United States.

Crisps — are potato chips. Note the meaning of chips in Ireland above.

Culchy — This is a Dubliners' word for a country person. Perhaps the American equivalent would be "hick," or, less favorably, "redneck" or "yokel."

Current Account — This term in banking refers to what Americans call a checking account. Note, too, that checks are spelled cheques, and that they are not ordinarily sent back to the person who wrote them.

Cute — Anything "cute" refers to cleverness of a nefarious kind. A con operation is cute; Selling Irish trinkets made in Hong Kong is cute.

Cutting the Grass — This wonderfully explicit term is used instead of the vague American "mowing the lawn."

<u>*Dáil (Dáil Eireann)*</u> — This is the all important lower house of the national legislature, corresponding to the British House of Commons.

Demo — This is a popular abbreviation for demonstration.

Deposit Account — This means a savings account.

Detached — This means a house standing without being joined to another. Such houses are much more ordinary in the United States in suburban areas than in Ireland. Semi-detached houses, meaning that they are attached on one side but not the other, are numerous in Ireland.

Directory Enquiries — This refers to what Americans call telephone information.

Divider — This is the line or strip in the middle of the road dividing traffic.

Dole — These are welfare payments, usually to unemployed persons. "On the dole" usually means being chronically unemployed.

Donkey's Years — This slang phrase implies a great length of time, as in "He hadn't seen her for donkey's years."

Dressing Gown — This is the word used in Ireland for bathrobe.

Dual Carriageway — This is the term used in Ireland for a divided highway.

Dust Bin — This means trash bin or can.

Dustman — This is the name for a garbage collector or garbage worker.

Elastic band — This means rubber band.

E.S.B. — These initials are for the Electricity Supply Board.

Estate car — This is the word used in Ireland for station wagon.

Fag — This means cigarette or sometimes a dreary

task. It is not a slang word for homosexual. "Nancy boy," "pouf" or "queer" are used in Ireland as slang for a homosexual.

Finished — This word is used in place of the American 'done,' as in "I am all done." In Ireland this means being on the verge of death.

First Floor — This is really the second floor in America. What Americans call the first floor is the ground floor in Ireland.

Flan — This is a pie that has no top crust.

Flat — This is the ordinary word for apartment.

Football — The American game of soccer is called football in Ireland, where it is immensely popular. American football is called just that. It is rarely played in exhibition games when American teams visit Ireland. Irish television gives some coverage of American football.

Form — This word is used to designate what Americans call "grades" in school, as in: "He is in the fifth form."

Fortnight — This means two weeks.

Full Stop — This means period.

Gaol — This word is pronounced exactly like "jail" in American English and it means the same thing.

<u>*Garda Síochána*</u> — Guarda is one of the very few words from Irish which has eclipsed the English word, police. Literally it means guard, and the full title is guardian of the public. The plural is *Gardái*.

Gateau — This is a rich, fancy cake, but the term has come to be applied to cakes in general.

Ghaeltacht — This refers to Irish speaking areas of the country. Gaeltacht is another spelling.

Give Way — Signs reading "give way" on Irish roads

are direct equivalents of yield signs in the United States.

Goods Lift — This means freight elevator.

Goods Lorry — This means a truck carrying freight.

Goods Train — This means freight train.

G.P.O. — These initials stand for General Post Office.

Greengrocer — Shops that sell fruits and vegetables are greengrocers' shops. Usually they do not sell other staples.

Greens — This term refers to green vegetables.

Half — In telling time, Americans often say "thirty" for the half hour, or half past. Irish people omit the "past," so "half five" means 5:30.

Handbag — This means purse. So does "bag" by itself.

Have a Go — This is ordinary slang for "try" or "try it."

High Street — this high street of a town or a district is the equivalent of "main street."

High Tea — This means a late afternoon meal.

Hire — To hire means to rent.

Hire Purchase — This is the installment plan, sometimes called the "never never."

Holiday — This word is used in Ireland for "vacation." On holiday means on vacation.

Holidays — These are vacation periods for school children and in general.

Hoover — This means vacuum cleaner, whether it is a Hoover or any other brand. To hoover means to vacuum.

Horse's Roar — This is used as a phrase to denote great distance, as in "He was a horse's roar away from the scene at the time."

Ill — This word is used instead of the American word "sick." Sick in Ireland ususally means nauseous, and to "be sick" means to vomit.

I.T.U.C. — This is an abbreviation for the Irish Trade Union Congress.

Jackeen — This word is applied to Dubliners implying their smooth, slick tendencies.

Jar — This is slang for a glass of beer, usually containing a pint of liquid.

Joint — This is a piece of meat for roasting.

Junction — Americans prefer to use the term "intersection" when roads meet and junction for the places where railroads meet. In Ireland, roads have junctions.

Keep your pecker up — This is a classic phrase. It means "keep your spirits up" in Ireland and Britain and quite another thing in America.

Knickers — This is an archaic term for underpants, something like the word "bloomers" in America. It amuses Irish and British people. The phrase "Don't get your knickers in a knot" means don't get distraught.

Knock Up — This means to look someone up or wake up someone instead of the American slang for impregnating someone.

Lecturer — This is the general title for college professor in Ireland. Most university teachers hold this rank. Very few become professors, which is a term of considerable distinction.

Left Luggage — This is a checkroom for luggage.

Lift — This means elevator.

Loo — This is a genteel but colloquial word for toilet.

Lorry — This is the word for truck in Ireland.

Lot — "The lot" means all of it, or everything. "Your lot" means all of your group. Americans often say "the works."

Lough — This is the Irish word for the Scottish loch, or lake. It is pronounced the same as loch. A second definition is an arm of the sea.

Mackintosh or *Mac* — This is a heavy raincoat.

Maisonette — This is a duplex apartment, often part of a house.

Maths — Mathematics is always abbreviated in the plural, and not in the American singular, "math."

Mead — This is a potent sweet alcoholic beverage of fermented honey which is served at Irish medieval banquets.

Mean — This word means "stingy" in Ireland, rather than hurtful or nasty.

Mews — This is usually an old alley that has become quaint or fashionable.

Minced Meat or *Mince* — This is what Americans call chopped beef or hamburger meat.

Mixed Grill — This is a main dish consisting of several diverse kinds of grilled meat often served with some vegetables.

Mot — This is Dublin slang for a girlfriend.

Motor — To motor means to drive a vehicle.

Mr. — Oddly enough, higher ranking doctors, surgeons, and dentists often bear the title of Mr. instead of Dr. Americans sometimes mistakenly think that they are lower ranking professionals.

Nancy or *Nancy Boy* — These are slang terms for homosexual, as are "pouf" or "queer."

Nappy — This word is used for diaper in Ireland.

Nearside — This is the word used in Ireland for the part of the road that is near the sidewalk.

Nil — This means zero or nothing.

Nipple — In Ireland, this term is usually just for part of the breast. The word "teat" refers to the nipple on a baby's bottle.

Number Plate — This means license plate in Ireland.

Off License — This means liquor store.

Offside — This word is used in Ireland for the part of the road that is away from the sidewalk.

Oireachtas — This Irish word is the official name of the Irish Parliament, which consists of the Senate, or upper house, and the *Dáil,* or lower house, which is similar to Britain's House of Commons.

Old Boys and *Old Girls* — These are the people that Americans call alumni and alumnae.

Paddy — This is often an acceptable colloquial term for an Irish person, but its proper use depends on the context. The term "Mick" is not, because it is often used as a derogatory term, especially in Britain.

Pants — This word usually refers to underpants in Ireland. The word "trousers" is ordinarily used for what Americans call pants.

Petrol — This is the term always used in Ireland for gas or gasoline.

Pint — This means a pint of beer which is slightly larger than an American pint. It fills a hefty glass.

Pissed — This is slang for being drunk.

Plaice — This is a flat European fish that resembles and tastes like a flounder.

Plimsols — This is the name of canvas shoes, or what Americans call track shoes, or, to the amusement of Europeans, sneakers.

Point or *Power Point* — This means electrical outlet.

Poteen — This is an illegally brewed white whiskey, comparable to moonshine and celebrated for its outstanding potency. (Pronounced pot-sheen)

Public Bar — This is the part of some old fashioned bars used by ordinary people. In such places, there is a slightly costlier lounge, which is supposed to be used by visitors and ladies. The lounge is sometimes called the saloon bar.

Public Liability Company — The abbreviation form, P.L.C., is the equivalent of Inc. in the United States and Ltd. in Britain. It means a corporation whose liability is limited.

Queue — This word means line, as in a line of people. It is pronounced "cue" and comes from the French word meaning tail. Queues are more carefully maintained in Britain than in Ireland, but "staying in line," as Americans would say, is important in both countries.

Quid — This is slang for a pound, just as "buck" is slang for a dollar.

Rag — as in a student's rag, means a time of high spirits and uproariousness, what Americans would call "a time to let off steam."

Reckon — This verb, which means to figure or calculate, is used in Ireland just as regularly as it is in old Western movies.

Redundancy Pay — This is the equivalent of severance pay in America.

Redundant — This odd sounding term means being unemployed. The number of redundancies refers to the number unemployed.

Return — This word is a short form of return trip,

which Americans call a "round trip." So in Ireland, ask for "return" tickets to get round trip tickets.

Ride — To ride is an obscene term, supposedly derived from "to writhe," a euphemism for sexual intercourse. Americans who talk about transportation by asking people for a ride or offering the same can encounter difficulties.

Ring Up — is used in place of "call up" on the telephone in America.

R.T.E. — This stands for the Irish radio and television service, *Radio Telefís Eireann.*

Rubber — This refers to an eraser and does not have the American meaning of slang for condom.

Rugby — This is a game vaguely resembling American football that is immensely popular in Ireland, Britain, South Africa and other parts of the world.

Scent — This word is used in Ireland for perfume.

Scotch Egg — This is a hard boiled egg embedded in a brownish pastry crust.

Screw — This is a slang word for salary, now archaic.

Scrubber — This is a slang word for a person with very poor standards of behavior.

Semi-Detached — This term refers to a house that is attached to another house on one side but not on the other side.

Send Down — This means to expel or suspend a person from a university.

Service Flat — This is an apartment which is cleaned and serviced.

Shepherd's Pie — This is a dish of ground meat and onions covered with mashed potatoes.

Sick — This word means to be nauseous. To be sick

means to vomit. The word "ill" is used for those situations when Americans would use sick.

Single — At a ticket window, this means a one way ticket.

Sitting Room — This word is used for what Americans would call the living room.

Slag — To slag someone is to give a bad name in jest. It is a form of teasing.

Solicitor — Ireland has two kinds of legal professionals. Solicitors do ordinary legal work, much of it paperwork. The barristers plead cases in the higher courts.

Spanner — This is the term for wrench.

Stalls — This term refers to theatre seats on the ground floor.

Stand for Office — In Ireland, politicians stand for office; in America, politicians run for office.

Starters — These are the items on the menu that Americans call appetizers or the first course.

Sticky Wicket — This refers to a difficult situation and comes from a sporting expression.

Stout — This is a heavy, dark, sweet beer, a famous Irish export. Some claim that it looks like motor oil capped by foam.

Supporters — This is the word in sport for those whom Americans call "fans."

Surgery — This is the medical doctor's office. If a doctor is in surgery he may be in to see his patients.

Suspenders — This is the word for garters. What Americans call suspenders are called braces in Ireland.

Sweet — Sweet can mean either dessert or a piece of candy. The plural form, sweets, means candy.

Taoiseach — This is the Irish title for the prime minister, the leader of the government. The pronunciation is something like "tea-shock."

T.D. — This is the abbreviation for a member of the *Dáil, Teachta Dala*. It is the equivalent of M.P., or Member of Parliament in Britain or member of Congress in the United States.

Teat — This is a nipple on a baby's bottle. The term nipple is used exclusively for part of the breast.

Telephone Box — This is used instead of telephone booth.

Terrace — This refers to a row of houses joined together.

Terrace House — This is one of the houses in a row of houses joined together.

The (as a missing article) — Irish people leave out "the" and "a" or "an" when discussing such institutions as universities. For instance, a student is "at university" instead of "at the university." the same applies to hospitals: One is "in hospital" in Ireland.

Through — In a phone conversation, this means connected, not finished. When an operator asks, "Are you through?" this means "Are you connected?"

Tin — One meaning of this word in Ireland is tin can or can in America. Therefore "tinned" means "canned" in Ireland.

Tinkers — This is a derisive term for Ireland's itinerant minority who are properly called "traveling people." (See below.)

Ton — This is 2,240 lbs. in Ireland and Britain. An American ton of 2,000 lbs. is often called a short ton.

Torch — This word means flashlight.

Tower Block — This means a high-rise apartment building.

Traveling People — This is the preferred term for Ireland's itinerant minority that move about from place to place, carrying on odd jobs and dealing in scrap metal as well as family begging. "Tinker" is a derisive term for them.

Trunk Call — This is a long distance phone call.

Turf Accountant — This is what bookmakers or bookies are called.

Underdone — This is the equivalent to "rare" in American restaurants.

Utility — This refers to something that is simple and cheap. The American equivalent is "generic."

V.A.T. — This is the value added tax, which functions like a sales tax. It is often wise to ask whether it is included.

Verge — This word is used to denote the strip of grass on the edge of a road. Americans would call it a shoulder and expect it to be paved.

Waistcoat — This means "vest" in America.

Washing Up — This ritual chore in Ireland is what Americans used to call "doing the dishes."

Watermelon — This is a derisive term for an Irish person who is "green on the outside and pink on the inside," meaning that he or she is really British on the inside. Pink is the color used to depict British areas on the map, usually.

W.C. — This is an abbreviation for water closet. It really means toilet. It is now used internationally.

Week — When this word is put after a day, as in "Monday week" or "Tuesday week," it means next Monday or next Tuesday.

Well Done — This is what is said to congratulate any striking accomplishment, such as a feat in sports or a good speech.

Wellingtons or *Wellies* — This refers to a high, waterproof boot, similar to galoshes.

West Briton — This is an Irish person who is disparaged for being too British in either lifestyle or attitudes.

Whiskey — Note that the Irish spelling has an "e" and the Scottish and American spelling does not. The Irish claim it was an old Gaelic word originally.

Work to Rule — Unions apply this to slow up and disrupt activity by rigidly adhering to rules and regulations.

Zed — This is what "Z" is called in Ireland.

CHAPTER FOUR

Geography, Economics and Society

GEOGRAPHY

Dublin's Importance

A consideration of Ireland's geography ought to begin with Dublin because it is so large, unique, special and so important to Ireland. In fact, it can be said that the whole country can be divided into two parts: Dublin and the rest of it.

Dublin is Ireland's only population center of a million inhabitants. Cork is the next largest city in the Republic, with fewer than 150,000. By taking in a generous sweep of suburbs and commuter habitations, it can be said that Dublin is the home of one out of three Irish people. The largest metropolitan area of the United States, including the New York City area, eastern New Jersey, southwestern Connecticut and western Long Island, contains fewer than one out of every fourteen Americans. An American metropolitan area containing a third of the nation's population would have over 80 million people. But Ireland is a small country, and the metropolis of Dublin actually has a smaller population than greater metropolitan Phoenix, Denver, Cincinnati or Kansas City.

Even though Dublin may be a medium-sized city by American standards, in Ireland it functions as the dominant city. Its importance to Ireland is comparable to all the urban areas from Boston to Washington plus San Francisco and Los Angeles in the United States. Dublin is at once Ireland's capital, center for trade, center for the arts, center for manufacturing of all kinds, as well as its center for finance, publishing and communications. It is indisputably Ireland's London or Ireland's Paris.

The city has been a magnet for country folk over the centuries. Dubliners call them "culchies," roughly the equivalent of "hick" and non-Dubliners have called the Irish of the capital "jackeens." Jackeens are supposed to be shrewder, smoother, harder and more crafty than the rest of Irish people. Countryfolk tend to be on their guard when they are in Dublin, wary of the inhabitants' trickiness and greed. This tension between country and city is age old, naturally. There has to be a vast difference between say, a sophisticated, urbane, well educated Dubliner and an unaffected, poorly educated and relatively uncomplicated individual from a village in Kerry or County Galway.

Dublin's particular way of life, rich in speech and redolent of the odors of pubs, has inspired a legion of writers and musicians over the centuries. "Dear, dirty Dublin" is how the city has been hailed, and "a great beauty in a dirty shawl" is how it has been described. Despite its poverty, filth, noise, and stretches of urban blight, Dublin remains a creative environment that is filled with shouting, laughing, gesticulating people, an environment teeming with exciting life.

The Interplay of History and Architecture in Dublin

One of the supreme ironies of Irish history is that Ireland's capital has long been regarded as the least Irish part of Ireland. Like many other coastal cities, it was founded by Scandinavian Vikings in the early Middle Ages. When the Normans occupied large portions of the island, Dublin became an important Norman stronghold. Very little is left of medieval Dublin, except for parts of the cathedrals and a few parts of Dublin Castle. Nothing was left above ground of the very earliest habitation, the Viking settlement, and the remains below ground had to be excavated at great speed by archaeologists before their location was entombed by the concrete of modern government buildings set down upon the site. This oldest part of Dublin was Wood Quay, near the cathedrals, where buildings looking like giant cliff faced blockhouses are now located.

During the several centuries that it took for the Normans to become the English, Dublin was the center of alien rule. The Viceroy presided from Dublin Castle and an English controlled Irish Parliament met in the city. By the 18th century, Dublin had become the second city in the British Empire after London. Its status and importance was celebrated by the erection of vast expanses of Georgian architecture. Georgian takes its name from British kings of the 18th century who had George as their first name. The great public buildings of the era are replete with symbols of British imperialism, such as crowns, lions and unicorns. The Custom House, Four Courts Building and the Bank of Ireland building across from Trinity College as well as many major buildings in Trinity College itself are the best examples. But most of the Georgian heritage is from the private residences of the wealthy and powerful Protestant elite who ruled the countryside and had town houses in Dublin. South of the River Liffey, especially along Merrion Square and Fitzwilliam Street, they are still resplendent. North of the Liffey, too many Georgian buildings have suffered the ravages of the wrecker's ball. If anything gives Dublin its distinctive style and appearance, it is its Georgian architecture, especially the streets of graceful four-story brick buildings with elaborate doorways containing solid, brightly colored doors.

In 1800 Dublin's importance was lessened when the Act of Union attempted to make Ireland into another part of the United Kingdom similar to Wales or Scotland. Ireland's Parliament, which had become increasingly independent in the 18th century, was shut down, and many important government functions were taken over by London. Consequently Dublin was less important in the 19th century, and many parts of the city, including many of its Georgian streets, fell into decay. New streets of cheap Victorian brick were hastily built around the old center of the city. So much of this brick from the era of Dickens remains today that British filmmakers often move their operations to Dublin when Victorian scenes are shot. By the turn of the 20th century, James Joyce and countless other writers had a somewhat seedy but wonderfully charming city to inspire them. Shortly thereafter, the Rising of 1916 and the civil wars wrought destruction to the center of Dublin, literally devastating O'Connell Street, the main thoroughfare. Some of it was restored.

After World War II, a surge of affluence brought demolition, rising speculation in property and the erection of what have been condemned as architectural monstrosities. Architecture has been a controversial subject for a long time and in many countries. It should be noted that many structures celebrated as achievements today, such as the Eiffel Tower, were once derided as atrocious. Yet even after taking this into consideration, it seems difficult to see how Dublin has been enhanced by a number of huge concrete and glass structures which have been deposited here and there in the city. For an example, consider Dublin's only "skyscraper," the sixteen story Liberty Hall along the Liffey, all too close to the gorgeous 18th century Custom House. It is capped by a rather silly crinkly roof. Close by is the Busaras, a sprawling glass and concrete terminal, once hailed for its progressive design. What are perhaps the worst modern additions have already been mentioned, the massive grey government buildings on the south bank of the Liffey on top of what was Viking Dublin.

Location as well as design work against appreciation

of some of Dublin's newer buildings. Many of the big modern buildings sit on Dublin's streets incongruously. Some of these buildings may have looked more pleasing in a suitable setting, with space around them, or in a district built exclusively or primarily in modern style, as can be found in many American cities. But in Dublin they often spring up with startling glass and concrete angles right in the middle of a street that has graceful classical lines and proportions from earlier centuries. All by themselves, modern buildings stick out here and there like sore thumbs.

Dublin's Districts

One pattern of Dublin's development has remained constant. Dublin has built outwards from the Liffey, north and south. The Liffey bisects the city, flowing from west to east, opening into a sheltered, busy harbor and, beyond, a scenic bay. Over the centuries Dublin has grown as an expanding circle of habitation, stretching north and south along the bay, and moving away from the river. A general rule of thumb is the closer to the river, the older the habitation.

Dublin has had two periods of rapid expansion and building. One was during the 18th century, when the population increased fourfold. By 1800 Dublin's population was 200,000, making it one of the chief cities in Europe. But it did not grow rapidly during the 19th century, when other important European cities multiplied their populations. Ireland's famine and emigration and Dublin's reduced status as a provincial city all contributed to this situation. By 1900, Dublin had only 300,000 inhabitants, making it smaller than Belfast. The second period of rapid expansion did not occur until late in this century, when a flood of people leaving agriculture, lower emigration rates and higher birth rates all caused the city to push outwards at a rapid pace and add thousands of acres of built up suburbs.

The old boundaries of Dublin were clearly marked by the curve of what were two important waterways in the past, the Grand Canal in the south, and the Royal Canal in the north. Today two major motorways encircle the oldest core of Dublin, each paralleling the old canals. They are the North Circular Road and the South Circular Road, although the latter takes different names as it proceeds, which can be confusing for non-Dubliners. Growth toward the south made the River Dodder a boundary for a time, but today urban development has gone beyond it and continues to edge toward the Wicklow Mountains.

The Liffey remains as an important divider of social geography. More of the nicer, safer, more expensive, more fashionable and richer districts are to the south of the river, and more of the poorer and more dangerous parts are to the north. For example, the Ballymun area is on the northern fringes and contains some housing projects associated with high crime rates. Several poorer districts with high crime rates also exist south of the river, especially Dolphin's Barn and the Liberties, but the south is generally associated with affluent, peaceful suburbs, such as Sandymount, Churchtown, Rathfarnham, Ballsbridge and Rathmines.

Shopping districts reflect the generalizations about Dublin north and south of the river. The south is upscale along Grafton, Dawson and Nassau Streets, more downscale along O'Connell, Mary and Henry Street north of the Liffey. The most prestigious area for establishing the headquarters of an agency or a company is in the district circumscribed by Trinity College, St. Stephen's Green, and Merrion Square. This area is the most prosperous and important part of the central city today.

Ireland's Physical Geography

Ireland is a small island of only 32,595 square miles, of which 27,136 are in the Republic and 5,459 are in Northern Ireland. South Carolina and Maine are each within 2,000 square miles of being the same size. Indiana is 3,500 square miles larger than Ireland. California is about five times larger and New York State is one and a half times larger. Ireland's greatest length is 302 miles and its greatest width is only 171 miles.

The surrounding ocean is a dominant physical feature conditioning life in Ireland because it determines the climate and provides beautiful scenery along a coastline so irregular that it actually comprises several thousand miles. No location in Ireland is more than 70 miles from the sea, and no location is free from abundant, frequent, oceanborne rainfall from the prevailing southwesterly winds. Warm ocean currents drawn out of the Gulf Stream, waters that drift up towards western Europe from the equator, grant Ireland a mild climate. Without this flow, the island might be as cold as Labrador, the region which is at the same latitude as Ireland on the other side of the Atlantic. Despite Ireland's location in the north Atlantic, its maritime climate is so mild that some varieties of sub-tropical vegetation can grow along the western shore.

The ocean flow warms Ireland in the winter, cools the island in the summer and keeps it moist all through the year. Irish people who complain that they cannot tell the summers from the winters cite the coolness of recent summers and the mildness of recent winters. Nevertheless, in a typical year the variations from season to season are not very pronounced, certainly when compared to the wide swings of inland, continental areas, such as the American Midwest or the Russian plain. Typically, the average temperatures of the coldest months, January and February, range between 39° and 45° (Fahrenheit). July and August are the two warmest months, with averages ranging between 57° and 66° (Fahrenheit). A temperature of 77° indicates a heat wave in Ireland, and any snow in winter is rare. Overall, the summers are cool and wet and the winters are chilly and wet.

Ireland's lush greenness is a gift from the Atlantic moisture. Heavy rainfall levels have created excellent pasture, or, as one wry observer put it, Ireland has a first class climate for plants and animals and something less than that for people. For up to 300 days per year Ireland is overcast or receives rainfall. Most of the time that it is not raining it looks as if it could or will rain. On what the Irish call "soft" days, a foggy mist fills the air, yielding gentle moisture like dew that is hard to distinguish from rain. Ireland remains bright green all through the winter, a time when the landscape is striking to those arriving by air from frozen North America. Greenness all through the year contributes to the diminution of the differences between seasons.

There is an important difference between the physical geography of eastern Ireland and western Ireland. Rainfalls in the west are twice as intense as they are in the east, averaging 60 inches per year, while the very driest portion of the east coast area has only 30 inches. It is too wet for wheat in the west but not in the east. While the west may have more lonely and dramatic scenery as a result of its barren, rocky conditions, farming is obviously at a disadvantage. Farms in the east, a region which looks more domesticated, are larger and richer, based on better soils for plowing or pasture. Farms in the west tend to be much smaller and much poorer. In the west, a typical farmstead might have around 30 acres marked out by walls of rocks taken from the fields.

The very significant division between eastern and western Ireland can be demarcated roughly by the long north to south flow of the Shannon River. The Shannon and other Irish rivers have a tendency to meander about because the higher land in Ireland is mostly along the rim of the island. Coastal land does not slope to the sea in many places, so rivers have contributed to the creation of marshy areas on the central plain. Over the passage of thousands of years, an organic material called peat or turf has formed from rich ancient vegetation. The peat rests in bogs consisting of a few acres to a few square miles. It was hacked out in the old days by hand and now, increasingly, by machine. It is left to dry in heaps, sometimes along the roadsides. Dried peat is sold and burnt all over Ireland and serves as a kind of low grade coal. It is even used to produce steam in some electric power stations. Nearly all of Ireland's peat comes from the wide, marshy plain that covers most of the center of the island. This part of Ireland is comparatively dull in terms of both history and scenery.

Most of Ireland's mountains loom on the edges of the island, often close to the sea, which enhances their

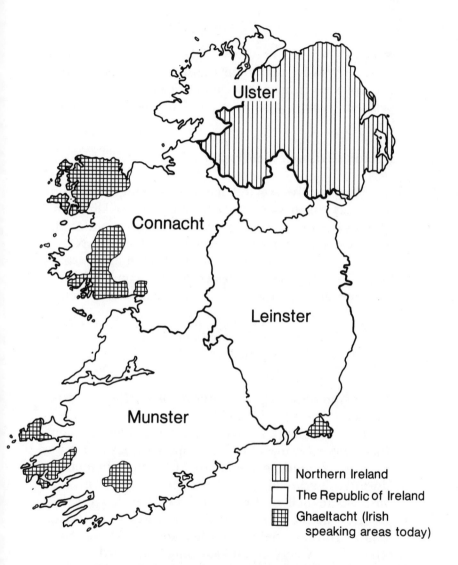

Ulster

Connacht

Leinster

Munster

||||| Northern Ireland

☐ The Republic of Ireland

⊞ Ghaeltacht (Irish
speaking areas today)

**The Historic Provinces of Ireland
and the Partition of the Island**

beauty. They are not very high, but they look much more impressive than their statistics imply because they rise upwards from a base close to sea level. The highest peak in Ireland is in Kerry, and measures only 3,414 feet.

Ireland's Historic Geography

Historically, Ireland has been divided into four provinces which were at some time former kingdoms. Besides acting as entities for some sports clubs, the provinces have no administrative significance. Nevertheless, they remain realities in the Irish mind. Perhaps the terms "Midwest" or "Deep South" conjure similar responses in Americans. An old jingle describes them:

> Ulster for a soldier
> Connacht for a thief,
> Munster for learning,
> Leinster for beef.

A variation declares that Ulster is for war; Munster for art; Leinster for wealth and Connacht for learning. Naturally, these jingles have some truth behind them. Rocky, poor Connacht did have monasteries and it was the place to send people banished for punishment. An old English admonition to Irish people faced with exile was "Go to hell or Connacht." Leinster has the best pasture, the most beef and the most wealth in Ireland today. Munster contains Cashel and Cork and many other places where art and learning flourished.

Ulster is a special case. It certainly remains beset with soldiers and civil war today, and historically Ulster is known for dogged resistance to invaders. The province is something of a geographical entity, since it is surrounded by sea on three sides and on the fourth side by groups of humped back hills called drumlins. People living in Northern Ireland tend to use the terms Ulster and Northern Ireland interchangeably, but this is not geographically accurate, because three of Ulster's nine provinces are in the Republic of Ireland, where Northern Ireland is frequently referred to as the "Six Provinces."

In the 19th and early 20th centuries Ulster was much more industrialized than the rest of Ireland, but in recent decades industrialization in the eastern part of the Republic has developed so considerably that the real economic division in contemporary Ireland is between east and west rather than north and south.

In the west of Ireland counties are much larger than elsewhere, just as states in the American West are larger. Weather conditions are just the opposite, however. Ireland's west is noted for exceptional wetness and the American West for exceptional dryness, although this does not apply to the American Northwest. The location of several western counties are worth noting because they are distinct and significant for tourism and Irish emigration to America. They comprise a tier, running north to south on the western and southern coast of Ireland: Donegal, Sligo, Mayo, Galway, Clare, Limerick, Kerry and Cork. Except for Clare, Kerry and Mayo, they are named for the county's major city. It is in these counties that more of old Irish traditions, language and culture have survived than anywhere else. The *Ghaeltacht* is etched along the west coast.

Geography has been a key element for much of Irish history and the source of important dilemmas. On

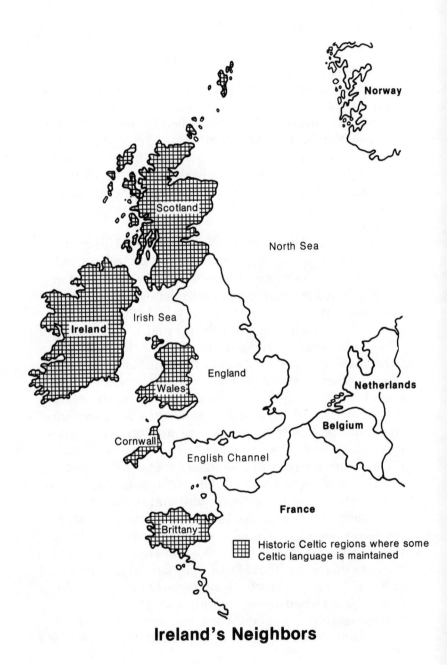

Norway

North Sea

Scotland

Irish Sea

Ireland

Wales

England

Netherlands

Belgium

Cornwall

English Channel

France

Brittany

Historic Celtic regions where some
Celtic language is maintained

Ireland's Neighbors

a European map, the island looks very close to the island of Britain and very far from other countries. Britain appears to shield or hide Ireland from Continental Europe. To this day, most Irish goods get to Continental Europe by going through Britain first. Ireland has been too close to Britain to be independent, either politically or culturally, for much of its history. Yet the salt water all around Ireland has served as enough of a barrier to help keep the island from full political or cultural integration with Britain. To put it succinctly: the island has not been near enough to become another Wales nor far enough to remain an entirely separate entity.

The physical separation between Britain and Ireland varies from 60 to 120 miles across the Irish sea, but at the narrowest point in the north, across the North Channel of the Irish Sea, the distance shrinks to within a dozen miles. Northern Ireland gradually shades into Scotland across a sprinkling of islands. People have moved back and forth over these islands for thousands of years. For people in this part of Ireland, Glasgow in Scotland seems closer than Dublin. Ironically, the very northernmost point on the island, the peninsula of Malin Head, is in the Republic or Ireland rather than in the political entity of Northern Ireland.

ECONOMICS

The Nature of the Irish Economy

A common contemporary assumption is that in modern society economics is now at the forefront of intellectual concerns the way theology and history used to be. This generalization may be less true in Ireland than elsewhere, but it still must be admitted that most people in Ireland seem to have more daily concerns about Ireland's economy than anything else. Therefore comprehension of the main facts about Ireland's economy is a very worthwhile endeavor.

First of all, what kind of economy does Ireland have? For centuries, Ireland's economy was dominated by agriculture, producing exports of beef, horses, pigs and grain. Ireland still has an important agricultural sector, but manufactured exports now exceed agricultural exports in value. This shift can be seen clearly in employment figures. In 1949, agriculture employed 43% of the workforce, which dropped to 17% by 1983. Meanwhile, industry employed 21% in 1949 and 29% by 1983. Ireland's important industrial base ensues in large measure from the operations of foreign firms that have been aided in one way or another by the Irish government. Even so, the largest number of jobs are in the service sector, indicating that at least an important part of the Irish economy can be called post-industrial.

While most of the Irish economy is capitalistic, an important public sector contains the health and welfare services as well as a number of public or state corporations. So the best answer to the question of what kind of economy Ireland has is that it is a mixed economy of both capitalistic and socialistic components, with substantially developed service, manufacturing and agricultural sectors.

Ireland's Natural Resources

Besides a lush green countryside, Ireland is not rich in natural resources. Small amounts of gold have been produced since ancient times, but there have been no discoveries of the black gold of the 20th century, oil, despite extensive and costly searches for it. Some natural gas has been found, and some modest amounts of basic minerals are mined. Because of the heavy use of wood for fuel over the centuries, and also because of extensive farming, very little of Ireland is forested today, just over 5%, which is the lowest percentage in Europe, but it is up from the 1% of 1920. Ironically, trees grow faster in Ireland than anywhere else in Europe, even Scandinavia, so there is hope that Irish forests can be expanded rapidly to satisfy more of the nation's needs for wood products. Another hope is that the fishing grounds west of Ireland can be developed extensively. They have been called the last fertile grounds left in Europe.

Bereft of rich natural resources, Ireland has had to rely upon agricultural and manufacturing exports to pay for needed imports of fuel, raw materials and some finished goods. A favorable balance of trade, that is, more value in exports than in imports, is critical for Irish prosperity, much more so than for the less vulnerable economy of the United States. It has not been an easy economic arrangement for the Irish to operate. Ireland's traditional exports have been beef, cattle, horses, butter, tweed, glassware, whiskey and beer. Newer exports are in the form of high tech industrial goods, nurtured by foreign firms in Ireland. Britain remains Ireland's main trading partner, receiving the largest amount of exports from Ireland and sending the largest amount of imports to Ireland. Britain's share in the Irish economy is decreasing. The rest of the European Economic Community is second and the United States is third.

Ireland's vulnerable economy depends upon utilizing the skills of Irish people effectively. Trained, educated people can be cited as Ireland's most precious resource of today and of the future. Keeping them from emigrating out of Ireland is one of the most important and difficult challenges that Ireland's government has to face.

The Agricultural Base

Ireland's agriculture is still a vital part of the economy, even if it is not the dominant sector it used to be. According to recent figures, it generates 11% of Ireland's gross national product, employs 17% of the workforce directly and generates many jobs in other sectors, such as the food processing industry. About half of Ireland's agricultural production is exported, which comprises a quarter of all Irish exports. The great advantage of agricultural exports is that they use Irish raw materials. Various kinds of manufactured goods for export are likely to have a component of previously imported materials in them.

Livestock products, particularly beef, butter and horses, are the major agricultural exports. Surprisingly, close to two million more cattle are on the island than people. Barley, wheat and sugar beets are grown, but potatoes are only a very minor crop now.

Expectations are high that closer integration in the European Economic Community will bring added benefits to Irish farmers and allay the widespread discontent with the condition of Irish agriculture. Farmers complain about low land prices and the need to go into debt. Urban dwellers, the overwhelming majority of Ireland's population today, over 75% by one set of calculations about what is urban, complain that farmers defraud taxpayers by not paying their share of taxes.The inefficiency of Irish agriculture is also cited, sometimes by pointing to the clean Continental vegetables that have taken over so much of the Irish urban market, particularly in the new supermarkets.

Another lamentation over the decline in the relative importance of Irish agriculture is cultural, not unlike the grave concern over the loss of so many farms in America. An old and treasured vision of an independent Irish Republic depicted a numerous class of small landowners as the backbone of national prosperity and the guarantor of political stability. Small family farms were idealized by many politicians as forming the bedrock of a healthy Irish democracy.

Ireland's Human Resources: Population and Emigration

Emigration has long been described as the scourge of Ireland, draining away the young and strong and creating an Irish diaspora, or dispersal, all over the world. The strength of the flow as well as the ability of the Irish to reproduce overseas is attested to by population figures from several countries. Forty million, or roughly 16% of the American population, have some Irish ancestry. The same percentage can be found in New Zealand. In Canada, Irish-Canadians are second only to French-Canadians among ethnic minorities. Australia has the highest percentage of Irish descendants of any nation, 30%. Irishness has had a bearing on Australian life from the time Irish political prisoners arrived as convicts to recent decades when a series of

Irish-Australians have become Prime Ministers. Smaller numbers of Irish emigrants went to places as far away as Poland in Europe and Argentina and Chile in South America.

The defeats of Catholic forces by Protestant forces was the main cause of the earlier migrations. Young Irish of military age, called the "Wild Geese," flocked to the armies of Continental Catholic states. In the 19th century the great push outwards came from the ravages of famine on an overpopulated island. A truly massive and desperate migration resulted. In the 20th century, spurts of migration have taken place since independence because not enough jobs could be created in Ireland. In the late 1940s, Irish laborers arrived in Britain to help rebuild what was ravaged by the war. In the 1950s, a surge of generally unskilled workers departed, most of them going to Britain where large numbers were able to learn skilled, well-paying trades. Many of them were very grateful for these opportunities. The most recent migration, which many Irish regard as a perilous national hemorrhage, is partly a "brain drain" of well educated, energetic younger people, including professionals, who want to make more money and avoid heavy taxes. Aggressive newspaper and television advertising from abroad has targeted certain groups, such as Irish nurses, offering them good salaries in Arabian or American hospitals. Recently up to half of the newly qualified nurses have departed. Many doctors and engineers have been lured overseas also. Understandably, many more of these professionals promise to return to work in Ireland than actually do so.

The pattern of Irish population history has diverged from that of the rest of Europe. The 19th century

The River Liffey. (*Courtesy Irish Tourist Board*).

Kilkenny Castle. (*Courtesy Irish Tourist Board*).

St. Canice's Cathedral *(Courtesy Irish Tourist Board)*.

Rothe House, Kilkenny *(Courtesy of author)*.

Gallarus Oratory *(Courtesy Irish Tourist Board)*.

Gallarus Oratory *(Courtesy of author)*.

King John's Castle, Limerick *(Courtesy of author)*.

King John's Castle, Limerick *(Courtesy Irish Tourist Board)*.

Georgian Fitzwilliam Square *(Courtesy Irish Tourist Board)*.

Georgian Fitzwilliam Street *(Courtesy of author)*.

Clonmacnoise, Round Tower and Celtic Cross *(above)* and aerial view showing River Shannon. *(Courtesy Irish Tourist Board).*

St. Mary's Cathedral, Limerick *(Courtesy of author)*.

View of Dublin Bay *(Courtesy of author)*.

Cahir Castle *(Courtesy Irish Tourist Board).*

Entrance to Newgrange tomb *(Courtesy of author).*

saw a surge in the populations of European countries, such as England, which went from five million to 40 million. Ireland's population did rise steeply until the peak population of eight and a half million was reached in 1845, just before the devastating onslaught of the potato blight and consequent famine. Six years later, in 1851, the population was down to six and a half million because two million had died or fled the famine's ravages. Ireland's population continued to erode thereafter, during a time when the rest of Europe grew in numbers. This erosion continued to 1961, when Ireland reached a low point of 2,818,000 in the Republic and many references were made to the vanishing Irish.

Suddenly, in the 1960s, an Irish baby boom surged simultaneously with the European achievement of lowering population growth close to zero. Ireland's population had again gone in the opposite direction from the European pattern. New prosperity, economic boom and a growing Irish population all coincided. For the first time since the 1840s, Ireland's numbers had ceased to decline from a combination of emigration and low birth rates.

At present the whole island has roughly five million people, but that is the same number of inhabitants on it in 1800. The Republic itself had 3,440,000 citizens by 1981 and, according to recent estimates, the figure is now up to 3,624,000. So many babies were born in the 60s, 70s, and 80s that Ireland has a Third World demographic structure, meaning that a relatively small percentage of older people are around and there are teeming masses of youngsters. Close to half of the population is under 25 and almost a third under 15.

Tens of thousands of new jobs have to be generated

in Ireland each year just to keep up with the annual flood of young people into the job market. Many looking for jobs have degrees in engineering, science and technology which were earned at considerable expense to the state. It upsets Irish people to see well educated youngsters leave Ireland to take high-paying jobs in Britain or Australia. Critics charge that the Republic failed its young in the 1950s and is failing them again today. This helps to explain the almost desperate anxiety in Ireland to create new jobs to keep these young people at home. Meanwhile the population growth has leveled off once more, bringing back anxieties once again over whether the Irish population will begin to drop once more in the future.

Tens of thousands of Irish emigrate to the United States each year, legally and illegally. Newer and tighter emigration laws have made the Irish compete to get into the country on the basis of family ties and skills. Many, especially those semi-skilled or unskilled, become illegal immigrants and suffer the lack of job security, social security, and the risk of exploitation through receiving lower pay, in cash, of course. If they try to return to Ireland for a wedding or a funeral they may be apprehended and may not be able to return to their American jobs.

Despite all of these disadvantages, thousands of young Irish people conclude that it is better to be an illegal alien in America than to be on unemployment compensation, called the dole, in Ireland. Once in the United States, they fit in rather easily, disappearing in the remaining Irish American ethnic enclaves which offer them shelter. Some of these immigrants bring angry views about Irish politics, particularly in regard to the situation in the north, which sometimes helps to reinforce militancy of some Irish Americans. Estimates of the number of illegal immigrants from Ireland in America go as high as 200,000 and have prompted complaints recently that little is done about them in comparison to the crackdowns which befall illegal Hispanic immigrants.

Vulnerable Aspects of the Economy

From the depression of the 1930s until 1957, the Irish government practiced protectionism, meaning that tariff walls were kept up and efforts were made to produce Irish goods behind them which would substitute for foreign imports. The sluggishness of the economy did not lift after the worldwide depression ended, and the lack of prosperity resulted in the tide of emigration in the 1950s. A dramatic shift came during the premiership of Sean Lemass, who opened Ireland not only to foreign investment but to foreign companies which were given tax breaks and other incentives to set up operations in Ireland. More emphasis was put on exports for markets overseas and less emphasis was given to the domestic market. The hope was that Ireland would become a major exporter of high tech manufactured goods, functioning as a Silicon Valley in Europe.

Opening Ireland to foreign firms did create a turnabout which generated jobs and led to dazzling growth and prosperity by the 1960s. A number of non-polluting industries requiring high levels of skills, many of them American and many of them multi-national, established themselves with the encouragement and assistance of the Irish government. Huge tax remissions were important incentives. Moreover, special preferential treatment was given to firms willing to put up factories in less developed parts of Ireland. The electronics, pharmaceutical, light engineering and chemical industries expanded rapidly as a result.

New jobs and better incomes spread optimism across Ireland in the 1960s. Irish households had more babies, television sets, electric appliances, washing machines, and many other new consumer goods, many of them acquired by hire purchase, which is what buying on credit is called in Ireland. Optimism for Ireland's economic future peaked in 1973, when Ireland joined the European Economic Community, also called the Common Market. It meant that this small country had a market open to it greater than the huge internal market of the United States.

In recent decades negative effects from these developments have been felt. Part of this situation can be explained by the worldwide economic recession of the early 1970s, brought on in part by the "oil shock" of rising petroleum prices, which was felt severely in Ireland because the nation has to import its entire supply. Less than half of Ireland's overall energy needs are met by indigenous sources. Faced with recession, many companies pulled out of Ireland. Those which stayed repatriated most of whatever profits they made. To confuse matters, other companies from abroad came in and took over Irish companies, while some Irish companies put their capital into more lucrative foreign acquisitions.

Short of funds, the Irish government borrowed heavily instead of cutting back on expenditures or raising taxes. Nevertheless, those employed during the recession paid a high rate of taxes and the cruelest unofficial tax of all, steep inflation. Moreover, much of the money collected from taxes was allocated to paying interest on money borrowed previously, putting Ireland in an economic situation similar to that of most Third World countries.

The weaknesses of Ireland's economy are perpetual topics of animated interest. One sweeping conclusion sometimes heard is that Ireland is a kindly society but a disorganized one, so disorganized that output costs are excessively high, thus making Irish exports too expensive. Contributing to this disorganization are frequent strikes, difficulties firing the inefficient, and a lax work ethic that is reflected in sloppy service and careless overpricing. Another factor contributing to economic drag are high costs of transportation for exports, a legacy of Irish geography.

After enjoying a period of optimism, expansion and prosperity in the 60s, the economic problems of the 70s and 80s seemed all the worse. In absolute terms, there is no question that problems were severe. Unemployment in the 80s touched almost one out of five workers, and fairly recently it was still up near 18%, far above the average rate for the European Economic Community. It could have been as high as 30% if up to 100,000 citizens did not leave annually. Inflation struck simultaneously with unemployment, running as high as 21% at the worst.

Most recently, the beginnings of a turnaround have appeared. Emigration is down to 32,000 annually and an Irish style austerity program has been attempted by the government. Exports have crept up and a trade surplus has occurred recently. Despite these encouraging reports that the worst is for the time being over, the continuing vulnerability of Ireland's present day economy is a constant preoccupation.

Wealth and Poverty

Among the 160 or so nations in the world today, the Republic of Ireland is in the top fifth, in the category of rich nations. Within the European Economic Community, an organization composed of highly affluent nations, Ireland is close to the bottom. Within Ireland itself there are wide differences between the richest and the poorest citizens, which is a common characteristic of many modern capitalistic states. The exact figures are hotly disputed, but a tiny segment at the top owns more than half of the personal wealth in Ireland. One recent calculation by Irish sociologists proclaims that 1% of the population owns 33% of the personal wealth and the top 5% owns between 60% and 63% of it.

Even if these figures can be challenged convincingly, it is obvious that a relative few in the Republic have enormous wealth at their disposal, which is ironically the charge that had always been leveled at the Protestant ruling elite during the time of union with Britain. The liberal democratic ethos declares that governments should actively use the tools of taxation and expenditure to redistribute wealth from the wealthiest sector to the poorest sector. As it has worked out in Ireland and elsewhere, the rich have found ways to shelter their fortunes and the burdens of taxation have fallen more heavily on the group in the middle. Middle class resources rather than upper class resources have been more readily transferred to the poor. This has led to a middle class outcry in Ireland against "Scandinavian" levels of taxation, noting that rates go from 35% to 60% of income, and, on top of that, indirect taxes, such as sales taxes on retail goods, take another hefty bite.

Middle class professionals voice loud lamentations over this state of affairs. Indeed, middle class professionals and business executives take home approximately half the income of their American counterparts. Even senior executives may make only £40,000 per year, excluding the perks of an expense account and travel pay. By the time taxes, deductions for pensions, voluntary health insurance and social insurance are subtracted, the executive will take home less than half of this income. The cost of living in Ireland is not cheap, especially in Dublin, which ranks with London and New York in cost of living. For example, the cost of food in the stores seems to be close to double what it is in most of the United States.

The poor have more cause for complaints. Most of Ireland's poverty stems directly from the high level of unemployment. Some of it is very obvious, in the form of disheveled beggars in the parks, and some of it is hidden away behind the closed doors of houses that look substantial from the outside, but on the inside children may have cornflakes for the main meal of the day.

As in the United States, the number of poor people in Ireland is staggering, and their actual number is a matter of keen political debate. Those who emphasize the problem cite a million poor, give or take two hundred thousand or so on either side of the figure. Even those who think that this number is far too high tend to concede that at least one person in five in the Republic of Ireland is born into or falls into poverty. Some social critics have gone so far as to declare that there are two nations in Ireland, the nation of the rich and the nation of the poor.

Measuring poverty is difficult, and many disagreements occur about where to "draw the poverty line," that is, where to begin counting people as poor. Nevertheless, the bottom fifth of the population clearly receives a very small percentage of the gross national income, and the resulting poverty bears most heavily on the children. Two out of five Irish children are said to be in this category, according to recent studies. Of course, poverty can be measured by many more indicators than income: those in poverty are unlikely to have bank accounts, cars, telephones, central heating or vacations. Some may have to share toilets or may not have indoor toilets.

Without jobs, the poor depend upon social welfare. The number of people dependent upon the state in some way is possibly as much as two fifths of the population, and certainly over a third of it. Like other modern societies, Ireland does have a safety net for the less fortunate, meaning that none of Ireland's poor have to starve to death or go without housing and health care because comprehensive social security is provided.

The State Sector

Providing for the large number of poor people is only one aspect of state operations in the economy. As in other developed societies, a large state sector coexists

with the private sector. Theoretically, nationalized organizations accomplish tasks and provide services for
society that private enterprise does not regard as profitable. Many parts of the Irish economy are socialized, or
under state control, in the manner of the United States
Post Office, or in the form of entities capable of considerable independent activity, comparable to the United
States Federal Reserve Board. Certain critical industries
are also government operations, usually in the form of
public commercial enterprises. In some cases they were
established to take over failing ventures in the private
sector.

In Ireland the government operates the harbors,
telecommunications, gas supply (*Bord Gais*), television
networks (R.T.E. 1 and 2), electricity supply (Electricity
Supply Board), rail service, bus service, international
airline (*Aer Lingus*), and ferries to Britain (the B and I
Line) and France. The Irish National Petroleum Corporation deals in the crucial international oil market and
operates refineries, while peat is handled by the Peat
Development Board. An Irish Sugar Company handles
sugar and produces other foods as well as agricultural
machinery. Other government agencies exist to attract
investments, encourage tourism (*Bord Failte*) and sell
Irish exports. The state is also active in promoting re-
search, developing fisheries and in helping to handle
corporate finance. It is no wonder that the number of
people employed in the public sector has doubled from
the 60s to the present.

At the local level, local authorities manage public
housing, collect waste, and provide various amenities,
including swimming pools, theatres, libraries, museums,
parks, open spaces, art galleries and recreation centers.

National Health Services

The State Health Services provide socialized medicine, but the coverage is not nearly as comprehensive as it is in Britain or in other European Economic Community countries. Those who have low incomes are issued medical cards which enable them to receive free health care. Cardholders are entitled to doctor's services, hospital services, medicines, some dental services and some optical services without cost. Those who earn a modest income are entitled to a more limited number of services which includes free hospitalization in public hospitals. Those with good incomes can still have some public hospital services but they must pay the doctors' fees themselves. Ireland's wealthy tend to have their own health plans and their own physicians anyway. Ireland's wealthy take up the limited number of beds available in the few high quality, American-style private hospitals, such as the Blackrock Clinic or Mater Private Hospital. Doctors can choose to take private patients or public patients or a combination of both.

Complaints about the State Health Services have been numerous. Doctors and facilities are overworked, treatment techniques lag behind other nations' programs, patients are crowded in hospitals, and long delays have to be endured for elective surgery. One critic has summed up the whole situation by saying that it is a ramshackle system giving inadequate care. Yet the system does its best in a relatively poor country, functioning with strained resources to meet the needs of all citizens.

Since the State Health Services are not comprehensive, meaning that a financial means test must be taken before a medical card is issued by the government, some individuals deceptively claim to have less income than they really do. Also, rumors are widespread about politicians who help their constituents acquire cards to which they are not entitled.

While overworked medical resources may contribute toward the relatively unhealthy condition of the Irish population compared to the rest of Europe, social behavior also plays a major role. Widespread smoking, drinking, unhealthy diets, and a lack of exercise are major factors leading to such phenomena as the high rate of heart disease, which is the fourth worst in Europe behind Northern Ireland, Finland and Scotland.

RELIGION

The Strength of Roman Catholicism

Ireland's Roman Catholicism remains an overwhelmingly important phenomenon in Ireland during an age when secular orientations have come to prevail in other European societies. Catholicism has given the Republic the strength of cultural homogeneity by imparting a common outlook and a common set of values to almost all of its citizens. Nearly all families, friends and colleagues share the same beliefs or religious attitudes. Ireland is spared most of the domestic conflicts that flare in the United States stemming from the wide diversity of religious and nonreligious beliefs and groupings.

Statistics show that in 1981 93% of the population declared themselves to be Roman Catholic. The three main Protestant churches taken together, the Pres-

byterians, Methodists and members of the Church of
Ireland claim only 3.35% of the Republic's population.
The Jewish population is a miniscule .06% and only 1%
stated that they had no religion at all.

Irish Catholics are noted for practicing their religion more diligently than any other European group.
Over 90% attend church weekly, compared to just half
of the Protestants in the Republic. A quarter of the
Catholics go to church more than once per week; two
fifths have family prayer; and a high percentage go to
confession. The so-called "rites of passage," birth, marriage and death, are almost exclusively religious ceremonies. For example, there are only a few hundred civil
marriages in Ireland each year. In addition, First Holy
Communion and Confirmation are important and costly
family occasions.

The cloth of a priest still commands respect and
gives the wearer authority in Ireland. Concern and advice from priests and bishops in matters of family and
sexual morality are generally accepted as legitimate and
important. Many social occasions, especially in rural
areas, are simply not complete unless the priest attends.

The Catholic Church is deeply involved in social
services. Catholic hospitals staffed by nuns, orphanages,
and a number of charities that bolster the state welfare
services are all significant. Nuns take care of the aged
and alcoholic, responsibilities that secular workers
would take on in other countries. The Catholic Church
controls or strongly influences most of Ireland's schools.
Segregation by denomination takes place in both the
Republic and in Northern Ireland, and most people
seem to want to keep it that way. Some schools belong to
the Catholic Church, but even state schools usually have
priests as school managers and members of religious

orders on the staffs. The dedication and discipline at work in these schools is noteworthy and appreciated in most cases by the local inhabitants.

A religious hierarchy and various religious orders give structure to the Catholic Church. Ireland is divided into four ecclesiastical provinces, each presided over by an archbishop. The most important of them, the Archbishop of Armagh, who is usually a cardinal as well, has the title of Primate of All Ireland. Armagh is in Northern Ireland, by the way. The provinces are subdivided into dioceses presided over by bishops. Each diocese is itself subdivided into a number of parishes, each with one or more priests. Many of these territorial divisions date back to the 12th century. Numerous religious orders of priests, brothers, and nuns are based in various places throughout Ireland. Dublin alone has up to 60 different orders of nuns. Overseas, thousands of Irish missionaries in various orders work in over 80 countries. Moreover, many Catholics join lay religious organizations, which tend to be more conservative than the church hierarchy.

The strength of Catholicism was well illustrated by the visit of Pope John Paul II in 1979. On the morning of his arrival, over one million people attended Mass in Phoenix Park in Dublin. Before he left, over half of the entire population of the Republic had attended at least one of the ceremonies in person and almost all of the rest watched some of them on television.

Popular Manifestations of Faith

Many small social graces clearly indicate that Ireland is indeed a very Catholic country. "God bless" is heard as a greeting; people make the sign of the cross

when they pass a church or a graveyard or when they say
grace; the handicapped are called "God's special people"; and various objects are officially blessed, including
Aer Lingus planes. More tangible indications of the
pervasiveness of Catholicism are found in homes and
shops in the form of religious imagery, jewelry and
writings. Priests and nuns can be seen almost everywhere. National radio and television stations call the
nation to prayer morning, noon and night, leading one
wit to remark that this prayer, the Angelus, is the only
event in the country that adheres to a reliable schedule.
In addition, some stations conclude the broadcasting
day with a priest's homily.

Many undertake what are sometimes difficult and
painful pilgrimages to famous religious sites in Ireland.
Plans are underway to make Knock an important international shrine, or, as it has been called, the Irish
Lourdes. Many persons believe that miracles do happen
on pilgrimages. Even without miracles, these religious
exercises are thought to be good for the soul, an ascetic
experience that will help to purge contaminations of the
modern world. When miracles are reported, the Catholic Church responds with extreme caution. Reports of
such phenomena as rural girls in a state of ecstacy,
seeing and speaking to the Virgin Mary, or some parishioners seeing a statue move, talk or bleed in a church are
greeted with skepticism and the announcement that the
matter is "under investigation" is likely to follow. Television news covers popular excitement at the scenes where
miracles are supposed to have taken place, sometimes
showing people in states of ecstacy or gatherings of
people awaiting the repetition of a miraculous event.

Changes and Challenges in the Catholic Church

How did the Republic become so overwhelmingly and actively Catholic, to the extent that Ireland has been called "more Catholic than the Pope"? The Roman Catholic Church in Ireland has a very special history that is inextricably intertwined with the history of Irish nationalism. For a long period, one way of expressing resistance to the conquest by Protestant England was to remain a staunch Catholic. Catholic resistance of this sort goes back to the 16th century during the reigns of Henry VIII and Elizabeth I and continued until this century. Many of those who embraced ardent Catholicism to resist English culture and power also affirmed many of the ancient Irish cultural traditions.

Resistance to England only partly explains the enduring strength of Irish Catholicism. During the time that a Protestant elite ruled, the whole Catholic Church, priests, nuns and especially anyone above their rank, was persecuted. This underprivileged and oppressed Catholic Church had to struggle and improvise, and in doing so the sympathy and empathy of the underprivileged Irish masses was enlisted permanently. A reservoir of loyal support was built up for the Catholic Church as clergy regularly stood up for the rights of the poor peasants and shared their suffering.

Oppression helped to make the Catholic clergy tough and disciplined. By the 19th century, priests who graduated from the main seminary at Maynooth were noted for their strict and conservative community leadership. They attacked local vices but refrained from excesses of nationalistic ardor. The clergy gave a severe, almost puritanical stamp to Irish Catholicism that differentiated it from the more lax and genial Mediterranean varieties. As an indication of their severity, over 10,000 books were banned over the years, mainly because of explicitly sexual passages.

Some of the historic nature of the Catholic Church has been altered in recent decades to the extent that some old stereotypes are no longer creditable. Some of the change stems from the liberalizing teachings of Vatican II, and some change reflects the different nature of modern Irish society, as more and more Irish people live in an urban, industrial environment rather than in a rural, agrarian setting. Another factor has been the return of many Irish people from abroad, including priests and nuns, who have lived in much more secular and skeptical societies.

For some urban Irish people, religious preoccupations and practices have lost some significance in recent decades. Although attendance at Mass remains the highest in Europe, there is a small but steady and perceptible decline, particularly among younger people. Some claim that religious practice is stronger in Ireland than religious belief, which is just the reverse of the condition encountered in many European countries. Going to mass is more of a social convention for some people, who are likely to seek out the shortest Mass and who have been known to grumble audibly when priests take what they regard as too much time. More demonstrable than the small decline in attendance at Mass has been the decline in the number of people willing to dedicate their lives as priests or nuns. This phenomenon is worldwide, of course, but it is particularly disturbing in Ireland because the country has long been known as a prime recruiting ground for the Catholic Church.

The situation is compounded by sharply differing attitudes among churchmen. Most of the hierarchy has tended to be conservative, loyal to the papacy, and "brick and mortar" oriented, meaning that they put top priority on erecting buildings. The hierarchy has not been inclined to incorporate the laity or women into directing the affairs of the Catholic Church. In short, much of the hierarchy has followed an old, authoritarian tradition. More radical views have now been interjected by priests and nuns who have served overseas in the Third World. For many of them, no matter how conservative they may have been when they left Ireland, they returned outraged at social injustice in the Third World and eager to change the structure of society in those places. Their anger at Third World dependency, particularly in Latin America, has made them to a degree anti-American. An example of this occurred when former President Reagan visited Ireland in 1984 and radical priests and nuns stirred up controversy on behalf of Latin American causes. They also show up on Irish television to make such comments as: "The Church has been too preoccupied with the sins of the bedroom rather than the sins of the boardroom," of "If I feed the poor I am looked on as a saint; if I ask why they are poor, I am looked on as a communist."

Separation of Church and State, the Vanishing Protestants and Ecumenicism

No matter how vital, diverse, preponderant and all pervading Catholicism may be in the Republic of Ireland, separation of church and state is officially proclaimed in the constitution. What is more, the constitution prohibits clergymen from sitting in the legislature. It proclaims freedom of conscience in religion and the free profession and practice of religion subject only to rules of public order and morality.

Has the extremely small Protestant minority in the Republic been able to enjoy these rights peacefully? Yes, indeed. The Protestants in the south are generally people who have high standards of living, often through inheritance of the fortunes created during the time of British rule when Protestants ran the island. Unlike Northern Ireland, a large working class Protestant group does not exist in the Republic. Therefore the nation is free from the struggles of working class Protestants against working class Catholics over jobs and housing that have caused such grief in the North.

The number of Protestants in the south has been dwindling, down from 19% to just over 3%. Many emigrated to Britain in the 1920s and another contingent left in the 1950s. With such small numbers remaining, the pool of Protestant marriage partners is so limited that many young Protestants have married Catholics. The strictures of the Catholic Church concerning the raising of offspring from mixed marriages as Catholics is always cited as a major cause for the Protestants' swift numerical decline.

Discrimination has not been a factor in the Republic. The state has always emphasized that religious discrimination would not be tolerated, and has backed up this stance with constitutional provisions. Appointments to the Senate were to assure Protestant representation in that body, and a complicated system of proportional representation served to safeguard minority rights in the elections to the lower house. Protestants in the Republic have continued to prosper without hindrance. In fact, two of them have been elected President of the Republic, an office that is largely ceremonial, since the *Taoiseach,* or Prime Minister, wields executive powers. Nevertheless, Presidents of Ireland do have prestige and influence.

It can be argued that Protestants have advantages in the Republic similar to affirmative action in the United States today. Government and businesses are often proud to have them as employees. Good treatment of Protestants in the Republic sends a message to the million Protestants in the north that the Catholic majority in the Republic plays fair, and that they too may do well as a minority in an Ireland of the future possessing 32 counties, north and south combined, in some sort of constitutional union.

Beyond political considerations, Catholics in the Republic seem genuinely tolerant and benign towards non-Catholics. For example, Ireland's tiny Jewish population has recently produced two Lord Mayors of Dublin and several Jews have been elected to the lower house. Perhaps Ireland's Catholics, so secure in their overwhelming majority, simply regard not believing in their faith as a personal misfortune to be treated with kindness and sympathy! Ecumenicism seems to go hand in hand with these tolerant attitudes. Some time ago, bishops advised Catholic parents not to send their children to Trinity College, which was regarded as a Protestant educational bastion. Today, Trinity College has several Catholic faculty members. Meanwhile, at the major Catholic seminary in Maynooth, lay students and female students attend along with seminarians, and one faculty member is a Protestant woman. Large numbers of nuns will attend special services at Protestant Cathedrals. Some Protestant Cathedral parishioners have the option of attending services in the Irish language and some parishoners devote time to studying the language.

Although it owns churches and property all over the Republic, the numbers attending the Church of Ireland are down to fewer than 100,000. In Northern Ireland there are almost three times as many members of the Church of Ireland than in the Republic. The Presbyterians are even more concentrated in Northern Ireland than the Anglicans. Over 95% of the island's 350,000 Presbyterians live there, half within fifteen miles of the center of Belfast. Methodists and several other Protestant denominations are also concentrated in Northern Ireland and have only a sprinkling of adherents in the Republic.

EDUCATION

Ireland has a system of "National" schools for primary education, which is also called the "First Level System." Most Irish children go to school at four, and must go at six. Two years of kindergarten and six years of elementary school are the norm for most Irish youngsters. The government owns the buildings, has paid most of the costs of constructing them, pays most of the teachers' salaries and the costs of maintenance. Government inspectors monitor the schools, and if they fall short of expectations, funds can be withdrawn. The state also sets up the school curriculum.

Despite this state involvement, separation of church and state is hard to discern in Irish education at the local level. In fact, some claim that the state system is really a parochial system because the Catholic Church is so actively involved. The state does support local initiatives in education, such as the desire to build a new school building in a certain place. but local initiatives emanate from parents who are led by their priests. The Catholic Church is likely to contribute perhaps 10% to 15% of the building costs. Once operational, the school is governed by its own Management Authority, composed of priests, teachers and representatives of parents. These boards are said to be less threatening to teachers than the boards of parents elected in the United States. The clergymen are powerful figures on Irish boards, where they sit as "managers" of the schools, or what would be called principals in America. Their authority is reinforced by the fact that some or all the local teachers will likely be in religious orders. These arrangements lead to the widely held view that the Catholic Church runs most of the schools in the National System.

Where they have children in sufficient numbers, Protestants and Jews in the Republic have their own National schools, willingly paid for and maintained by the state. A few sophisticated Dublin neighborhoods have "multi-denominational" schools, which result from local petitioning efforts. Outside of middle-class Dublin, schools are segregated by denomination. The same holds true, of course, in Northern Ireland. Since so much religious strife has marked the history of the region, segregated education is particularly unfortunate because young people could learn so much from mingling. If they were exposed to various points of view in such subjects as history this would undoubtedly mitigate against community bigotry.

The secondary school system, paralleling the junior high school and high school arrangements in America, is called the "second level." Its teachers must have a university degree and a postgraduate diploma in education. The students are from twelve years and older, and school remains compulsory until age fifteen, when some drop out. There are three basic types of second level schools, called secondary, vocational and comprehensive community schools. The secondary schools draw in two-thirds of Ireland's teenagers, including most of those who are in the academic stream. There is a "junior cycle" of three years and a "senior cycle" of two years. Graduates gain a "Leaving Certificate," the basic qualification to go on to what is called "third level" education, what Americans call a college education or higher education. The term "college" is used differently in Ireland and may confuse Americans. Many secondary schools have "college" in their names. Almost all of the secondary schools are private and controlled by the Catholic Church. Nearly all of their funding comes from the state, except for some schools that are called "fee-paying," which receive tuition payments from parents as the famous British private secondary schools do.

The vocational schools provide technical education and are owned and run by the state. So are the comprehensive community schools, which try to educate all the students locally, those going on to third level as well as those committed to learning a trade. Nevertheless, relatively few who graduate from these state owned second level schools go on to higher education.

Overall, a small percentage of Irish students go on to third level or higher education. While two thirds of Irish adolescents graduate from the secondary level, only one out of four goes on to third level. This percentage is about average for western Europe, but higher than the 15% that go on in Britain and much lower than the 40% to 50% that go on in the United States.

Ireland has two huge state universities, the National University with university colleges in Dublin, Cork and Galway, and Dublin University, which has its core in Trinity College. There are also two complexes of the National Institute for Higher Education, one in Dublin and one in Limerick. They may become full-fledged universities in the future. They offer highly technical instruction in certain fields and degrees up to the doctorate level.

At the third level there are some marked differences from American higher education. A three-year program rather than a four-year program ordinarily leads to a bachelor's degree. Another difference is that professional schools operate at the undergraduate level. Entrance to them is determined by highly competitive examinations in six subjects required for the School Leaving Certificate. It is very difficult to gain admission to them, hence only the students with the very highest scores can become, for example, lawyers or doctors. Some students insist on taking their leaving certificate examinations over again to boost their scores.

The cost of education at all levels provides hot topics for debate in Ireland. Some parents deny the existence of free public education, citing pressure to make "voluntary contributions" to defray special costs and the necessity to pay for books, travel, uniforms and sports equipment. At the third level, only students whose grades are good and whose parents are of modest means can have their fees, or tuition, dropped and receive maintenance grants to support them while they study. Close to a third of the Republic's students at the third level qualify for these grants. Allegations of parents underreporting their incomes are rife. Farmers and the self-employed, in particular, are accused of hiding much of their income in order to have their children qualify for grants, which are ultimately paid for by taxpayers.

Other European countries do not have a means test to qualify for maintenance grants. All students get them, a practice based on the assumption that students will pay society back through their work and taxes after they graduate. In Ireland as in the United States, the idealistic goal of free higher education for all is far from being achieved. The same can be said for the goal of educating able children of all classes and backgrounds at the highest level of aspirations. Offspring of the professional and managerial classes are heavily overrepresented at Irish universities and working class youths are heavily underrepresented.

THE CHANGING IRISH FAMILY

The family has been of such extreme importance in Irish society that both the Catholic Church and the state have made vigorous efforts to guide and protect it. Nevertheless, the demands and pressures of dynamic modern urban life have had a powerful impact upon this basic institution even in Catholic Ireland.

The state's solicitous concern for the family was written directly into the Irish Constitution. At one time the Irish Constitution praised women for staying at home and raising children rather than working outside the home. Divorce is illegal in Ireland because the Constitution declares that the state cannot enact any law that provides for "the grant of a dissolution of marriage." In a recent complicated referendum about constitutional sanctions on divorce, a clear and large majority of voters rejected the idea of divorce, thus showing not only the strong influence of Ireland's bishops but also indicating that in matters of family life Ireland was not rapidly evolving towards a pluralist society. The fact that divorce is illegal only in Ireland and Malta in Europe says a great deal about the special regard for the family and the power of the Catholic Church.

There are legal separations, however, which make provision for child support, and the state does provide allowances for wives who are deserted. Nevertheless, separated individuals cannot remarry legally in Ireland, and if they do, offspring are illegitimate without rights of inheritance. Many Irish people have had to spend time and money obtaining foreign divorces and legal safeguards for new offspring.

Until very recently, birth control devices were banned in the Republic. Protests in favor of the sale of contraceptives by groups of women and by doctors were widely covered in the newspapers up until a short time ago. Ever since a new law on contraceptives was passed in 1985, they have been readily available at many outlets, but in most situations they are not on display and they have to be asked for, much in the same way that many Americans had to ask poker faced druggists for them in some states in the 1950s.

Unlike contemporary America, Ireland is not racked by debates over abortion. It is simply out of the question as an issue, given the strength of practicing Catholics. Curiously, abortion is also prohibited in Northern Ireland, where hardlining Protestants are adamantly against it. So Irish women who want abortions, whether they come from the north or the south, must travel to Britain, where abortions are readily available upon demand. Each year thousands of women who register for abortions in Britain give Irish addresses.

Like so much else in contemporary Ireland, the family is in transition. As it might be expected, in general the urban middle class families have changed the most and the rural families have changed the least, but the forces of change are at work all over the country, eroding old style family arrangements. Although many Irish families remind visiting Americans of life in the United States in the 1950s or before, the dynamics, pressures and problems of contemporary life are altering Irish families relentlessly.

The traditional Irish family has patterns of behavior that date far back into Irish history. Fathers were strong; households were likely to hold three generations; force was used to encourage children to be passive and silent. Clear division of male and female tasks was understood, and these roles were believed to be in accordance with the natural order of the universe. On farms, the husband did the heavy work and the wife dominated the household; in urban areas the husband went out to a job and the wife stayed at home and attended to the house and to raising the children. Since the famine, Irish people tended to marry late, the average age for men was 33 and for women 23, as late as the 1950s. Many people never married at all, including the large number of young people who took up religious vocations.

Today gender divisions remain strong and continue to permeate social relationships and the workplace. Many more women now have jobs, although the percentage is much lower than in other European Economic Community countries. Also, Irish women are less likely to return to work after having children than their British or American counterparts. Women still show up in disproportionately large numbers in traditional female jobs, such as clerical jobs, or lower ranking jobs in health and education. Women continue to work for lower pay in jobs with lower requirements for skill and few prospects for advancement. A few women have been celebrated for their success in climbing to the top of their chosen fields, but women remain as a tiny percentage of the persons in important positions of various kinds empowered to make significant decisions. On the other hand, full participation in the European Economic Community fosters improvements because Ireland must accept legislation providing for such benefits of modern life as mandatory equal pay for men and women and paid maternity leave.

Today there are signs everywhere that traditional family practices are fading. As people have been getting married at younger ages, greater variety has begun to exist in the relationships between husbands and wives. On one end of the scale, some treat each other as partners in all things. Many husbands, usually the better educated urban individuals, share some housework. Close to half of Irish households now consist of an American-style nuclear family of husband, wife and

children. A growing number of single parent households has emerged also. Therefore in many Irish families the feared old family patriarch has become a figure
of the past. The power of the grandfather over the
parents has declined in many families simultaneously
with the decline of the power of parents over children.
Some parents and children actually negotiate their roles
in a fluid setting.

Despite the emergence of new and varied patterns,
the family remains the bedrock of Irish society, something that is of paramount importance to nearly all of
the Republic's citizens, to its predominant Church, and
to the state and its Constitution. The sad irony about
modern Ireland is that families are being torn apart not
so much by modernization but by emigration. There are
simply not enough jobs being generated to go around to
all of the sons and daughters coming into the job market, and so they depart across salt water, usually to
Britain, following a pattern generations old.

IRELAND'S UNDERCLASS: THE
TRAVELING PEOPLE

Although they are less than one half of one percent
of the population, approximately 20,000 in the whole
island, Ireland's traveling people are painfully conspicuous as an underclass whose squalid living conditions
closely resemble poverty in the Third World. Unkempt
women and dirty children show up on the streets of
Dublin to beg, at a time when begging has become rare
elsewhere in Europe. Their scattered illegal campsites

along the roadways are ugly collections of vehicles and junk that can startle foreign motorists.

Traveling people is the name they prefer for themselves. They disparage other terms, such as "itinerant," because they are condescending, or those such as "knacker," an abusive term which refers to their old trade in horses, or 'tinker,' which refers to their old trade of mending pots and pans.

Traveling people are Ireland's gypsies, the descendants of those groups that migrated about the country in colorful horse and wagon caravans. Their exact origins remain unclear, but dispossession and eviction probably led them to take to the roads. Although their lifestyles have resembled those of gypsies, traveling people are nothing else but ethnic Irish who, for one reason or another, have lived in a sub-group that has resisted integration into ordinary Irish society up to the present day.

Various attempts have been made to change their lifestyle by getting them to settle down, educate their children, hold regular jobs and thereby merge into ordinary Irish society. High unemployment and ferocious neighborhood opposition to them have stymied these well meaning attempts. When a settlement site for them is proposed, neighborhood residents are likely to protest vehemently, frequently by marching and by putting pressure on the local council by various means in order to have the traveling people move on to somewhere else. What motivates ordinary Irish people to mobilize against the traveling people is a stereotype that depicts them as lazy, drunken, dirty and dishonest. "They will steal the foam off of your stout if you look the other way" is one typical saying. Consequently, some Irish

people who are generous to unfortunate but distant
Third World people turn out to be unwilling to help
these poor Irish in their midst. Others try to help everyone.

The government has made persistent efforts to in-
tervene and alter the traveling people's lifestyle. As a
result, half of the traveling people today live in one
place, an official site, and only move around for part of
the year. The other half moves from one illegal site to
another. They pick up odd jobs when they can, and
most deal in scrap. Fantastic stories about them abound.
Some of them are depicted as having become extraordinarily rich from loan sharking, and displaying their
wealth in the form of several expensive cars. Another
tale describes how the funerals of important leaders
reach a climax when the leader's vehicle is set on fire
with the corpse inside of it.

CRIME

While poverty is found in rural and urban Ireland,
crime is predominantly an urban phenomenon. Crime
rates in Ireland are on the rise alarmingly. In just over
two decades, 1961 to 1984, recorded crime has risen
600%, according to several authorities. Nevertheless,
Irish rates are still far behind those in America. Crime is
more prevalent in Dublin than anywhere else in
Ireland, naturally, but Dublin's rate is far lower than that
of major American cities. The difference is qualitative as
well as quantitative. Most crimes in Ireland are property
crimes, an overwhelming 96%. The majority of crimes
in America are property crimes also, but the percentage

is lower, 88%, meaning that many more crimes are against persons. American homicide rates simply horrify the Irish. Ireland has just over two dozen murders per year. The sexually motivated murder of one Dublin girl in 1988 was front-page news for days. Irish people are shocked and astounded by news of widespread assaults, rapes and muggings in America, and by the random mass shootings by deranged individuals and ghastly serial murders.

Since nearly everyone lives peacefully in the Republic without fear of violence directed against them, the spectacle of widespread violent crime in America is hard to comprehend. An indication of the sense of security Irish people enjoy is given by the number of females who hitchhike everywhere. Also, women walk alone in the country and in the city and do not have to glance about furtively and apprehensively as they usually do at night in so many places in the United States. Some muggings do take place in Ireland, of course, and some districts of Dublin have a statistically higher likelihood of such crimes than others. Hard drugs are on the streets, which has contributed to a rise in the rate of crime against persons, but Dublin still has a long way to go to reach American inner city rates.

Most crimes in Ireland are committed by young, unemployed working class males operating in urban areas. Much of it falls into the category of the "five finger discount," or the quick, clever theft. Housebreaking is another very prevalent form of stealing. So is breaking into cars. Ordinarily, criminals do not carry guns and try to make sure that people are gone before trespassing. Burglary is so common that alarm companies do a booming business. Unfortunately alarms go off all the time in Dublin, in almost all cases accidentally, and usually there is no rush to turn them off or even to investigate.

Bank robberies do occur with some frequency, leading banks to build fortress-like enclosures around the places holding cash. The author once came upon the scene of a bank robbery seconds after the thieves had made their getaway. Three desperados had charged in carrying one large rifle, which was apparently their only weapon. In the rush to leave, the large hat of one robber fell to the pavement. Moments later, a group of police surged into the bank, running right over the hat and pushing aside a number of American students standing in the entrance who had not only witnessed crime but who had taken down the license plate number of the getaway car. Many minutes later the police emerged to take down the vital information from the witnesses outside and to pick up the hat.

Ireland's typical Guardian of the Peace, or *Garda Síochána* in Irish (plural *Gardai*), is a friendly, likeable police person that goes out of his or her way to do such things as chat with lonely old ladies. Most of the police look like local fellows and girls dressed up in uniforms for a show or a pageant. Most just do not have the stern, suspecting demeanor so common among American police, and most of them saunter about unarmed. They are not without critics. Some claim that they are too tolerant of bending the law here and there, and that they are not good at crowd control. One of the most amusing programs on Irish television is the "Gardai Report," describing crimes, suspects and stolen property. The show displays recovered stolen property in the hope that the owners will come forth and make claims. The camera

pans across caches of television sets, VCRs, and fur-
niture. Once four dirty, mud splattered stolen tires were
featured!

SPORT

Ireland enjoys sports of all kinds. Racetracks for
horses and greyhounds and golf courses are found all
over the country, and rivers and streams attract droves
of foreign and local fishermen, while windsurfers and
sailors take advantage of Ireland's marvelous irregular
coastline. Team sports are exceptionally numerous because Ireland can draw upon both the English and Irish
traditions.

Irish people are said to suffer from hippomania,
the excessive love of horses. It cuts across all class lines,
from the richest Anglo-Irish breeder to a poor youth on
a scruffy pony. Horseraces mesmerize in Ireland, undoubtedly because betting is a national preoccupation of
epidemic proportions. Lush pasture makes Ireland the
Kentucky of Europe, the exporter of fine steeds to Arab
countries and to Britain. Half of the horses in Britain
today are said to be of Irish origin.

In international competitions, Ireland has produced athletes who excel in bicycling, running and box-
ing. But the Irish enthusiastically support any Irish
person who competes internationally, win or lose. A case
in point was the Irish showing in some swimming events
in the recent Olympic games. The announcer on Irish
television concentrated on the Irish entrant in one
qualifying race, almost screaming with rapture when he
broke the Irish record for that distance. Yet the swim-

mer finished behind several other contestants, and eventually the announcer had to acknowledge, after much exultation, "Good as it was, he failed to qualify for the final heat."

An old saying proclaims that soccer is a gentleman's game played by hooligans and rugby is a hooligan's game played by gentlemen. The Irish add that hurling is a hooligan's game played by hooligans. Hurling is one of the Gaelic, or old Irish games, said to be the fastest game played on dry land. It is somewhat similar to lacrosse, since it is played with a stick and ball, but it differs from that sport because the stick has no net and resembles a hockey stick. What is more, hands and feet can be used to supplement the action of the stick. How players keep from splitting each other's heads open regularly remains a mystery to the uninitiated. The pattern of play is similar to rugby or soccer. The object is to make goals at the end of the opponents' side of the field. Gaelic football is also similar, using a round ball that can be played with hands or feet. Gaelic games have been immensely popular, regularly filling Croke Park in Dublin with capacity crowds of 70,000 people.

Gaelic games have significant political connotations. Originally they were to be played as Irish substitutes for English games, which were deemed alien by militant nationalists. Members of the Gaelic Athletic Association were not supposed to play what were called "foreign" sports. For a time they were not even supposed to watch them. Today teams and championships are "all Ireland," meaning that all 32 counties are unified in participation in these sports, foreshadowing the dream of many militant nationalists for a united Ireland in the future.

Despite the popularity of Gaelic games, the Irish

continue to relish the sports brought over by the British. For Europeans in general, soccer, which is called 'football', is immensely popular. The equivalent to the World Series or the Super Bowl is international professional championship competition. Soccer therefore serves to link Ireland with Europe and Britain. Nimble cockneys play on Ireland's national team and Irish boys dream of playing on professional British teams. Many celebrated Irish players have seen those dreams come true. Some Irish players wear the uniforms of British professional teams and others have played for Italian, Spanish, Portuguese and Belgian teams.

Rugby, a game popular wherever the British Empire flourished, retains an amateur status in Ireland. It has an all Ireland organization, with each of the four historic provinces contributing players to a team that competes internationally. In the past, rugby was thought of as the favorite sport of well educated young Anglo-Irish gentlemen. Even today it is associated with middle class players. Cricket draws from a similar pool of sportsmen. In midsummer in suburban Dublin it is not uncommon to come upon cricket players enjoying the odd gyrations of that most British of all sports on the green grass of Ireland, an echo of the recent past.

CHAPTER FIVE

Politics

POLITICS IN THE REPUBLIC

Ireland's Symbols

Like all modern states, Ireland has symbols of nationalism that foster national enthusiasm, cohesion and loyalty. The Irish flag was first introduced in 1848 by the Young Ireland movement and recognized as the national flag when it flew over the rebel stronghold at the Dublin General Post Office in 1916. It is a tricolor of green, white and orange, with the green closest to the staff. The green represents the Gaelic and old Anglo-Norman element of the population. The orange represents the descendants of the Protestant planters, most of whom live in Northern Ireland today. The white signifies the permanent truce between orange and green in the Republic.

The harp is a Medieval symbol for Ireland and is seen everywhere in the Republic, from coins to statues. It is comparable to the eagle of Germany or the *fleur-de-lis* of royalist France or the lion of Britain. Hibernia is the female figure representing Ireland who is usually depicted bearing a harp. The green shamrock is perhaps the most well known of all the symbols for Ireland. Legend has it that St. Patrick plucked a shamrock so that he could explain the Holy Trinity to his listeners.

Ireland's Democracy

The Republic of Ireland is a small, peaceful country enjoying the blessings of social justice and political stability through the free operation of the democratic process. Personal freedoms are guaranteed under the constitution: freedom of speech; freedom of assembly; equality before the law; freedom of religion and freedom from discrimination.

Voting for Ireland's representative government via secret ballot begins at age 18. The electorate is also called upon to vote on constitutional amendments, and certain controversial matters are submitted to them in the form of referendums. A complicated system of proportional representation as well as frequent redrawing of constituency boundaries in order to keep them equal serve as guarantees of fair representation. There is also a Supreme Court to judge whether or not certain laws are constitutional. In addition, a public ombudsman, or citizen's advocate, is charged to investigate misconduct in government after receiving citizens' complaints.

Ireland's civil service is required to be strictly professional, meaning that it must be above and separate from politics. Positions in the civil service are acquired on the basis of success in competitive examinations. Each department of government is staffed by these professionals, and their head is called the Secretary of the department. The elected political leader who is given the portfolio for the department is called the Minister. Both the Secretary and the Minister must work in tandem. If these arrangements seem very British, it is because the British civil service smoothly and peacefully became the Irish civil service in 1922.

Free and democratic governments are based on law instead of the power of persons. In democratic societies, leaders come and go, but the laws remain as the basis for the rules by which society is supposed to function. Like American law, Irish law has its origin in English common law that evolved over centuries. In fact, all of the statutes passed by the British Parliament before 1921 have the force of law in Ireland unless they have been specifically repealed by the Irish Parliament, the *Oireachtas.*

Another carry over from the British system is the independent judiciary. Judges cannot be removed from office unless there is a charge of misbehavior or incapacity, and only then by a resolution passed in parliament. Still another carry over is the division of the legal profession into solicitors and barristers who share the responsibilities that lawyers take on in America. Solicitors deal with paperwork outside of the courts, such as the transfer of property and the setting up of companies. Barristers are the stars who conduct cases in the higher courts, retained and advised by solicitors. Poor

Irish people have free legal aid available to them in criminal cases and for some civil cases.

Ireland's Parliamentary System

Like many western European democracies, Ireland has a parliamentary form of government based upon the Westminster model which evolved in England from centuries of experience. To emphasize the Irishness of the system, Irish names were given to its parts and officers. The national parliament is called the *Oireachtas,* and consists of a President; an upper house, the *Seanad;* and a lower house, the *Dáil Eireann,* or simply the *Dáil,* which is pronounced something like "dole." The *Dáil,* consisting of around 170 deputies, concentrates and exercises political power in the nation, as does the British Parliament's lower house, the House of Commons. Elected members to the *Dáil* are called *Teachtai Dala,* or T.D.s for short, corresponding to M.P.s, or Members of Parliament in Britain. T.D.s are addressed as "Deputy."

Just as the British House of Commons selects the Prime Minister today, Ireland's *Dáil* selects the Irish Prime Minister, who is called the *Taoiseach,* which is pronounced something like "tea-shook." The Taoiseach is the head of the government, or the cabinet of ministers who run the state. He is not the head of state, who is the President. The Irish President is elected by the public to a seven year term in what is largely a ceremonial office corresponding to that of the Monarch in Britain. West Germany has a comparable system, where the President of West Germany has ceremonial functions and the Chancellor has the real power derived from his base of operations in the legislature. The Irish President does have a few responsibilities, besides cutting ribbons and laying cornerstones, that are worth noting: He can send some bills to the high court to test their constitutionality and he can set up others for popular referendum.

The power of the *Dáil* is such that government is almost unicameral, or one chambered, functionally. The *Seanad*, or upper house, corresponds to the British House of Lords, and has almost no real power. The *Taoiseach* nominates many members of the *Seanad* directly and the rest are elected indirectly from panels of candidates representing special interests, such as culture, education, agriculture, labor, industry, administration and the universities. Only a few hundred electors drawn from those who have special political credentials select most members of the upper house.

The function of the all important *Dáil* may be confusing for Americans unfamiliar with how Europe's parliamentary systems work. There are no checks and balances between the branches of government: the executive comes right out of the legislature and is always responsible to it. This means that the party with the most members of the *Dáil*, or the party that can link up with minority parties to form a majority coalition, has its leader become *Taoiseach*, or Prime Minister, the leader of the government. As it has been pointed out, government is a word used in a narrow sense in the parliamentary system. It means the Prime Minister and the ministers chosen by him or her in consultation with other party leaders. Each minister runs a department of the state, such as the education department or the defense department. The ministers form a group called the cabinet which meets privately under the auspices of the Prime Minister. When they are in the *Dáil*, the government members must sit on the front bench of one side, where they are faced right across the way by the front bench of the opposition party. Thus situated, parliamentary business can become exciting and dramatic, and meanwhile the time consuming and frustrating American style struggles between the executive in the White House and the legislature in Congress are avoided. The executive is right there in the legislature, drawn from the dominant party or from a dominant coalition, so the leaders of the executive are the strongest members of the legislature at the same time.

Whenever the *Taoiseach* and his government do something highly unpopular, or if a grave scandal breaks out, they run the risk of losing their majority and falling, particularly if the majority is composed of a major party in coalition with smaller parties. Party discipline usually ensures that this does not occur. What is more usual is an attempt on the part of the *Taoiseach* to extend the government's tenure of office by dissolving the *Dáil* so that new elections can take place. This is ordinarily done when the government senses a strong tide of opinion running in its favor. Such a move can be made any time during the government's five year term. The hope is that the party's seats in the *Dáil* will increase, but the tactic can backfire. The majority might be lost in an election and a new *Taoiseach* and government will be selected from the victorious opposition.

Ireland's Political Parties

English speaking democracies have tended to have an alternation of two major parties in office. Ireland is no exception. *Fianna Fáil*, roughly translated from the Irish as "band of warriors," and *Fine Gael*, roughly translated as "the Irish family," take turns at forming the Irish government and presenting their leaders as *Taoiseach*.

Both parties trace their origins to the difficult aftermath of the Anglo-Irish War of 1919–1921, and neither party has been able to free itself from this context so far. *Fianna Fáil* grew out of the Irish Republican Army group that rejected the treaty of 1921 with Britain, the treaty that partitioned Ireland into Northern Ireland and the Irish Free State. Officially it was founded by de Valera in 1926. *Fine Gael* goes back to the group that accepted the treaty of 1921 and took over from Britain as the Irish Free State government. A civil war between pro- and anti-treaty forces followed the establishment of the Free State, a sad, bitter struggle in which many patriotic Irish nationalists died at the hands of other Irish nationalists. Even today, over half a century later, the two main groups of Irish politicians find it impossible not to look back to their grim origins without recriminations.

Telling these parties apart is a difficult task for an outsider, just as difficult as telling the difference between America's Republicans and Democrats would be for an Irish person. Nevertheless, the attempt has to be made, despite the risk of offending some Irish people who are active in politics and who may dislike sweeping generalizations about what they may regard as much more subtle and complex matters.

Fianna Fáil has been described as a populist nationalist party. Some have compared it to the Gaullists in France. The party does tend to take more of a hard line on issues of Irish nationalism. It is noted for being more vigorous in standing up to Britain and the Orangemen up north over the vital question of uniting all of Ireland eventually. At the grass roots level, a 32 county Republic is an important goal for many *Fianna Fáil* voters. The party depends upon a Catholic and socially conservative rural electorate that can be fiercely loyal, an electorate that demands a conservative stance towards such moral issues as divorce and contraception. *Fianna Fáil* also distinguishes itself by being more committed to keeping the Irish language and culture alive. Over the years the party has been willing to follow Keynesian policies of government spending to generate economic growth. *Fianna Fáil* attracts more working class voters than any other party.

Fine Gael is a party more open to the vision of a pluralistic Ireland. Consequently the party is not as keen on fostering the Irish language and tends to be more moderate on issues touching nationalism. Fine Gael has tended to become the voice of the bigger farmers, those in the professions, large merchants and old money. It has the image of being the employer's party. *Fine Gael* is also less ardently Catholic than *Fianna Fáil*, having more non-Catholics and non-practicing Catholics in its ranks than *Fianna Fáil*.

Actually both parties are what could be called center or center-right parties. Since they are not class based parties, to many voters they can seem like tweedledum and tweedledee. What determines elections between them often boils down to a matter of everyday economics, not ideological matters. A large number of Irish voters, similar to a large number of American voters in recent elections, are likely to respond on the basis of a party's perceived record over such issues as wages, inflation and unemployment. In recent years, *Fine Gael* has come to power in coalition with one or more of the smaller parties, in particular with the Labour Party. This is ironic in light of the reputation of *Fine Gael* as the slightly more conservative of the two major parties and as the party more prone to represent business interests. *Fianna Fáil*, by contrast, always tries to stand alone, either in office or out of it in opposition.

Ireland's Labour Party was founded in 1912. Some of its founders gained impeccable republican credentials by participating in the 1916 Rising. Like Britain's Labour Party, it is committed to the democratic process as the means to achieve socialistic goals. It, too, has intellectual leaders who are sometimes disparaged as "smoked salmon socialists," as well as leaders who have come up from the mills and factories.

There is also a Workers' Party that is more in line with left-wing European parties. A branch of the Workers' Party broke off in the late 1960s to form the small provisional *Sinn Féin* party, which means "ourselves alone," thereby resurrecting the name of a party famous in the struggle for Irish independence. *Sinn Féin* has links with the outlawed Irish Republican Army and aims at uniting workers in the south and north to create a secular, socialist republic.

The Style of Irish Politics

Irish politics are loud and raucous, full of oratory and emotion. Ireland is credited with having the fastest talking politicians in western Europe. The opposition is ever ready to point to government wrongdoing, and uproarious laughter can break out at any time, especially when some contradiction or irony is discovered.

The smallness of Ireland is manifest in its political style. Politics are immediate, folksy and chummy in Ireland to a degree impossible in the United States. Leaders are not distant, surrounded by aides and bodyguards. They are immediate and accessible, more like ordinary people. Even ministers regularly meet with, talk to and joke with large numbers of ordinary people. One former *Taoiseach,* who is also a former professor, wanders unshielded in the stacks of a university library. Another *Taoiseach* has been noted for doing such spontaneous things as calling up a Dublin talk show host personally during a program in order to invite himself to a party he has heard about.

Several organized, institutionalized groups put pressure on political parties and individual politicians: the trade unions, the farmers' organizations, and business groups. Businessmen have a particularly close relationship with the state, and are said to be influential out of proportion to their numbers. The same is said of farmers. In addition, much pressure is put upon T.D.s by voters in their home constituencies, as might be expected. To serve the home voters, T.D.s arrange such things as farm subsidies, improvement grants, and cards to acquire free medical services. In the west of Ireland they are also likely to deal with such local matters as poaching, trespass, assault, tax evasion and summonses of various kinds.

Foreign Relations

Ireland is unique among the states of Europe. Several other states were colonizers in the past, but Ireland itself was in many ways a colony. Among members of a

military alliance, N.A.T.O., Ireland is steadfast as a neutral, the only neutral country in the European Economic
Community so far. Among secular states, Ireland is
religious, despite official separation of church and state.

Irish foreign policy can be described quite simply. It
has two aims: one, to keep Ireland out of trouble, expressed as neutrality; and two, helping other nations get
out of trouble, which is expressed as peace-keeping.
Ireland has been a vigorous participant in United Nations peace-keeping efforts, sending troops to what was
then the Congo (now Zaire), the Middle East, Cyprus,
West New Guinea (now West Irian), India, Pakistan,
Iran and Iraq. In general, Irish troops have been very
welcome and often praised for their professional conduct. Incidentally, Irish peacekeeping troops have
found the Irish language very useful for keeping communications indecipherable by hostile forces.

Regardless of the appearance of Irish military con-
tingents in so many places, Ireland has scant military
power to draw upon compared to other European
states. The whole of Ireland's all-volunteer defense
forces add up to around 14,000, and under 17,000 are
in the reserves. The air corps, which is operated by the
army, has only around 800 in uniform and approximately 37 aircraft, including ten helicopters. The navy
has a total strength of around 900, manning five patrol
vessels and two minesweepers. Naval forces are assigned
to protecting the fisheries and guarding against oil pollution.

Considering that Ireland is a small country with a
high rate of unemployment, Irish responses to calls for
contributions to unfortunate situations in the world
have been remarkably generous and compassionate.

The Irish Catholic agencies and the Irish government have targeted some of the poorest countries in the Third World for aid, including Lesotho, Tanzania, Zambia and the Sudan. The Irish tend to specialize in what their own compatriots needed so desperately in the last century: food security and agricultural development.

IRELAND AND BRITAIN

The Closeness of Ireland and Britain Today

The most important questions of Irish foreign policy involve relations with Britain and Northern Ireland. These matters are so important that they deserve separate and detailed consideration. Republic or no Republic, Britain and Ireland are indissolubly linked through geography, economics, shared history and ties of family. Ireland has had only one close neighbor and one adversary through the ages. After almost seven decades of Irish independence, the connection between the two islands actually seems closer and stronger than ever before.

Television, the most important form of media in the late 20th century, illustrates how the two islands have drawn closer together. The British Broadcasting Corporation (BBC) and independent British television stations are picked up in the most remote corners of Ireland, either by antenna or by cable. Irish viewers are bombarded by British shows, news, advertisements, perspectives and attitudes. The wall of Catholic censorship was blown open by British television, which is often preferred over the two more stodgy Irish television channels because it is more racy. The BBC and independent stations regularly screen high quality news broadcasts and interesting documentaries, but also programs with nudity and raw language which would be censored by networks in the United States. Under the impact of competition from British channels, the Irish television stations have loosened up considerably and now even they will show material that American network censors would cut.

The same holds true for British newspapers, particularly tabloids, which are sold all over Ireland. Many Dubliners read a British newspaper as part of their regular morning ritual. Most curious is the abiding interest of citizens of the Republic of Ireland in the British royal family, particularly Princess Diana's latest clothes, activities, or hairstyles. It is said that in some places her picture on a woman's magazine will guarantee a sellout.

So much else in Ireland is obviously British in origin: drinking tea, driving on the left, weights and measures, the parliamentary system, and most language use. Irish people will say such words as schedule (pronounced "shed-yule") or laboratory (pronounced "la-*bor*-a-tory") in an entirely British manner. Cover-ups of British practice are also revealing, because they display strong nationalistic urges to be separate from British culture. John Q. Public has become Sean Citizen and Peter Rabbit has been transformed into Sean Bunny. Red British mailboxes and buses have been painted green. Arch British names such as Queen's County (Ofally), King's County (Laois, pronounced "leash," as in dog's leash), Queenstown (Cobh), and Kingstown (Dun Laoghairie, pronounced "Dun Leary"), have been changed.

Despite such transformations, the distance between Ireland and Britain has continued to shrink, culturally and physically. Measured in the time it takes to get from one island to the other, the truth of this assertion is obvious. Until fairly recently northwestern Europe was one of the most expensive parts of the world for air travel, measured in cost per mile. Ordinary people had to take a ferry from Ireland to get to Britain and then a train from Wales to get to England. Today cheap air fares, either from Aer Lingus or its privately owned younger rivals, make it possible to travel from the Dublin airport to a London airport in about an hour. The skies are filled with Irish and British people going in both directions.

There are no barriers or delays for these travelers. The Irish going to Britain are not treated as aliens. They do not even have to show a passport when entering Britain from Ireland. When they enter from abroad, they must show their Irish passports, but they are encouraged to get into the lines for British and Commonwealth passports. In a way, treating the Irish as *de facto* Commonwealth subjects does seem to deny the existence of an entirely sovereign, separate Irish Republic, and it annoys some Irish people.

This special status for Irish people probably does not annoy those who live in Britain and enjoy its advantages. Getting a foothold in Britain is easy. The more prosperous parts of Britain have been absorbing a stream of Irish workers from the largely unskilled to the highly educated graduates of Irish universities. There are no work permits for Irish citizens or other requirements that vex aliens from other countries. Once residency is established, Irish citizens can vote in Britain like anyone else. In other words, an Irish citizen in London, let us say, would be treated no differently than a Scots or a Welsh emigrant to the metropolis.

British employers do not complain about the special status of Irish immigrants either. A competent person behind a computer screen who speaks with an Irish accent is just as welcome as any other competent person. Some of the unemployed and underemployed roughnecks of England are the people most likely to be hostile to Irish immigrants, but such types harbor hostilities for various other groups to say nothing of civilization in general. A more subtle middle class disparagement of Irishness has been expressed in Britain for a long time, often taking the form of Irish ethnic jokes. Nevertheless, British cosmopolitanism, especially in London, and the already established Irish neighborhoods in many cities and towns, all make it relatively easy for the Irish immigrant to sink roots in Britain. Besides, countless millions of Britons genuinely like the Irish. What is more, countless millions of Britons are Irish descendants themselves!

Strong, indissoluble bonds of blood tie the two islands together. Nearly every family in Ireland has some members living in Britain. Family members visit back and forth more regularly now because of the cheaper fares and higher wages and salaries. Moreover, large numbers of Irish immigrants marry into British families and produce British grandchildren for Irish grandparents. In America the descendants of Irish immigrants still call themselves Irish, but the offspring of Irish parents in Britain rightly call themselves British. Being British has, after all, a cultural connotation.

For the folks back at home in Ireland, the progress

of a son or daughter in Britain is watched with close anticipation. Sending bright and promising youngsters off to London to make their fortune is an old Irish tradition. Many of the greatest Irish names in literature followed that path. Today popular singers and rock musicians anxiously await their success on the British charts, and should they reach the top over there they feel that they have reached the pinnacle in music. Some may even anticipate being named in the Queen's Honors' List. The same striving for recognition in Britain holds true in education. Oxford and Cambridge degrees are more esteemed than any others and academic standards for Irish universities are keyed to Cambridge standards. Many Irish citizens enroll themselves in degree programs at Britain's Open University, including, strangely enough, some Irish Republican Army prisoners in jail in Northern Ireland.

Some flow of population goes the other way. Sometimes an East London cockney accent or a smooth Oxbridge accent can stand out in Ireland, usually along the coast and usually in a very attractive location. The lure of the quiet charm as well as the inexpensiveness of Ireland has brought a trickle of British immigrants to the Republic. Their skills win them jobs or they live on a retirement income, and they do seem to get on quite well. Their Britishness seems to be quietly accepted and tolerated by the Irish, who know how important tolerance for the Irishness of some friend or relative in Britain might be. Besides, it is likely that many of the Brits who settle in Ireland had an Irish ancestor who moved the other way some time ago. These islands which have exchanged such substantial numbers of people back and forth as far back as prehistoric times are unlikely to slacken the pace in this age of an hour's travel between London and Dublin.

Close relations remain in economics, dictated as always by geography, just as Canadian and American relations must be interdependent. In 1965, an Anglo-Irish Free Trade Area Agreement was signed, which provided for the elimination of all protective duties between the two countries. Britain remains the most important buyer of Irish exports and the most important seller of imports to Ireland. Britain also remains the greatest single source of foreign capital invested in the Republic. Although Ireland is currently increasing the percentage of exports and imports to and from other E.E.C. countries and decreasing the percentage with Britain, the total value of goods traded with Britain continues to rise.

Irish Nationalism and Britain

Regardless of all of the manifestations of contemporary closeness, British and Irish people continue to feel ambiguous towards each other, the legacy of centuries of strife and misunderstanding going all the way back to the English conquest. The key factor was that Irish culture, particularly Catholicism, could never be entirely uprooted and replaced by British culture. Assimilation always remained incomplete and frought with strife. Generations of British statesmen, officials and landlords came to Ireland and were baffled and frustrated by Celtic resistance that ranged from the subtle and devious to outright bloody atrocities. Coercion was their answer to resistance, leading to struggles between the Catholic populace and British led police and military power. Such sad scenes as the eviction of Irish tenants who could not pay their rent became commonplace. Frustrated British authorities declared, "Every time we figure out an answer to an Irish question, the Irish have changed the question." For themselves, the British unhesitatingly assumed that they brought to poor, backward Ireland the very height of civilization known to humankind. These struggles and perceptions left many indelible impressions that becloud British and Irish relations down to the present day.

Although a large Irish and Irish descended component in the population of the United Kingdom is taken for granted, both positive and negative feelings can still be evoked by Irishness. For example, on the positive side, Irish wit and humor always charms the British public, as attested to by the great popularity of Irish comedians on the British stage and on British television. An example on the negative side is the reaction to outrages perpetuated by the Irish Republican Army in Britain and Northern Ireland. Ordinary Irish people in Britain are profoundly disgusted by such incidents as bomb explosions, and have no sympathy with the I.R.A. Yet many seem to sense that some British co-workers will imply that they are somehow linked to the event on account of their Irishness, or they may hear such things as someone quoting the historic saying that the Irish were "the men that God had made mad." Of course, there are some Britons who are blatantly prejudiced against the Irish, clinging to the stereotype of Ireland as the home of drunks, gunmen and pigs. Somewhat more subtle, but similarly biased, are those Britons who will toast the rebels of 1916, explaining that they "eventually freed us from the responsibility of trying to govern these ungovernable people."

Irish feelings toward Britain are similarly ambiguous. Many Irish people claim to dislike the English at the very time that they consciously strive to imitate them. Those who are very successful in imitating Irish nationalists call "West Britons" or, more recently, "watermelons," green on the outside and British pink on the inside. One Trinity College student expressed Irish ambiguity toward the British very succinctly: "We hate the bastards and we love the bastards."

At the same time that British models and standards are held up to Irish people for emulation, Irish nationalism demands that Britain be loathed as the national enemy of Irish history. Patriotic songs about martyrs and rebels continue to be passed down through the generations, featuring the British as the vicious villains. Cromwell is still singled out as the scourge of ancient Irish civilization, a veritable Hitler. Guides in great historic houses may be likely to declare that the landlord families were "English," even if they had been in Ireland for three to six centuries and called themselves Irish. They were landlords, therefore they were English. This is how nationalistic stereotyping operates. Anti-British sentiment can take a more overt form. As recently as 1972 a mob turned out to burn down the British embassy in Dublin as a protest against particularly grim killings in Northern Ireland. Most recently a protest developed against Irish people who wore red poppies on Remembrance Day for the war dead. Most of those honored died in British uniforms during World War I, when Ireland was part of the

United Kingdom, and some died in British uniforms during World War II, when Ireland was independent and neutral. Many Irish volunteered to fight for Britain from 1939 to 1945 anyway. Irish nationalists do not like to be reminded of the fact that in the 20th century more Irishman died fighting for the Union Jack than for an independent Ireland.

Part of the effort of nationalism has been directed at clearing away the symbols of British rule. Some remain as part of the decor of historic buildings, but statues have been targeted for destruction. Huge statues of Queen Victoria have been removed by heavy construction equipment. Admiral Nelson's statue that graced O'Connell Street was deftly blown off its pedestal by the Irish Republican Army in 1966. The rest of the pedestal was blown away less skillfully by the authorities, whose blast broke many windows in the vicinity. The Duke of Wellington's monument remains probably because of its sheer mass and possibly because Wellington was born in Ireland. Even so, when someone said he was Irish because of his birthplace, Wellington tersely replied that just because someone was born in a stable, that did not make him a horse!

For a considerable length of time when Ireland was under British rule, Irish nationalists blamed the British for most of what had gone wrong on the island. When independence came, many social and economic problems did not magically disappear, and many Irish came to share an uncomfortable realization with many postcolonial peoples in the Third World, that the departure of the colonial authorities does not automatically bring about a golden era of peace, justice and prosperity. Here and there in the world, and now and then in Ireland too, a few quiet voices may dare to whisper that life was better under the old system.

For a considerable period of time, up until 1922, the Irish were widely classified as a submerged nationality. A submerged nationality is one that lives on despite a lack of national sovereignty and despite the fact that another nation enjoys sovereignty over it and may push for assimilation and the destruction of its culture. A submerged nationality will try to keep alive its own language, if it has one, its own historic tradition, and its sense of its own separate culture. Armenians, Kurds, Ukrainians or Estonians can serve as examples of present day submerged nationalities. Poles or Czechs are examples of former submerged nationalities that have been able to achieve statehood in this century. At the time of the Celtic revival, in the late 19th and early 20th centuries, Ireland was a submerged nation to some extent, and a few years after the conclusion of World War I, the Irish nationality found expression in a sovereign Republic. Even so, sharing of British culture continued pervasively, in language, common concerns, values and institutions. In many ways, Ireland gained sovereignty at the top but was still part of the United Kingdom below, on the cultural level. Every contemporary Irish person has had to be at least something of a West Briton, like it or not.

Perhaps this is why so many Irish people in official positions emphasize the Irishness of Ireland by putting great stress on the differences from the United Kingdom. This might explain such things as the passionate struggle of Irish language enthusiasts in what appears to be a lost cause. In other words, the separateness of Ireland must be supported vigorously precisely because the push toward a common culture is so strong in this shrunken world. It is, in some ways, similar to the way Canadians emphasize the uniqueness of Canada in the face of the massively pervasive culture and economy of the United States. This is an analogy worth pondering, considering that Canadians are outnumbered by Americans in roughly the same proportions as the Irish are outnumbered by the British. But this analogy should not be pushed too far, because except for a few invasions and nasty little border and fisheries disputes, Canadian and American relations have been relatively good and free from a heritage of conquest.

Despite all of the hatred and admiration between the Irish and British in the past and present, and regardless of the passion of Irish nationalism, as well as the consequent ambiguities, the destinies of Ireland and Britain must continue to be linked in the future. Family ties, commerce, and culture are inextricably interwoven across the two islands. British influences and interests are so pervasive that they are impossible to uproot, even if all the Irish shared the urge to do so on the level of the most committed nationalists. In the future the cultural and physical closeness of the two islands may be the basis for growing friendship, closer cooperation and shared prosperity. But much depends on how the problem of Northern Ireland is resolved.

THE QUESTION OF NORTHERN IRELAND

The Magnitude of the Problem

The Irish and British in the 20th century have been compared to a couple going through a painful divorce. There has been an outpouring of resentment from both sides and the inability of each to see the point of view of the other. The divorce has been infinitely complicated by a long custody struggle over Northern Ireland, a region more analagous to a lusty, willful adolescent than to a child.

There are no simple answers for this problem. It is as tangled as the Middle East or southern Africa today. Americans, who have such a predilection for solving problems and issuing solutions quickly, tend to become exasperated and frustrated by intractable problems such as this. It preoccupies people all over the island as an incessant topic for worry, concern, discussion and argument. It would not be going too far to say that Irish people are so mesmerized by events, personalities and politics surrounding Northern Ireland that it has become an obsession. Irish people tackle it, play with it, and chew it like a dog with a big bone. Perhaps the reason behind this preoccupation is that the problem of Northern Ireland is the last logical continuation of the centuries old struggle with Britain over authority in Ireland. Perhaps part of it is the explanation offered by cynics that Northern Ireland makes it possible for smart Irish politicians to divert interest from problems in the Republic.

Regardless of the reasons for it, American visitors

are more than likely to be exposed to this Irish obsession. It is therefore important to know something about it beforehand. The following sections attempt to present the basic facts about the region, the conflict, and some of the views of various groups of participants in the ongoing struggles. It is presented in the hope that it will seem both unbiased and clear.

Nationality and Nationalism in Northern Ireland

What kind of people live in Northern Ireland? What is their nationality? These are difficult questions. Something over one third, perhaps up to 40% of the estimated population of 1,568,000, are Roman Catholic, and nearly all of them look to the Republic in the south as the government to which they wish to owe allegiance. The other two thirds, or just about one million people, are Protestants, most of whom are keen on flying the Union Jack and keeping Northern Ireland out of the clutches of the Republic.

The ancestors of most of the Protestants came from Scotland and England in the 17th century, populating "plantations" in areas confiscated from Catholic earls who had resisted the British crown. As one old Catholic nursing home resident recently put it, "You have got to realize that these bastards didn't start coming here until 1607." Once settled, the Protestants proved to be tough, hard-working farmers. Confrontation with the Catholics who had remained in the region began with rival rural gangs of Protestants and Catholics who practiced intimidation and violence against each other over three hundred years ago.

A considerable number of the descendants of the

Protestant immigrants to Northern Ireland emigrated to the United States, where they were known as the Scots-Irish. They gained reputations as formidable frontiersmen, and their ethnic stock produced a number of American presidents, including Woodrow Wilson, and numerous heroes, including Stonewall Jackson.

They are not called Scots-Irish in Northern Ireland today. Just what this Protestant majority is called is a matter of debate. "Orangemen" or "Ulsterites" are terms they often use for themselves, and are code words for being Protestants and against the concept of one Ireland. In the eyes of some, they are "British" as well as Irish, British being a general term that can be used to indicate a Welsh or a Scottish as well as an English person. Can it also be used to indicate a person from Northern Ireland? Is there a separate Northern Irish Protestant nationality that can be added to these other British groups? Catholics tend to argue that these northern Protestants are essentially Irish and not British. British authorities and politicians have been accused of encouraging delusions of Britishness in the north when it suited their needs. For example, the Britishness of Northern Ireland was stressed to inspire patriotic efforts during World War II and to make election issues in Britain more emotional during the last two decades. Many British people nonetheless cannot believe in the Britishness of Northern Ireland Protestants because they have been so violent and so disinclined to compromise, two traits they deem very un-British.

Geography does underline a connection with Scotland, which is in sight of Northern Ireland, less than a dozen miles away. For many, Glasgow seems closer than Dublin. Geography by itself does not demand that Northern Ireland has to be unified with the Republic. Just because the United States and Canada share North America does not mean that they must merge to become one country.

The key question is nationality. If the Protestants of Northern Ireland truly are a separate nationality, the right of national self-determination by the majority in Northern Ireland may keep it separate from the Republic of Ireland permanently, or for as long as they can maintain their majority among voters. If, on the other hand, the Protestants of Northern Ireland are Irish rather than British, then surely some sort of accommodation with the Republic ought to take place, perhaps some sort of federation. Either way, it is absolutely essential that minority rights be protected: Catholic rights in Northern Ireland today and Protestant rights in a possible federal or united Ireland.

Such generalizations about the problem of Northern Ireland can never be made without running into further complications. First of all, the Protestants in the region do not function as a united block and do not share the same goals. They do not even belong to the same denomination. The two most important groups are the Anglicans, or Church of Ireland members, and the Presbyterians. There are also some smaller Protestant groups such as the Methodists and the Quakers. The Presbyterians themselves have divided into Free Presbyterians, followers of the controversial Ian Paisley, and the regular Presbyterians.

One view that most Protestants share today is that they do not want to be absorbed in the Republic because they perceive it to be a backward, sectarian state. It is the same view that their forefathers held in 1914, when Ulster appeared to be poised to rebel against British law rather than to be included in an Ireland that was about to be granted Home Rule, or Dominion status. "Ulster will fight and Ulster will be right" was one of their defiant slogans. "Home Rule is Rome rule" was another.

While contemporary northern Protestants are united on this point of resisting control from Dublin, they differ among themselves about plans for the region's future. Those belonging to the official Unionist Party want to have greater integration with Britain, so that Northern Ireland can become another Wales or Scotland. Their position is called "integrationist." The Democratic Unionist Party, Paisley's party, wants Northern Ireland to have its own Parliament and uncompromising majority rule, meaning no power sharing with the Catholic minority. These people are called "devolutionists" because they want British power to devolve on the province.

Nationalism in the Catholic minority in Northern Ireland adds complications. The Constitution of the Republic of Ireland was written for all 32 counties, but it has allowed a "temporary suspension" for the six counties in the north. Many Catholics living in Northern Ireland feel that they owe true allegiance to the Republic nonetheless, and they are often unwilling to obey the authority of the government of Northern Ireland unless coerced to do so. Therefore they are regarded as disloyal traitors by many of the Protestants, who consequently feel guiltless about denying all Catholics political and social rights. Many Catholics have been accused of "loyalty to the half crown," an allusion to the old coin called the half crown. It means that they are perfectly willing to live off of the British government's welfare and unemployment compensation, which is more lucrative than the payments offered in the Republic for similar circumstances.

Northern Ireland actually suffers from two superimposed minority problems: The Protestants are a minority in Ireland and the Catholics are a minority in Northern Ireland. If all were forced into one state, how could four million Catholics possibly coerce one million angry, unwilling Protestants into loyalty to a state they loathe? Conversely, how can one million Protestants coerce half a million Catholics into loyalty to a state that they loathe? So far viable answers to these minority problems have not been forthcoming.

The Game of Telling the Sides Apart

People in Northern Ireland constantly play intricate games to tell who is Catholic and who is Protestant. Coming right out and asking another person about their religion is regarded as boorish and it can kill a conversation immediately. So more subtle means must be employed. The game is challenging because people in Northern Ireland look alike and share their own very noticeable way of speaking English. The northern accent came originally from Scotland and it is now spoken by Protestants and Catholics alike. People in the south recognize it instantly, and northerners who try to change their accent usually find it a very difficult process.

Some indications of religion can be given by names. First names tell more than last names. Usually names such as Declan, Sean or Patrick will be given to Catholics, while Protestants usually bear names such as William, David or George. Since many mixed marriages have occurred over the centuries, some Protestants bear ostensibly Catholic last names, such as Kelly, and vice versa. A Catholic may have the surname of Adams or Johnson.

Other indications can be given by neighborhoods. Belfast and other towns have distinct Protestant and Catholic residential districts, so finding out where a person grew up or where a person lives can be an important move in the game. Failing that, finding out details of a person's education can be revealing because nearly all schools are voluntarily segregated by denomination right up to but not including the university level. If a school has "Saint" in its name, it is probably Catholic. If it has "Royal" in its name, it is probably Protestant.

The name used for one particular city in the north is frequently a good indicator. Catholics call it Derry, the old Irish name, and Protestants call it Londonderry, the name given when London fostered settlement of the town in the 17th century. Some individuals who do not want to give the game up will actually say "Derry-slash-Londonderry" in conversations. The very name used for Northern Ireland can be another giveaway: Catholics will say "the north" and refer to the Republic of Ireland as "the south," implying thereby that both are parts of one country. They might also say "the six counties" to avoid recognizing the entity bearing the official name of Northern Ireland. A Protestant will call Northern Ireland "the province" or "Ulster." Technically the Protestant is wrong, because three of the counties of Ulster, Donegal, Monaghan and Cavan, are in the Republic. The six historic Ulster counties that are in

Northern Ireland no longer exist officially. They have been replaced by a large number of administrative units.

Some minor cultural phenomena can identify the sides. Protestants will tend to say "Roman Catholic," while Catholics will simply say Catholic. One reason why Protestants add "Roman" is that Church of Ireland members claim to be catholic themselves, using a lower case 'c' to denote the meaning of 'universal.' Even the loyalties of sports fans can indicate religion. Protestant soccer fans will tend to support the Glasgow Rangers while Catholics will follow Glasgow Celtic. Glasgow, like Belfast, contains a large Catholic minority. Body adornments can be giveaways also. Catholics will wear certain kinds of crosses and rings and working class Protestants might indulge in tattoos.

Local graffiti clearly shows what side a neighborhood takes. Republican symbolism, featuring the tricolor and allusions to 1916 show up in Catholic districts. So does F.T.Q., initials for an unpleasant expletive about the Queen. F.T.P., initials for an unpleasant expletive about the Pope, is the rejoinder found in Protestant neighborhoods, along with orange symbolism about William of Orange and the Battle of the Boyne in 1690. "No Surrender" is a Protestant slogan which stands for no compromise with Catholics now, just as their ancestors used it when they held out during the seige of Londonderry. Of course, in the small towns and villages of Northern Ireland such symbolism and the various games of identification are simply unnecessary because people know and recognize one another and are well aware of who is on what side.

The game of identifying Catholics and Protestants

is played so intensely in Northern Ireland that it even can carry over to visiting Americans. "What part of the world are your ancestors from?" is a typical ploy. Americans naturally tend to regard this preoccupation as ridiculous, since religious tolerance, ecumenicism, and widespread secularization in the United States has made the question of who is a Catholic and who is a Protestant quite passé. To put it simply, most Americans do not care what religion their neighbors choose to follow. Consequently, Northern Ireland looks like a boiling cauldron of passions left over from the intolerant period of European religious persecution of around three hundred years ago. It is more than that, however. In most cases, being a Protestant or a Catholic in Northern Ireland today stands for belief in one of two different national destinies, each with its own interpretation of Irish history and British history and each with a presumed different way of life.

Simple Answers That Will Not Work

The Irish Republican Army and its offshoot organizations, the Provisional I.R.A., or Provos, and the INLA or Irish National Liberation Army, have a very simple solution for the problem in Northern Ireland that consists of two words: "Brits out." For them the struggle in the north is the last chapter in the long effort to rid Ireland of British rule. From their point of view, violence was the only thing that worked to get the British out of the 26 counties of the Republic and it will be the only thing that will work now. Maintaining a steady urban guerilla war of attrition will make the British exasperated, disgusted and tired. Eventually they will find some way to quit and get out of Ireland forever.

The key presumption behind this simple solution is that British withdrawal will lead to peaceful absorption of the north into the Republic. One million angry Protestants, many of them armed and all of them heirs to a militant, violent tradition, could release a full scale civil war. In many districts Catholics would be hopelessly outnumbered and outgunned. A fearful bloodbath did occur when British forces withdrew quickly from India and Pakistan, as Churchill and others predicted. A similar horror could befall Northern Ireland, bringing untold suffering to the innocent on both sides.

Surely millions of British taxpayers are inclined to want a "Brits out" solution also. They have been pumping money into the infrastructure and the peace keeping operations in Northern Ireland for decades. Northern Ireland has long been a heavy drain on the British exchequer. British parents, siblings and wives who have loved ones in the British army in Northern Ireland also earnestly wish that "Brits out" were possible. The hard fact behind British involvement is a legitimate commitment to maintain peace and order in Northern Ireland. No matter how difficult and stubborn many Protestant leaders may have been, they represent a people declaring allegiance to the United Kingdom, a people who demonstrated their loyalty and patriotism to Britain by heroic sacrifices in blood and toil in two world wars. How can the British possibly get out when they have made solemn pledges to underwrite the national will of the majority in Northern Ireland?

The simple solution heard in some Protestant circles is "Catholics out." Why don't they just pack up and move across the border into the Catholic dominated Republic? Population transfers have occurred between hostile communities in history. The Greeks and Turks and the Hindus and Moslems can be cited as examples. Yet from a Catholic point of view, why should they move? Their roots are deep in most cases. Their ancestors may have lived in Ulster since ancient times. Most have families, neighborhoods, and an appreciation of the beauties of their region. Most have jobs, too, but those who are unemployed or on welfare receive higher social security payments, as mentioned, than the payments offered in the Republic. In short, Northern Ireland is the home of over half a million Catholics, despite the presence of over a million Protestants, many of whom are hostile. Besides, many Catholics have hopes that the situation may improve immensely in the future.

Their higher birth rate is a source of optimism. The Catholic minority is getting larger and the size of the Protestant majority is a smaller perecentage with each passing year, and the median age of the Protestant community is steadily advancing. The most optimistic Catholic prediction is that they may have a majority by 2020. Recently the Catholic birth rate in Northern Ireland has dropped, but the Protestant birth rate has dropped even further during the same time span. Perhaps the different birth rates will, at some distant date, cause the unification of Ireland, once a majority of Catholics of voting age is achieved. On the other hand, Catholic migration out of Northern Ireland to the Republic, to Britain and overseas remains high, so high that it offsets the higher birth rate. Therefore many predict that a Catholic majority in the future is unlikely.

Another simple solution is the offer to redraw the border to more closely approximate local wishes, thereby allowing the Catholic sections to join the Republic and the Protestant sections to stay as part of the United Kingdom. After all, the boundary drawn in the treaty of 1921 was originally a temporary line, which was to be more accurately drawn by a new commission. When it met, it decided to take the easy way out and accept the temporary line as the permanent border. If a plebiscite were held in each of the old six counties, or in the new administrative districts replacing them, at least two counties and many districts would be likely to vote for union with the Republic because those places contain Catholic majorities. The Protestant population is very concentrated in an area around Belfast, and more thinly spread elsewhere in Northern Ireland. Local plebiscites would in all probability cause geographical nightmares. Large pieces would be carved out of Northern Ireland, making it an odd shaped, fragmented little state of dubious viability. It would also divide cities and create situations reminiscent of West and East Berlin. All that might be left of Northern Ireland might be a virtually ungovernable collection of bits and pieces. Besides, armed and angry Protestants would fight any territorial revisionism every step of the way.

Violence in Northern Ireland

Two facts about violence in the north deserve emphasis: First, there is nothing new about it, and, second, the region is very far from being as violent as it is depicted on television.

Sectarian violence in Ulster goes all the way back to

the 17th century butcheries between Catholics and Protestants. Rival sectarian rural gangs fought each other in the 18th and 19th centuries. Belfast was the scene of bitter strife in the 19th century, when people were burned out of their homes and beaten to death on account of their religion. The recent strife is therefore just the latest chapter in ongoing violent confrontations. This recent phase began in 1968, when a peaceful Catholic civil rights movement was thwarted by baton-wielding police who were mostly Protestant. It escalated to a height in the early 1970s and then dropped off to what a British minister has strangely described as "an acceptable level of violence."

This level is certainly less than that accepted in large American cities regularly. For example, the homicide rate in Los Angeles in the early 1980s was over four times that of Northern Ireland, and it has gotten worse in Los Angeles since then. Homicides in Washington, D.C., occur much more frequently than in Belfast. This impression of the scale of violence changes when Northern Ireland's violent deaths are compared to the population base of 1.56 million inhabitants. More than two decades of violence have claimed over 2,500 lives. The equivalent number of deaths for the American population base would be 400,000, or about eight times the number of dead suffered by the United States in all the years of the war in Vietnam.

There are groups committed to violence on both sides. The Irish Republican Army claims to have emerged in Catholic neighborhoods in order to protect the population. The Provos, or Provisional I.R.A., took over in places where the regular I.R.A. was perceived to be ineffective. There have been other splinter groups as well, some of them extremely violent. Help for the I.R.A. and its offshoots has come from a variety of sources, including the Irish Northern Aid Committee, known as Noraid, which regularly issues disclaimers of such support, and Gaddafi of Libya.

Northern Ireland's police has employed paramilitary forces. The now disbanded "B Specials," who were really armed and uniformed Protestant partisans, were notorious for cracking down on Catholics and looking the other way when their Protestant compatriots broke laws during sectarian strife. More recently, British authorities have striven to recruit Catholics in the Royal Ulster Constabulary, a heavily armed peace-keeping force. They have had some success, since the unemployment rate has hovered close to 20% from time to time. Applications for this dangerous work have far exceeded the number of positions available.

The police forces are backed up by the British army, whose patient, thorough patrols go on everywhere. When they first arrived, Catholic communities welcomed them because they were in dire need of protection from the onslaughts of the hostile, largely Protestant police. Unfortunately, any regular army tends to be clumsy, overarmed and prone to overreaction when engaged in a low grade, chronic, urban guerilla war. Armies have not been designed to do the tasks of urban police. A number of tragedies and misunderstandings have cost the British army the initial support of a large number of Catholics.

Civil rights have been sacrificed in Northern Ireland, as is usually the case when military authorities operate in violence prone areas. Organizations that advocate violence, Catholic and Protestant, have been denied the right to broadcast their views. Also, suspects can be detained by the authorities without the rules of evidence and other judicial processes that prevail in Britain. Many I.R.A. suspects have been imprisoned for long periods without trial, and their claim to be treated as prisoners of war has been ignored. Highly dramatized hunger strikes and some deaths from them have occurred.

The toll of thousands of casualties in the north has been accumulated over a twenty year period. The level of day-to-day violence is greatly exaggerated because the media zoom in on it like vultures. Irish people note with sarcasm that foreign reporters or anchor persons might break a three month silence on Northern Ireland with a thirty second film clip about an outrage. Unfortunately, this is almost invariably the only news that is ever carried about the north. Meanwhile, nearly all of more than a million and a half inhabitants go on with normal lives and adjust to the military patrols, electronic searches, hand searches, barricaded police bunkers, metal fences surrounding downtown Belfast, and the areas where cars cannot be parked without someone in them because empty cars will be blown up on the spot by authorities fearing car bombs.

The Politics of Confrontation, Despair and Hope

Discrimination against the Catholic minority over jobs, housing, and voting was the initial cause of the present phase of sectarian violence. Gerrymandering is the practice of drawing constituency lines to maximize the political power of one group at the expense of the other. It was practiced energetically by the historically dominant and Protestant oriented Unionist Party. For example, Londonderry or Derry, with a clear Catholic numerical majority of two to one, once ordinarily returned two out of three respresentatives who were members of the Unionist Party. Catholic votes were simply not allowed to count for as much as Protestant votes because of the way the voting districts were drawn. Therefore Catholics were perpetually underrepresented in the old legislature for Nothern Ireland, the Stormont.

Job discrimination was rampant and not thought of as particularly wrong by the Protestants, who felt they were merely taking care of their own. Jobs often passed from father to son. Belfast's skyline is marked by the great cranes of the Harland and Wolff Shipyard, once a dominant industry which had almost an entirely Protestant workforce. Elsewhere throughout the region, the employers tended to be Protestant and to favor hiring Protestant workers first and Catholics last, and reversing the order when it came to laying workers off in hard times. Even as late as 1981, after many efforts of the British government to end job discrimination, the unemployment rate for Protestants stood at 12%, while the Catholic rate was 30%.

Not enough public housing was available to meet the needs of the lower income population. Local councils were to determine allocations. Considering that the Protestant majority controlled politics in nearly all places, is it any wonder that they also controlled local government councils? Naturally, in most cases, Protestant families got the first crack at what was available.

To protest against such discrimination, Catholics began to march and sing the hymn of civil rights protests in America, "We Shall Overcome." Their efforts were greeted by assaults from the police themselves. Violence begot counterviolence, and outrages were committed by both sides when tough, irregular combatants emerged to defend their respective sides and to launch attacks on their opponents. In politics those on either extreme started to pull away from moderates in the middle. *Sinn Féin,* the political ally of the I.R.A., began to receive a very substantial part of the Roman Catholic vote as Ian Paisley's extremist Democratic Unionist Party gained an increasing Protestant vote.

Paisley and his followers preoccupy Catholics all over Ireland. To many Americans he seems rather silly—his prejudices are so deep and his bigotry so pronounced that they cannot take this holder of a doctorate from Bob Jones University seriously. Irish Catholics do. They expect that after he departs from the political stage, like minded fundamentalist leaders will take his place. He stands for the Protestants who love to dress up in orange regalia and parade through Catholic areas, beating their drums in commemoration of historic Protestant victories over Catholics. Paisley has said that it is better to be dead than green, and he and his followers really seem to believe it.

The civil rights analogy compares the orange majority to whites and the Catholic minority to blacks during America's struggle against segregation. What spoils this analogy is that Catholics have another country to which to give their allegiance. The tricolor of the Republic is flown in the Catholic neighborhoods, shows up on wall murals, and attempts are made to drape coffins with it. Black and white Americans could relate to only one nation during the era of civil rights struggles.

A few signs of hope can be perceived in this gloomy, chronic conflict. Some smaller towns have many mixed marriages and freely integrated housing without incident. A charitable program exists to send young Catholics and young Protestants to America for their summer vacations, so that they can have the opportunity to live under the same roof. Some moderate political parties continue to attract voters. The Alliance Party is a small party that goes across community lines. The S.D.L.P., which stands for the Social Democratic Labour Party, is an outgrowth of the Catholic civil rights movement and believes in constitutional traditions of legal, peaceful opposition. What is more, brave individuals of both religions have stepped forth calling for peace and reconciliation.

Meanwhile, the British government has continued to pour money into Northern Ireland. As a result, the roads, social services, hospitals, schools, public housing, health care, public facilities and welfare system are generally in better shape than in the Republic. The effect of government grants, subsidies and underwriting can be seen everywhere. Literally billions have gone to help prop up Northern Ireland. If the Orangemen who want to function autonomously, that is, largely independent of Britain, have their way, their small state would probably collapse economically if they tried to continue the levels of expenditure provided by the British government.

A significant development in Republic of Ireland and British relations came with the Hillsborough Agreement of 1985, known also as the Anglo-Irish agreement. It set up an intergovernmental conference so that Britain, Northern Ireland and the Republic could cooperate in matters of security and administration. The Protestant Unionists were furious because they saw the Dublin government encroaching on them while the British seemed to be making devious, crablike movements of withdrawal. Some Catholic extremists were also furious, because it seemed that by entering into this agreement the Republic had recognized the existence of Northern Ireland and accepted the partition and its border as permanent until a majority voted to change the legal status of Northern Ireland.

Since this agreement, a few minor matters have been ironed out successfully through cooperation between the United Kingdom and the Republic of Ireland. Representatives continue to meet regularly. On the other hand, sharp differences have continued to flare between the two countries. Extradition of I.R.A. suspects indicted by British courts from Ireland to Britain to face trial has been a heated issue in both countries. British overflights of Irish territory in border patrol operations have also sparked controversy. Regardless of such sharp issues, the question of custody over Northern Ireland, that legacy of the divorce between Britain and Ireland, may be heading towards a very modern resolution: joint custody.

CHAPTER SIX

HIGHLIGHTS OF HISTORY

PRACTICAL APPROACHES TO IRISH HISTORY

The history of Ireland or any other country can be overwhelming if it is approached in the wrong way. History yields a daunting number of facts, names, dates and events. Travels in Ireland will inevitably expose the visitor to many formal and informal lectures on history, either by guides at historic sites, tour bus drivers, or by various individual citizens, some of them with axes to grind. Some of this volume of information will consist of solid history and some of it will be such bad history that it may seem like contrived fiction.

Much of the history that visitors hear in Ireland will go in one ear and out the other because it consists of an immense welter of details about what seem to be dim and obscure people and events. Knowing some of the basics of Irish history and gaining a limited, manageable number of reference points will help Americans in Ireland to get more out of the inevitable lessons on the subject that will be provided by many Irish people.

At its best, historical knowledge can liberate individuals from many of the confines and constraints of their own time and place. At its worst, history can oppress people today with the passions of yesterday. Many Irish people continue to be haunted by sufferings, wrongs, hatreds and grievances from the past. Most discussions about any current topic somehow manage to turn to arguments about the past. Since so much of Irish history is tragic, riddled with misunderstandings and scarred by episodes of savage violence, these arguments usually heat up very quickly.

What follows is a dispassionate account of Irish history stripped to the minimum. Only the major events, dates, characters and themes are included. The most recent period of Irish history is not presented in great detail because much of it has appeared in previous chapters, particularly under politics and economics. Whenever possible, periods of Irish history are keyed to places in Ireland where significant physical remains of the era still exist.

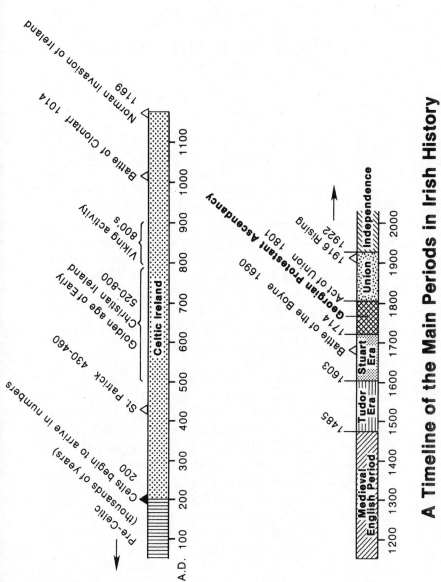

A Timeline of the Main Periods in Irish History

Pre-Celtic
(thousands of years)
Celts begin to arive in numbers
200

St. Patrick 430-460

Golden age of Early
Christian Ireland
520-800

Viking activity
800's

Battle of Clontarf 1014

Norman invasion of Ireland
1169

Celtic Ireland

A.D. 100 200 300 400 500 600 700 800 900 1000 1100

Medieval
English Period

Tudor Era
1485

Stuart Era
1603

Battle of the Boyne 1690

1714

Georgian Protestant Ascendancy

Act of Union 1801

Union

1916 Rising

Independence

1922

1200 1300 1400 1500 1600 1700 1800 1900 2000

PREHISTORIC AND CELTIC IRELAND

Prehistoric Ireland

Since history begins with written records, the prehistoric period for Ireland came to an end in the early Christian era, the time when St. Patrick and his followers began writing about the island and its inhabitants in the early 5th century A.D. Just how long Ireland was populated by prehistoric humans is still a matter of speculation. The prehistoric period for humankind in general comprises well over 99% of the existence of the species, but it was late in the prehistory of *Homo sapiens* when they moved into Ireland's cool, wet climate. Some authorities claim that evidence exists to show that humans lived in Ireland for over 10,000 years, and others declare that 6800 B.C. is the earliest date that can be given.

Before some time around 6000 B.C., Ireland, Britain and the Continent of Europe were all connected by land. After the rise of the oceans, settlers and invaders had to come by sea. The earliest Stone Age inhabitants lived off of nature's bounty by hunting, fishing, and gathering. Just where they emigrated from or how many of them there were is uncertain, although there could not have been many of them because prehistoric people not practicing agriculture must be spread extremely thinly in order to survive. Rudimentary agriculture, the growing of crops and the keeping of animals, developed with the new Stone Age people, or neolithic (lith means stone) people, who began to arrive in Ireland around

5000 B.C. They began the process of controlling nature rather than living off of it parasitically. They were short, dark-skinned people who may have originated in southern Europe or the Middle East.

Prehistoric Ireland is shrouded in myth, mists and legends. Certainly a series of conquests went on until recorded history. Warfare for territory was a norm for human groups in this region, and the victors could claim the better lands. There was something of a prehistoric arms race. Once metals were worked, the harder the metal the better the weapons' edges, and those with the best weapons were likely to acquire the best territory. Stone users were at a disadvantage facing those who had copper, and they in turn were at a disadvantage contronting those using bronze. The Bronze Age lasted until iron weapons put bronze weapons at a disadvantage. This evolution of metallurgy began around 1800 B.C. A byproduct of the arms race was the earliest Irish gold and bronze jewelry.

The Celts

All of prehistoric Ireland can be divided into two periods, pre-Celtic and Celtic. Celtic, by the way, is pronounced with a "k" rather than with the "s" sound used by the famous Boston basketball team. Who were the Celts? This is one of the more mysterious questions of history that has long been debated vigourously by historians. Identifying them among other prehistoric peoples is a major problem. some identify them by language, others by physical remains, especially those of a style named La Tène, and others rely upon classical

Greek and Roman sources describing Celts in central and western Europe.

Celts were a warrior people who came to populate France, Spain, Switzerland, Belgium, Britain and Ireland. Today Celtic tongues can still be heard only in a few fringes of European countries: in parts of Wales, Scotland, Cornwall in England, Brittany in France and, of course, western Ireland.

Celtic Britain was conquered by the Romans but Ireland was not. Latin influence came to Celtic Ireland not through the sword of the Roman legions but through the cross of Christian missionaries. The transition from prehistoric to historic Ireland took place without the conquest and overthrow of the Celts. Celtic Ireland continued to develop uninterrupted for centuries once it had fused with the culture of Latin Christianity. While the Romans were uninterested in sending expeditions to what they regarded as a cold, wet, distant, peripheral island, they did give Ireland a name: Hibernia. To this day Irish people in Britain and America are sometimes, if rarely, called Hibernians.

The long span of Celtic control of Ireland has been of fundamental importance to Irish nationalism. The Celts are perceived as the original Irish people, and their culture as the only pure and genuine Irish culture, uncorrupted and untainted by Englishness. In relatively recent times, avid nationalists have attempted to revive Celtic culture and purge it of the effects of centuries of English assimiliation. That is why the revived Irish language, old Irish folklore and Celtic art forms have been so important to zealous modern Irish nationalists. They exemplify the long centuries when Ireland was Irish and not English.

It is not an easy task to reconstruct an historically accurate account of Celtic life, especially in prehistoric and pre-Christian times. Celts came to Ireland a few centuries before the Christian era. Just when they arrived and how many of them effected the conquest of the pre-Celtic people remains unclear. So does the degree of violence imposed on the island by their settlement. It is certain that they invaded from Britain in waves, and some probably invaded from the coast of France. For a long time they fought and wandered around Ireland, a period called an heroic age, a time immortalized in great, bloody, aristocratic epics. These epics were finally written down hundreds of years after they originated and began to be passed from generation to generation by word of mouth.

While these Celts were divided up politically into fragments of local authority, they did have a cultural unity, meaning that they had a common language, outlook, technology, economy, and, in general, a common way of life. The Celts were noted for their skills in using iron, fighting from wheeled vehicles and living in fortified hilltop settlements. Classic texts describe them as tall in stature, with many individuals having flaming red hair. They were organized in tribes that tended to become or coalesce into small kingdoms as time went on. Each tribe was made up of several large extended families or clans, which were the essential social units. The extended families looked after their members, protected them physically and were responsible for their behavior.

At the head of Celtic society were warrior kings surrounded by warrior nobles. They were supported by the druids, who were priests, prophets and magicians,

busy with perfecting rituals and reading omens to fore-
tell the future. Some illustrious women poets were important in this society as well. Great sagas about kings
and aristocrats were recited by the bards, who committed vast amounts of information to memory, as do
storytellers in the few pre-literate groups that have survived long enough to be studied in this century. A considerable amount of fighting went on among the petty
kingdoms of Celtic Ireland. Fighting and disunity are
characteristic of heroic ages elsewhere also. Lesser folk,
some of them freemen and some slaves, are ignored in
these sagas. Yet they were responsible for the hard,
steady work of growing crops and tending cattle. As in
some pastoral east African societies today, wealth and
status were measured by the number of cattle owned.

A primitive form of writing developed after the
first few centuries of the Christian era, but before
Ireland itself was Christianized. It is called Ogham, and
consists of lines struck on stone. Reports of finding
Ogham on rocks in the United States are made from
time to time, but in all probability the scratches are
either fakes or such things as marks made by Native
Americans counting game.

What Can Be Seen of Prehistoric Ireland Today

The monuments of prehistoric Ireland are impressive and widely scattered across the island. The
most delicate and precious prehistoric objects in gold
can be seen in the National Museum in Dublin, which
has one of the world's finest collections of them.

Most of the Stone Age and Bronze Age monuments

are tombs and many Iron Age monuments were once
habitations or forts. A rather specialized vocabulary is
used for such objects. A megalith is literally a large
stone. Over a thousand examples of prehistoric mega-
liths have been found in Ireland, many in round circles
similar to but much smaller than Stonehenge, England's
most impressive prehistoric site. A dolmen consists of a
tripod of unhewn stones topped with a capstone, making it look like a table. Legends mentioned dolmens as
Druid altars, but they are really just a kind of megalithic
tomb. The body was buried below. They are found in
many places, but there are fake dolmens also, some
undoubtedly erected by students with a sense of humor.
The Shannon Airport has a "reconstruction" of a dolmen right outside one of the ultramodern plate glass
windows.

Court cairns and passage graves are more elaborate. A cairn is a mound or heap of stones. A court cairn
has a forecourt where ceremonies presumably took
place. A passage grave has a burial place at the end of a
long chamber. They date from 3700 to 2000 B.C. and
are Neolithic, or New Stone Age constructions. Newgrange, a location in the Boyne Valley and fairly close to
Dublin, is a large, impressive example of a reconstructed grave. It also reveals something of the beauty of
neolithic designs carved on stone. It is best to see it on a
weekday because the press of weekend crowds might
cause the interesting guided tour to be cut short.

Hill forts and ring forts date from the Iron Age.
The hill forts covered several acres and had a ditch
around them with a stone wall either inside or outside of
the ditch. Ring forts were smaller and usually on level

ground. They protected a small circular area with a stone or earthen wall surrounded by a ditch on the outside.

Tara is undoubtedly the best known hill fort. Later on it became the dwelling place for the high kings of Ireland. Later still it was the scene for St. Patrick's legendary contest in magic with pagan druid priests before an audience of Irish kings. Today it is crowned with a strange, decaying, cast concrete statue of St. Patrick dressed as a late medieval bishop. The outlines of various fortifications and a large building are still visible as mounds and ridges. On a good day the view from the top is supposed to encompass parts of all four historic provinces.

The most spectacular of all the Iron Age forts has already been described in the chapter on travel. It is Dun Aengus on Innishmore, one of the Aran Islands.

Crannogs were first built by prehistoric people and many were occupied well into the Middle Ages. A crannog features several small thatched buildings surrounded by a palisade on an artificial island built out in a lake some distance from the shore. The island was built up by piling up rocks and brush. A very realistic reconstruction has been made at the Craggaunowen Project near Ennis. The prehistoric site at Lough Gur near Limerick contains a discovered crannog.

Raths were habitations prepared for defense by building a bank and ditch. Some may have been only cattle pens, but many had houses as well as corral to protect cattle. Raths were occupied well into the historic period. Remains of them can be found all over Ireland. Before many of them were plowed over or bulldozed, remains of 50,000 may have existed. Over 100 have been excavated by archaeologists.

EARLY CHRISTIAN IRELAND AND THE GOLDEN AGE OF CELTIC CULTURE

According to tradition, St. Patrick brought Christianity and history to Ireland. Undoubtedly because of the contacts abroad through trade, some Christians lived in Ireland along the coasts before St. Patrick arrived. Nevertheless, his energetic mission brought the new teaching to many parts of pagan Ireland and led to the establishment of many churches. The main problem with St. Patrick is sorting out myth from reality, a problem compounded by the fact that only biographical fragments about him remain, pieces of the puzzle written down four hundred years after he lived.

He certainly did not drive snakes out of Ireland because Ireland in recent millenia has not been a suitable environment of these reptiles. He may or may not have used the shamrock to describe the Holy Trinity. What is well known about him is that he was first brought to Ireland by Irish raiders who kidnapped him from the island of Britain and made him a slave. He was probably a Celtic youth who had absorbed Roman culture along with Latin Christianity. He was in all probability not an Anglo-Saxon because these Germanic people had not yet begun to arrive in Britain in large numbers.

He first came to Ireland in the very early 400s.

After a dozen years as a slave in Ireland he escaped and somehow got back to Britain. After clerical training, he became resolved to return to Ireland to win the island over to the new faith. He was remarkably successful, as attested to by the fact that Ireland was converted without the creation of martyrs, a rare achievement in the history of Christian missions to pagan areas.

St. Patrick is revered in Ireland as the nation's most famous and important saint. Penitents go across rocks on their knees at Lough Derg, where St. Patrick was supposed to have seen a vision of purgatory. Incidentally, his color was blue, not green.

Other saints are revered also. St. Columba (or Columcille) went into exile as a penitential exercise and founded a monastery on the island of Iona. St. Brigid is supposed to look out for flocks, herds, butter and milk, leading some anthropologists to think that she was preceded in this role by a pagan goddess who cared for animals. Furthermore, some of Ireland's saints are said to preside over certain places, such as holy wells, thereby leading to the assumption that they replaced ancient pagan gods in local popular veneration.

Despite borrowings and adaptations from the pagan past, early Irish Christianity developed its own special form of organization: monasticism. The church had never before converted a large area inhabited by people who were un-Romanized, un-urbanized and un-commercial. Parish organization was suited to places that had at least some urban life, no matter how rudimentary. The usual hierarchy of bishops and archbishops was certainly designed to inhabit towns and cities. Ireland was simply too small, too poor and too pastoral to support a traditional church structure.

Therefore church activity was centered in monasteries, around which settlements eventually developed. This kind of church life was dominant until the Vikings settled and founded Ireland's first towns in the 9th century.

Ireland's unique monastic based Christianity had its golden age from the 6th to the 9th centuries, at the very time when the pagan Germanic barbarians who had ravaged and destroyed the Roman Empire and much of its culture were being slowly and painfully assimilated into western civilization. Roman Britain was destroyed by the floods of Anglo-Saxon invaders to the extent that Latin was lost permanently and Christianity was lost for several centuries, except on the fringes. Consequently, Ireland's links with Rome through Britain were cut off for a long period. For nearly all of Europe, the early Middle Ages lived up to its name, the "Dark Ages," but for Ireland, ironically, it was a time when Christian Celtic culture blazed with creativity and came to inspire western Europe.

Free from the scourge of Germanic barbarians, Ireland's monasteries trained exquisite creative artisans, scribes, illuminators, and craftsmen. Delicate and beautiful metalwork, richly illuminated manuscripts, high crosses and the preservation of the Celtic past were all products of this golden age. These monasteries provided the greatest contributions that Ireland has ever made to the artistic and architectural heritage of Europe. Monastic dynamism spilled over to other parts of Europe. Irish missionaries set up new monasteries on islands off the coasts of Britain and on the Continent, in what became France and Germany. Going abroad to be a missionary and thereby leaving the dear green island

was one of the most severe forms of penance a monk
could undertake. Abroad, Irish monks were noted for
their enthusiasm, industry and asceticism. Since Ireland
was such a small, sparsely populated island, the influence of the Irish in this era was disproportionate to their
numbers.

Some have speculated that one Irish monk from
Kerry, St. Brendan the Navigator, may have gotten to
North America. This feat may not be as far fetched as it
may seem at first. The Irish certainly had settlements in
Iceland, and it is farther from Ireland to Iceland than
from Iceland to Greenland and farther also than the last
lap of St. Brendan's presumed journey, Greenland to
Labrador. Some questionable evidence about the voy-
age exists in manuscripts kept in the national library of
France. Recently an Englishman made a celebrated two
year trip to North America in a reconstructed vessel of
the kind used in St. Brendan's day, a coracle constructed
of timber and hides. Even so, St. Brendan was never
equipped with the Englishman's compass, radio and
freeze dried food.

What Can Be Seen of the Early Church Today

Curiously, the earliest Christian structures remaining in Ireland are in the remote west rather than in the
more inhabited and fertile east. The reason for this is
that most of the earliest structures were of wood, and
wooden buildings do not survive over many centuries.
On the barren, windswept, treeless west coast, timber
for building was so scarce that stone was used from the
beginning. Churchmen in the fertile eastern region
turned to stone for their larger structures centuries

later, when the early period of the history of the church was over.

One of the best places to see some of the earliest remaining structures is on the picturesque and partly Irish speaking Dingle peninsula which juts out into the Atlantic from southwestern Ireland in County Kerry. Monks built so-called beehive huts out of stone for individual habitations. A cluster of them can be seen not far from Ventry, which is the first town to the west of Dingle, the main town on the peninsula of the same name. Other sites are scattered about, and finding out directions to them can lead to some interesting interactions with local people. One edifice on the peninsula not to be missed is the stark, striking Gallarus Oratory, already described in the chapter on travel. Its specific location is well marked on most maps.

The very adventurous may wish to hire a boat further south in County Kerry in order to travel to Skellig Michael, a deserted monastery on a stark, uninhabited island. Remains of very early monastic settlements can also be found on the Aran Islands.

Ireland's three wonderful monastic settlements of a later period, from the 9th to the 12th centuries, have already been introduced in the chapter on travel. Clonmacnoise, Monasterboice and Glendalough all have a round tower, high Celtic crosses and carved grave slabs.

Relatively few of the Celtic high crosses even in Ireland today actually date from the Celtic era. There was a revival of high cross sculpting in the 16th and 17th centuries and Victorians and other later admirers of them also built imitations. Celtic originals are found only in Ireland and northern Britain. Muireadach's Cross at Monasterboice is justly famous for its great size and elaborate depiction of simple stories from the Bible. The same can be said for the Cross of the Scriptures at Clonmacnoise.

Round towers are also hallmarks of Celtic Christian Ireland. They were built from 900, at the earliest, until the 12th century. Their five or more stories in height were originally capped by conical roofs. They served as bell towers and lookout platforms. Raised doorways reached by ladders seem to indicate defensive purposes, but a determined enemy could use fire to turn a round tower into a chimney. Some of Ireland's round towers, such as the one next to St. Canice's Cathedral in Kilkenny, can be climbed, but good physical condition should be a prerequisite to an ascent.

Several of the most gorgeous art treasures of the Celtic Christian era are in Dublin. The National Museum has the Ardagh Chalice and the Tara Brooch, both remarkably beautiful, and both revelations of Celtic excellence in metalworking and style. These two objects symbolize early Christian Ireland for many people and they regularly appear in various illustrated works about Ireland. Irish monastic illustrated manuscripts are magnificent and famous. The Book of Kells and other beautiful and intricate early illuminated manuscripts are kept at Trinity College in the Long Room of the Old Library.

IRELAND IN THE MEDIEVAL WORLD

Invaders of Celtic Ireland: Vikings and Normans

Celtic Ireland was spared invasions of masses of Germanic pagan barbarians, the hordes that brought down the Roman Empire. Later, Ireland did have to suffer the incursions of Scandinavian pagan barbarians, the Vikings, who stormed all over the seacoasts of Europe in the 9th century. At first the Vikings came as raiders and pillagers, destroying or stealing away many treasures from the Irish church. In fact, one of the best places to view early Irish art is in Norwegian museums. Since Ireland in the ninth century was justifiably known as *Insula Sanctorum et Doctorum,* or the land of saints and scholars, it was easy prey for the Vikings who could concentrate their sleek, shallow draft vessels to sail up Ireland's gentle rivers.

After a time the raiders began to overwinter and finally to settle as traders, choosing good natural harbors on the sea, usually at a river's mouth. Dublin was one such place, and although the city's millenium was celebrated in 1988, the Vikings probably established themselves along the Liffey as early as the mid-800s. The very oldest part of Dublin is called the district of Oxmantown, which is derived from Ostman, or men from the east, an early name for the Vikings. Wexford, Cork, Limerick, and Waterford also have Viking origins.

These Viking trading settlements were the first recognizable European towns to be built in Ireland, having streets, walls and timber houses. Hitherto the closest thing to any urban settlement in Ireland were the small clusters of habitations around monasteries. The Vikings brought much else: coinage, organized trade with the outside world, seamanship, and a new vitality for Irish art.

These advances came at a high cost in strife and bloodshed. Before this relatively small number of highly energetic Vikings settled down, numerous campaigns and wars were fought with various Irish rulers. After sporadic violence in the 800's and 900's, a large force of Vikings who had some Irish allies were trounced by an Irish king, Brian Boru, in the famous Battle of Clontarf in 1014. The victorious Irish hero king, like many great Irish heroes, became a tragic figure because he died while achieving his victory. The Battle of Clontarf did not ensure a departure of the Vikings. Instead, they collaborated with the Irish population, eventually blended in and were soon completely absorbed. Therefore any Irish person today might have genes that originally came from Norway.

The effect of the Vikings on the church was profound. First of all, old monastic settlements adopted the use of stone for buildings to avoid the danger of destruction by raiders' fires. High stone crosses were carved in order to explain Bible stories to these pagans. Once the Vikings settled in towns and converted, the church was able to build a more conventional organizational structure of parishes under the authority of bishops who became established in central locations.

While the Vikings eventually invigorated and further developed Celtic culture, the next wave of invaders, the Normans, sought to conquer the island and impose their own culture on it. The coming of the Normans marks the beginning of the connection with England because by the time the Normans arrived in Ireland they had already conquered England and Wales. Some historians have declared that their arrival was as important to Irish history as the coming of St. Patrick.

Who were these remarkable Normans? They were originally Scandinavians who conquered a province of France which was called Normandy, a name derived from an early name for them, Northmen. In Normandy they rapidly absorbed French culture and military skills. In 1066 they launched a successful attack across the English Channel on Anglo-Saxon England. Their leader, William the Conqueror, was able to gain a victory at the Battle of Hastings, an event that shaped English history for all time. Thereafter the conquered Germanic Anglo-Saxons had to work for the new Norman lords, but because there were so few conquerors and so many of the conquered, a two way cultural and biological diffusion between the two peoples took place, producing, when blended, the English people.

At the time of their arrival in Ireland, however, the Normans were still adventurous Frenchified Scandinavians. They had a reputation of being superb organizers, administrators and fighters. Normans fought on horseback, wearing armor made by blacksmiths. Once they captured an area, they threw up castles to defend it. They had a sinister reputation from having crushed resistance in France and Britain mercilessly and thoroughly.

One of the great old stories of Irish history, which is substantially true, is that the connection with England was brought about through an incident of Irish wife stealing. A king of Leinster, Dermot MacMurrough, abducted Dervorgilla, the wife of a rival ruler. The aggrieved husband, Tiernan O'Rourke, a minor king, was able to drive MacMurrough out of Ireland, at least temporarily. MacMurrough went to England to search for King Henry II and enlist his support in regaining his kingdom. Henry II was that vigorous monarch depicted by Peter O'Toole in classic films, one about the martyrdom of Thomas à Becket, and another about his domestic struggles with Eleanor of Aquitaine. Henry II was willing to back MacMurrough, providing that the Irishman recruit adventurers among the Normans in Britain himself. With this royal backing, MacMurrough struck a bargain with the Earl of Pembroke, known to history as "Strongbow," who agreed to lead an expedition of restless Normans from Wales. If they were successful, MacMurrough would get his throne back, but upon his death Strongbow would succeed him. Strongbow's force of Norman knights and lords were all willing to risk death for the prize of Irish estates.

According to some Irish commentators, with this invasion of 1169, "seven and a half centuries of plain and fancy hell" for the island began. The point of this lament is that from 1169, the date of the invasion, to 1922, the year the Irish Free State was established, some sort of English authority existed in what is now the Republic of Ireland.

For a time it was touch and go. Initially the Normans were hard pressed to hang on to a fortified foothold near Babingbun Creek, giving rise to the jingle "At the creek at Babingbun, Ireland was lost and won." One of the most ironic aspects of Irish history is that this invasion had the full backing of the pope, who regarded the Irish Church as disorganized and irregular. He wanted to bring the Irish Church in line to conform to the rest of Catholic Europe, and felt that a victory of Henry II's forces under Strongbow would make this goal feasible. The name of the Pope was Adrian, and the most remarkable fact about him is that he was the only English pope in the history of the Catholic Church!

Unlike the swift and thorough conquest of England, the Norman conquest of Ireland was much less organized, much more sporadic and much less forceful.

The Normans tended to take the best lands and control the rivers, leaving the less hospitable parts of the country, the woods, boglands and hills, to the Celtic Irish. Even so, Henry II was declared ruler of all of Ireland, and the island was made a fief, or possession, of England. The crown's control was never complete in the Middle Ages, however, because here and there Celtic chieftains and their followers held out against royal authority. Cultural duality was the result, an island partly of English culture and partly of Irish culture, a phenomenon that has endured permanently through Irish history.

The Rule of Medieval England

Where they were solidly established in Ireland, the Normans stamped it with the hallmarks of their civilization: castles went up; feudal manors or estates were organized; coinage was introduced; romantic literature became popular, some of it expropriating Irish stories; towns were built; cathedrals were erected; various new religious orders were imported, the legal system, including trail by jury, was introduced; so were mayors, coroners, town clerks and town councils. A variety of early English was spoken in these areas by those who had wealth, authority and power. Parts of Medieval Ireland truly began to look and function like Medieval England.

Another component was added to the Irish population in this process. The Normans in Britain became English while many of those in Ireland became Anglo-Irish, or, as they came to be called later on, "old English." Furthermore, many of the descendants of these Norman invaders actually became *hiberniores hibernis ipsos,"* or more Irish than the Irish themselves. The DeBurgos family in Connaught can serve as a case in point. Over time their Norman name changed to the Irish name of Burke. Edmund Burke, the 18th century philosopher, is their most famous descendant. Other supposedly typical Irish names, such as Joyce, Costello, Pendergast and Fitzgerald are all originally Norman names. They indicate the absorption of many Norman invaders over time.

England's power in Ireland waxed and waned in the Middle Ages. English kings were simply too busy and committed to wars in France and Scotland to spare resources for Ireland. So they allowed their authority to devolve upon great Irish families who gained considerable autonomy in the process. The Earls of Kildare, Desmond, and Ormonde ruled parts of Ireland in the name of English kings. The Earls of Kildare, members of the Fitzgerald family, were outstandingly powerful. Their power lasted for centuries and was called the Geraldine Supremacy.

Towards the end of the Middle Ages it was clear that there were two Irelands, the smaller part under English control and the larger part under Irish control. The Engish area, centered right around Dublin, was called "the pale" and gave rise to the expression "beyond the pale." By the 15th century, English authority reached its low point, and the pale was reduced to a beleaguered outpost extending only 20 miles west and 40 miles north of Dublin. Within that circumscribed area English government functioned, complete with a royal council, Parliament and Lord Deputy who exercised power in the name of the king. All of these functionaries used the English language, not Irish. This shrunken pale was the base for the expansion of English authority outwards to all of Ireland once the Middle Ages had come to an end.

The English in the pale fiercely resisted the seductive ways of Ireland, that is, the Irish culture's ability to absorb invaders and make them Irish. The English run Parliament in Ireland passed the Statutes of Kilkenny, which insisted that everyone in the pale speak English and follow English law and customs. Irish influences, including games, costumes and storytellers, were barred. The struggle between the two cultures has a very long history.

What Can Be Seen of Medieval Ireland Today

A large horde of Viking material has been assembled by the National Museum in Dublin, much of it gathered in haste before huge concrete buildings were settled on the best Viking archaelogical site in Ireland.

Stone castles and the Middle Ages are almost synonymous. Even so, the first Norman castles were of the motte and bailey type, the motte being a mound of earth with a flat top and the bailey an enclosure holding cattle and supplies. A wooden tower crowned the mound. The towers have long vanished, but in some places the mounds remain.

From 1200 on, the Normans began to build big, dominating castles to hole strategic points. See the section in the chapter on travel for details on Trim, Cahir and St. John's Castle.

Ireland's countryside is amply dotted with lesser castles, most in the form of the tower house, which was a rectangular stone fortified house. Since important local

Irish families followed the Norman families' penchant for building stone strongholds in the late Middle Ages, large numbers of these rather simple castles remain. Bunratty Castle is an example. The late-Medieval castles generally do not match the grandeur of the great castles built in the 13th century.

The Norman era was also the time that great cathedrals were built. Christ Church Cathederal and St. Patrick's Cathedral in Dublin have portions dating back to the Normans. Cathedrals in Kilkenny, Cashel, Limerick and Clonfert were built on a grand scale by the Normans. See the section on cathedrals in the chapter on travel for details.

The arrival of a style of architecture called Romanesque in Ireland predated the Norman invasion by several decades. Romanesque was the Medieval adaptation of the monumental style of the roman world. What makes Irish Romanesque churches different from those on the Continent is their smaller size. Irish churches were much smaller because they served smaller populations. Other features, rounded doorways, rounded chancel arches and lively decorations, are shared by Continental and Irish churches. Two of the best places to see examples of the Romanesque style in Ireland is at Cormac's Chapel in Cashel or at Clonfert Cathedral in County Galway. Cashel is actually a complex of church buildings and ruins majestically jutting up from the surrounding plains of Tipperary. Cormac's Chapel is noted for its stone roof supported by a great arch below it. Incidentally, Henry II summoned a gathering of church leaders at Cashel to acknowledge his lordship over Ireland.

The Romanesque style was succeeded by the Gothic

style, featuring pointed arches. Dublin's cathedrals and many Medieval cathedrals in the countryside were built in Gothic style. It was also a favorite of the Victorians of the 19th century who rebuilt churches in their own psuedo-medieval Gothic. The new orders of monks who arrived in Norman Ireland, the Cistercians, Augustinians, Dominicans and Franciscans, built many impressive abbeys that can be seen today as ruins in many parts of Ireland. Mellifont Abbey near Drogheda, north of Dublin, deserves special mention as an impressive ruin.

Portions of Medieval towns have not been preserved in Ireland as they have been in Britain, Germany, France and Spain. Here and there a portion of old town walls, or a gate or an individual building or just parts of such structures will recall the medieval period. Nearly everywhere newer houses have replaced the old and the town walls have been torn down. Even so, Kilkenny still does suggest its medieval past as a small Norman fortified trading town with a rectangle of streets within a ring of stone walls. For details, see the section on Kilkenny in the chapter on travel.

IRELAND IN EARLY MODERN TIMES

The Tudor Era, 1485–1603

A whole new era in English history and Irish history began in 1485 because in that year Henry Tudor became King Henry VII of England. In the century that the powerful, dramatic Tudor dynasty ruled, roughly the whole of the 16th century, the shrunken English pale around Dublin extended out in all directions and finally broke nearly all Irish resistance everywhere. This English expansion in Ireland was part of the worldwide extension of European energy and power that marked early modern times. It was part of a larger movement that also brought Columbus to America, a revolution in science, and a number of key inventions, including gunpowder, the telescope and printing with moveable type.

In 1485 few would guess that Henry VII would found such a dynasty, or, for that matter, even stay on the throne very long. Several previous claimants had short reigns and lifespans during the bloody Wars of the Roses in England. Henry was in a defensive position in both England and Ireland in the first part of his reign. The Earl of Kildare was the *de facto* ruler of Ireland. A story declares that Henry was told that "All of Ireland could not rule the earl of Kildare." Henry's wise reply was: "Then the earl shall rule all of Ireland." Whether or not these words were actually spoken, Henry did choose to accept the Earl of Kildare's position and rule indirectly through him.

Ireland was particularly troublesome for Henry VII because several rival Yorkist pretenders launched their campaigns against him from Ireland after the Irish parliament was pressured into recognizing them. Once Henry shrewdly and skillfully strengthened his position in England he turned to bringing effective rule to Ireland as well, so that Ireland's role as a base for treasonous plots against him could be ended.

The agent he chose for this mission was Sir Edward Poynings, who gave his name to Poynings' Laws. These laws came to govern Anglo-Irish constitutional arrangements for nearly three hundred years. Poynings put down rebels and pushed important new laws through the Irish Parliament. Among other things, Poynings' Laws stated that no Parliament could be held in Ireland unless specifically authorized by the English king and that legislation could only come before it after being specifically approved for their deliberation by the English crown. Meanwhile, all legislation passed by the English parliament was extended to Ireland automatically. The effect of this legislation was that the Irish Parliament was made subservient to the English government and could never become an autonomous, self-governing body. These laws had one end in view: the assertion of English control over Ireland.

Henry VII was not powerful enough to apply this control on a regular basis, but his famous son, Henry VIII, was. Unlike his father, he was never on the defensive, either in England or in Ireland. Henry VIII began a process of vigorous English expansion in Ireland that eventually led to the crushing of all resistance. Lessons learned in Ireland about expansion and colonization came to be applied elsewhere in the world by the English. For example, Sir Walter Raleigh and Sir Humphrey Gilbert transferred their knowledge of how to establish English plantations from Ireland to the New World. In the process, the tribal Irish were regarded and treated in much the same way as the tribal North American Indians. Tribal societies in both places were handled with lofty contempt as being obviously inferior to English ways.

Henry had the power to break the House of Kildare, and he did so. He was the first English king to garrison Dublin with an English army, a practice continued until 1921. Hitherto, English kings had borne the title of "Lord of Ireland." Henry VIII made himself King of Ireland also, and demanded that all Irish chieftains submit. Most of them did, because they regarded such salutes as harmless tactical maneuvers. What they really wanted was to be left alone, and if pledging allegiance to an English king from time to time was a prerequisite for non-interference by the English crown, they would do it willingly. What worked with other English kings did not work with Henry VIII.

Henry wanted to replace tribal organization with Tudor central administration. He called upon all chiefs to surrender their lands to him and he would then grant them back to the chiefs, thereby making the point that all the chiefs of Ireland ruled at the pleasure of the king. This Tudor policy, called "surrender and regrant," clashed with the old Celtic tribal law called Brehon Law, which regarded tribal land as the permanent joint property of the tribe, over which rule was temporarily exercised by a long line of Irish chieftains. It was a situation that faced North American Indians and Africans confronting Europeans who brought new conceptions of absolute property rights rather than community property rights.

Those chiefs who did not surrender their lands and have them granted back from the king were put down ferociously. When defeated, their lands were confiscated for treason and granted to loyal supporters of the Tudors, many of them English. Henry picked able and loyal deputies to rule Ireland for him, men who worked zealously to pacify Ireland through force and to Anglicize as much of Ireland as possible. Anglicization meant making Ireland more like England.

Religion became the key issue in the process of

Anglicization, a situation brought about by Henry VIII's notorious marital difficulties. Henry was desperate for a male heir to ensure a peaceful succession. To gain his ends, he divorced his wife, Catherine of Aragon, and married Anne Boleyn. He pressured the pope to annul the first marriage but Rome refused to cooperate, largely because of European political considerations. As a result, Henry had his marital difficulties settled his way in an English church court. Henry had to break with Rome and make himself Head of the new Church of England in order to bring this adjudication about. This opened the way to more changes in doctrine and practice which came about later on under the inspiration of Reformation leaders on the Continent.

Ireland's Catholic Church was supposed to become part of Henry's Anglican Church, and indeed new teachings were proclaimed in the main cathedrals and churches. The problem was that most people in Ireland could not understand these proclamations because they were made in English rather than Irish. What is more, transportation and communication with many parts of rural Ireland was primitive at best. In many places, thin populations were scattered over roadless bog and scrub. It took a long time for news from the outside to reach the interior. The net result was that only the most Anglicized areas, and therefore English speaking, were changed over to the Anglican Church. Elsewhere the practices and teachings of the old Catholic Church continued on, at first mainly because the Irish were inaccessible physically or because of a language barrier.

By the time the English got around to proclaiming their new Protestant faith to the Irish in their own language it was too late. By then the powerful Catholic

Counter-Reformation or, as some call it, the Catholic Reformation, had taken place on the Continent. The movement had Jesuit leadership and the overt aim to reconvert all of those who had broken from Rome. So by the time the English got around to try to convert Irish speakers to Anglicanism, the Jesuits were on the scene to strengthen resistance to the English in the name of the old Catholic faith. Also, friars travelled about to keep the old faith alive and eventually the pope appointed a new, rival hierarchy for Ireland.

Catholicism took on a new role: It was now both an affirmation of Irishness and a way to resist Anglicization. Irish history had reached another turning point. The dual culture of Irish versus Norman was perpetuated in a new form: Catholic versus Protestant, which often stood for Irish versus English. The partial conquest of the Normans was now followed by the partial Reformation of the Tudors. Because of the incomplete Reformation, the Tudor policy of assimilating all of Ireland to English culture failed, even if physical conquest eventually succeeded by the close of the reign of Elizabeth I. Many of the seeds of future Irish nationalism were scattered by these 16th century developments.

As the Reformation worked its way out under Henry's successors, it came to mean the destruction of the monateries, the replacement of Latin services with English services, a married clergy, and changes in several important doctrines pertaining to the Mass, purgatory, the saints and the Virgin Mary. The Church of Ireland, as the Protestant Anglican style church was called, became the church of the powerful establishment who were connected to English interests. Meanwhile efforts were made to root out Irish bards and Irish laws. Gaelic culture was under attack and barely survived. Oral tradition and Roman Catholic efforts kept it alive. The new learning and the new faith were bolstered in 1593 by the opening of Trinity College. It would become one of the better universities in Europe and remain a Protestant stronghold until this century.

Elizabeth I, Henry's famous daughter by Anne Boleyn, was able to conquer almost all of Ireland before she died in 1603. It became a military necessity for her because Ireland became a pawn between England and England's arch enemy, Spain. Spanish forces, crusading for the old religion, made several attempts to gain a foothold in Ireland. The island became the place to attack England through the back door, a point not missed by the French in the 17th, 18th and early 19th centuries, and by the Germans in the early 20th century.

Some Gaelic chiefs rebelled against Elizabeth and welcomed Spanish and Italian troops. The most dogged resistance to English power was manifested in Ulster under Hugh O'Neill, the Earl of Tyrone, once a charming courtier at the English Queen's court. A major defeat for Tyrone and his Catholic allies from overseas occurred at the Battle of Kinsale in 1601.

Elizabeth's captains treated the ordinary Irish ferociously, as if they were wild subhumans. Many English officers regarded the Irish as nothing more than filthy, barbarous beasts, and said so. As an example of English ferocity, consider how the royal deputy, Sir Humphrey Gilbert, cut the heads from the bodies of slain Irish opponents and lined the path to his tent with them. The purpose was to intimidate or "bring great terror" to the Irish with whom he had yet to deal.

Elizabeth herself wanted all Irish opposition broken, but she was not fanatical about what people believed. As long as they were loyal to her, the "Old English" families, who may have been in Ireland for centuries by that time, were allowed to remain in peace as practicing Roman Catholics. As time went on these "Old English" families merged more and more into the Irish population, now the population of their coreligionists. Meanwhile, priests were active all over the island, maintaining a rival and clandestine, or secret, Roman Catholic Church.

Elizabeth and other Tudor monarchs enlisted settlers from Britain to help control and transform Ireland. These settlers were installed on stretches of Irish territory, usually on land confiscated from rebels against the English throne. Such settlements were called plantations, the name given to some early colonies in the New World. In both places, natives displaced by plantations were generally treated in the same harsh way. Plantations were not as successful under the Tudors as they were under the Stuarts. The Stuart dynasty followed the Tudor dynasty when Elizabeth died unmarried and without children to succeed her.

The Stuart Era, 1603–1714

It is another irony of Irish history that the greatest loyalty to Britain today can be found in the province which was the scene of the most vigorous resistance to English rule and culture in the time of the Tudors. Up until the end of the 16th century, Ulster remained the least anglicized portion of Ireland. All that changed in the Stuart era, which was roughly the 17th century.

Ulster became thickly settled with anti-Catholic Protestants, setting the stage for the infamous conflicts of the present day.

After their crushing defeat at Kinsale, Irish earls from Ulster were allowed to settle down on some of their holdings, but this did not satisfy them. They suddenly sailed away to France aboard a French ship. This event of 1607 is known in Irish history as the "Flight of the Earls," and it opened the way for wholesale confiscation of Ulster land. Since they had fled, all the lands of the Ulster earls were confiscated by the crown.

To hold these extensive tracts of land, the crown sought to 'plant' large numbers of Protestant English and Scottish settlers. The ongoing dilemma of Northern Ireland began when these plantations were established. Protestants took the best land and Catholics were pushed onto poorer land. But Ulster could never become purely Protestant because too many Catholics remained. Many of them, in fact, provided valuable labor and rents for Protestant plantations. As early as the 17th century, the towns in Ulster began to have a "Scots quarter" and an "Irish quarter."

Various London companies took the responsibility of settling colonists in Northern Ireland, as did people called "undertakers," who literally "undertook" to settle parcels of land. Derry got the name Londonderry in recognition of London's efforts to settle the area with Protestants. In general, however, the English were less successful in Ulster than the Scots, who proved to be tough, industrious settlers, as they did in the New World thereafter. Proximity to Scotland made things easier, as well as the religious zeal of the Presbyterians, who were discriminated against in Britain by the dominant Anglicans. The Scottish settlers concentrated on arable farming, meaning that they plowed the land and grew crops rather than concentrating on grazing animals as the Irish in Ulster had done. Consequently, the plantations in the north came to feature neat, orderly farms. Elsewhere in Ireland the Protestants tended to be landowners and clergymen, but in Ulster all kinds of Protestants arrived, including artisans and workers. The north became the home of thousands of poor, ordinary Protestants, a fact about Ireland's population that remains unique in Ulster to this day.

Many Irish Catholics became discouraged by the flood of Scots and English into their region and followed the path of their earls into exile, offering their military skills to French, Austrian, Spanish and even Polish rulers. Their departure was called the "Flight of the Wild Geese." Many descendants of these voluntary exiles became noted citizens or subjects in their adoptive countries in later centuries. The Wild Geese provide another chapter in the great Irish diaspora, or dispersal, which began with the self-exiled Irish monks and continues to the present day.

In the middle of the 17th century, England became involved in a complex series of events that led to a civil war. There were many other civil wars on the Continent in this century, but they were usually marked by struggles between Protestants and Catholics. In England, two varieties of Protestants fought: the Anglicans and the Puritans. For a brief time the Puritans won, cut off the king's head in 1649, and established a republic under a military leader, Oliver Cromwell. After some years of experimentation and extremism, the Stuart dynasty was restored in 1660.

The nature of these complex and often confusing events in England need not be elucidated here, but their significant ramifications in Ireland deserve consideration. Actually, the outbreak of civil war in England was triggered by events in Ireland. Dispossessed Catholics rose in several places, including Ulster. The English king, Charles I, had to call a hostile English Parliament to ask for funds to pacify Ireland. His difficulties with Parliamentarians led to the outbreak of war between the king and members of Parliament.

In Ireland ugly massacres of thousands of Protestants by enraged Catholics took place. One such slaughter, at the bridge at Portadown, is still inscribed on orange banners today. Over a hundred Protestant men, women and children were seized at their homes, many of them robbed, stripped and raped, and then herded to the bridge where they were thrown into the water to drown. Those who could swim were clubbed from the boats. Other stories of atrocities recount incidents of people being burned alive. In the end, perhaps as many as 12,000 victims were claimed. Thereafter a permanent fear was held by Ulster Protestants, a fear that has never left. Many of them became convinced that there could be little safety for them in Ireland until the Catholics were permanently suppressed. This attitude set the stage for Protestant harshness in the future, including the brutalities of Cromwell and his troops and the ferocious discriminatory laws against Catholics in the 17th and 18th centuries. The deadly, dreadful cycle of alternating violence between Protestants and Catholics had begun.

Once the Puritan leader Oliver Cromwell emerged triumphant over the Protestant Anglicans in England, he turned to the pacification of Ireland. Cromwell commanded the best battle-trained and battle-hardened army in the world, the stern, austere, Puritan New Model Army. These fundamentalist, Bible quoting soldiers regarded Catholicism as a great evil, and zealously sought to destroy it. Cromwell casts a long, dark shadow over the historical consciousness of most Irish people. At worst, he appears to be something of an English Hitler, a destroyer, despoiler and a thief. Wherever ruins are found in Ireland they are likely to be attributed to Cromwell, even if destruction occurred centuries before he arrived!

Cromwell and his army gained their villainous reputation by slaughtering garrisons and priests after capturing towns. The most famous massacre was at Drogheda, after which Cromwell declared: "God alone shall have the glory." He justified his actions by declaring that he was avenging the massacres of Protestants and fulfilling God's will to have the Puritans triumph by crushing Catholic resistance. He also cited the 17th century rules of war about the right to slaughter garrisons that continued resistance beyond the point of hopelessness. Cromwell's bloody victories and massacres forged a greater unity among all Catholics, the Irish and the "Old English."

This sad period in Irish history includes another major turning point, perhaps not as important as the coming of St. Patrick or the coming of the Normans, but highly significant nonetheless. Put simply, the land of Ireland changed hands on a massive scale. As a result of Cromwell's victories over Catholic forces, most of the land on the island was forfeited to the Parliament of England, which made massive grants of estates to Protestant adventurers and Cromwellian ex-soldiers. Historians estimate that two-thirds of the land of Ireland was in Catholic hands before the Cromwellian conquest. After it, the amount shrank to less than one quarter. By the 18th century, the percentage was down to single digits. The very conquest of Ireland had been financed by promises of confiscated lands from Irish rebels. Therefore, those who risked money on the conquest were paid off handsomely in Irish estates. Meanwhile, Connaught became a dumping ground for dispossessed Catholic families.

Even after Cromwell died and the Stuart dynasty was restored in 1660, most of the revolutionary land arrangements remained fixed because Charles II, the Stuart king, owed his throne to the support and cooperation of Puritan generals. The pattern of Protestant landlords owning estates and deriving income from the rent of Irish Catholic peasants prevailed throughout Ireland during the later 17th, 18th and 19th centuries.

Since Charles II had no legitimate offspring, he was succeeded by his brother, James II. James II was an earnest Roman Catholic who wanted to put his coreligionists in position of power wherever possible in both England and Ireland, even if this meant bending or breaking the laws which specifically prohibited Catholics from taking such positions. James' deputy in Ireland put Roman Catholics in government jobs, packed the benches of courts with them, and got as many of them into the Irish Parliament as possible. Protestants were alarmed and fearful. Similar activities took place in England, where Protestants, particularly those from great aristocratic families, were much more powerful. James had two Protestant daughters from an earlier marriage,

Mary and Anne, and since he was fiftyish, he was not expected to be king for long, nor to have any children by his second wife, who was a Catholic. The plan of the great English Protestant aristocrats was simply to wait until he died. Their plans were upset by the unexpected birth of a son, who promised to continue a line of Catholic kings.

For a long time English politicians had been negotiating with James' daughter, Mary, and now they invited her and her husband to invade England and topple the Catholic king, pledging their support in the field. Mary's husband was William, Stadtholder, or traditional executive, of the Dutch Republic, and since he came from the House of Orange, he was known as William of Orange.

The plot succeeded easily and almost bloodlessly. Catholic James II fled to France and Protestant William III and Mary replaced him on the throne. This quick set of events gained the name of the Glorious Revolution of 1688, but it was really more of a *coup d' état*, a quick change of government at the top. It emphasized that a limited, constitutional Protestant monarchy had to have a limited, constitutional Protestant monarch at its head.

James II did not stay long at the French court. With French backing, he sailed for Ireland, the most Catholic part of his former realm. Once in Ireland, he asserted his hereditary right to rule once more, and used Ireland as a base to recover his English throne. All of this was part of a much larger European struggle, which pitted a powerful, expansionist France against the Netherlands, England, Spain and Austria. The main interest of William III, a Dutchman, was to preserve the Netherlands from French armies. William had Catholic allies, Spain and Austria, and he even had the support of the pope, who threw his support against the powerful France of Louis XIV. Therefore, when William of Orange sought to defeat James II in Ireland, a curious political situation ensued: Catholics in Ireland had a choice of supporting a Protestant Dutchman or a Catholic Englishman, both of whom claimed to be the rightful king of England.

James was resoundingly defeated at the Battle of the Boyne on July 1, 1690, by the old style calendar, and on July 12 by the new. Protestants still commemorate the battle on July 12 by dressing up, donning orange sashes, hoisting orange banners, beating drums and parading about in a solemn revelry, as if they themselves had personally won the battle. "Remember the Boyne" is a Protestant taunt still hurled at Catholics on the streets of Belfast or Londonderry.

The Protestant historical consciousness also centers upon the siege of Londonderry, where a number of young Protestant apprentices shut the gates in the face of an approaching Catholic force and joined the Protestant defenders in resisting a siege that lasted several months. Over this period of time the Protestants were often asked to surrender. "No surrender" was always the firm reply, and this phrase has become the watchword of Orangemen ever since, especially whenever they perceive Catholic aggression.

The war was finally concluded by the Treaty of Limerick, 1691, which marked the low point of Catholic power in Ireland. A minority of Protestants were now firmly in control, politically, socially and economically, all over the island, and they would remain in this position for a long time to come.

What Can Be Seen of Tudor and Stuart Ireland Today

Buildings from the Tudor and Stuart era are comparitively rare. Most are in ruins or long gone without remnants. The beautiful groups of black and white half timber buildings so noted in England or Germany are not to be found in Ireland. This makes the Elizabethan Rothe House in Kilkenny a special treasure. It was built by a rich Tudor merchant.

Fortified tower houses were built until the mid-17th century, long after such castle-like structures had ceased to be erected elsewhere in Europe. Monasteries and the churches connected to them that survived the onslaught of Henry VIII's Reformation were smashed, burned and looted by Cromwell. Although Irish people tend to exaggerate the destructiveness of the New Model Army, many ruins across the land are justifiably attributed to their violence. Since much of the fighting in Ireland revolved around holding strong points, the great old castles, such as King John's Castle in Limerick, played a part in the civil wars, sometimes changing hands several times. Nearly every old church or cathedral offers evidence of the changes of Tudor and Stuart times because they are Church of Ireland edifices and because their interiors have been altered. Notice how Church of Ireland locations tend to be more centrally located in the older parts of town than Catholic churches.

Classical architecture began to appear in Ireland in the later 17th century, stressing proportion, restraint, balance and often grand designs. The Royal Hospital in Dublin, near Kilmainham Jail, built from 1680 to 1684, is a fine example. Originally it was a home for retired soldiers, but now it has been restored and serves to display various exhibits.

Despite all of the Protestant drumming and celebrating about it up north, the actual site of the Battle of the Boyne is unmarked and almost completely ignored in the Republic for reasons that are understandable. Protestant banners and graffiti in the north remain bright orange, celebrating 1690 and William III, as if this Protestant hero were still alive today.

THE PROTESTANT ASCENDANCY OF THE 18TH CENTURY

In order to solidify the Protestants' position in Ireland and to keep the Catholics down, the British Parliament passed a number of harsh, discriminatory acts against Roman Catholics. Collectively they are known as the Penal Code, and individually the laws and provisions indicate how intensely the suppression of Catholics was pursued. Religious orders, Catholic schools and Catholic bishops were banned under this code. Priests could stay, providing that they took an oath abjuring, or denying the Catholic Stuart pretender to the throne. Anyone playing a part in politics had to take an oath against Catholic beliefs in the Mass, the Virgin Mary and the saints. Since no Catholic could make such a denial, only Protestants could be elected to Parliament, fill offices of state, be in the legal profession, establish schools or even vote. Intermarriage between Catholics and Protestants was discouraged. Protestant heiresses who married Catholics lost their estates. On the other hand, if one of several sons of a Catholic landholder converted to Protestantism, he would inherit his father's whole estate and leave his brothers landless. Protestants could follow primogeniture, which is giving an inheritance in land to the first born son only, so that the family estate could be kept together. Meanwhile, Catholics were required to divide their estates up among all of their male heirs. Catholics were also discriminated against over leases and mortgages. All of this meant that Catholics came to have control over less and less land. Also, Catholics could not have firearms, or horses worth more than five pounds.

By 20th century standards, the Penal Code was a most unjust and inhumane set of laws. The state was officially and ruthlessly anti-Catholic. While we are appalled at this today, we need to remember that the alternative to discrmination was persecution. Europe in the 18th century was still in an age of religious persecution, and much closer to the time when people had been burned at the stake or put on the rack because of their religion. England and Ireland did enjoy toleration in the narrowest sense of the word, meaning that people were allowed to worship a variety of religions without criminal punishment. Although this might not seem like much today, it was a giant step forward from the fierce, fanatical religious persecution practiced by both sides in the past.

The Penal Laws were inspired by the firm conviction of dominant Protestants that Catholicism was superstitious and idolatrous, and that people should be encouraged to become Protestant. Moreover, from a Protestant point of view, Catholics had been treasonous in the 17th century by rising barbarously and by supporting England's main enemy, France. Besides, if God did not want the Protestants to rule in Ireland, He never would have granted them their victories.

Ordinarily, discrimination involves the oppression of a minority by a majority. In Ireland, a majority was discriminated against by a minority. On the other hand, if the British Isles were taken together as one political unit, the Catholics were a minority, and most of them were poor and backward. The main question about the Penal Code is: How rigorously was it enforced? In most places at most times, the Penal Laws were not strictly enforced, particularly as the century wore on. Tactful circumventions were always practiced. Perhaps American laws about using turn signals, underage drinking, pot smoking, curfews or certain copyright laws can be compared. What remains on the books is not necessarily applied.

Protestant rule for all Ireland in the 18th century was assured in all important aspects, political, economic and social. The name "Protestant Ascendancy" has been used to describe their dominant status. Ireland in the 18th century has also been called "the Protestant nation."

Some of the Protestant estate owners lived on their lands in Ireland and others were called absentees because they lived in Britain and had stewards run their estates and collect rents for them. Some of these estates were gigantic, considering how small Ireland was. One particular duke owned 100,000 acres; an earl 86,000 acres, another duke 32,500 acres and a baron 41,000 acres.

Were the Protestants who lived on their family estates in Ireland Irish or English? It was a matter of debate. The English considered them Irish and the Irish considered them English. The name Anglo-Irish came to be applied as a compromise, a designation which was later defined by an Irish wit as "a Protestant on a horse." What compounds this question is the fact that many Protestants from the Ascendancy were keen Irish patriots. They felt that Britain treated them as colonials, and they wanted independence, much as Americans colonists did in the same century. Wolf Tone and Robert Emmett were two famous Protestant Irishmen who gave up their lives for the cause of Irish nationalism during the Ascendancy period. The ascendancy also provided famous literary and intellectual figures, including Bishop Berkeley, Oliver Goldsmith, and Jonathan Swift. Swift was so intensely patriotic that he once urged people to "burn everything English except their coal."

Despite official discrmination, some Catholics prospered in the 18th century on account of the generally buoyant and expanding British economy. Many Dublin businessmen and merchants who gained riches acquired the nickname "Castle Catholic," a sarcastic reference to friendliness with the British authorities who presided from Dublin Castle.

Dublin itself flourished magnificently in the 18th century. In one word, Dublin achieved elegance. (See the section on Dublin's Georgian heritage in Chapter One and the section on the interplay of history and architecture in Dublin in Chapter Four.) Over 100,000 inhabitants made Dublin the second largest city in the widespread and powerful British Empire. It had five newspapers, excellent theatre, good music and many bookstores. Handel composed the *Messiah* in Dublin, and the city was also the scene of its premier. The

Parliament, courts, and busy commerce all helped make Dublin the one important center for all of Ireland.

A prejudice of the 18th century was that true gentlemen had to draw income from land and be based in the countryside. Ireland's Protestant landholders have been compared to the 18th century gentry of colonial Virginia, to Thomas Jefferson and George Washington. Both groups certainly had similar feelings toward the mother country, wishing, like adolescents reaching maturity, that they were more loosely attached, more independent, more in control of their own affairs. Yet there was one inalterable difference between Ireland and America: the Atlantic Ocean was wide and the Irish sea was narrow. When the Americans were denied control of their own affairs they rebelled successfully. Those of the Protestant Ascendancy who chose to rebel failed.

The Ascendancy can also be compared with another group: the ruling whites of contemporary South Africa, a prosperous minority that controls a nation containing a large, generally impoverished majority. Certainly most rural Catholics in the 18th century were close to the subsistence level, living in squalid huts with thatched roofs. They had very few opportunities for even the most rudimentary education. There were only a few illegal Roman Catholic "hedge teachers" who worked furtively. Priests did what they could, often holding mass outdoors or in barns or in old ruins. Such shared privations built strong bonds between priests and laity which carried over into the next two centuries.

Despite privations, Irish culture endured. The Irish sense of humor and love of poetry and music certainly survived the years of the Protestant ascendancy. In fact, many rural Irish struck back in what Catholics called the application of a rough system of rural justice. Protestants called it rural terrorism. The Irish formed numerous secret societies, complete with oaths, passwords and pseudonyms for leaders. They delivered threatening letters, shot through windows, maimed cattle, and burned houses, hay ricks and barns. Their targets were those who evicted tenants, those who took over property after an eviction and those who gouged their tenants financially. Most of those targeted by secret societies were Protestants, but some Catholic gentry and landowners were singled out as well.

In Ulster in the 18th century, the Presbyterians were also discriminated against by the Church of Ireland establishment, even though the Presbyterians were fellow Protestants. The Presbysterians, after all, had belonged to the Puritan party which had fought the Anglicans in the English Civil Wars. Yet the Presbyterians were often excused for infractions, such as holding government offices illegally, much more readily than Roman Catholics guilty of the same misdemeanors. Still, Presbyterians had no seats in the Irish Parliament and the big government plums were inaccessible to them. In landholding they had more security and a better kind of contract for holding land, a policy called Ulster Tenant Right. In addition, Presbyterians supplied their own variety of rural terrorists who frequently fought with rival Catholic groups in a grim forshadowing of the troubles of the present day.

The outbreak of the American revolution strengthened the hand of the Protestant Ascendancy because the British army and navy were drawn off to fight the Americans, French and Spanish. While the Irish Parliament did have an undercurrent of sympathy for the American side in the struggle, it nevertheless passed a resolution condemning them as rebels. The possibility of an invasion of Ireland by England's enemies loomed. To face this threat, the Ascendancy created a popular militia, the Irish Volunteers. The Volunteers actually sought to parlay their loyal efforts to protect the British Empire to gain more independence for Ireland. They wanted Ireland to rule itself at home, which meant autonomy for the Ireland they dominated. Greater independence of the Irish Parliament was the key constitutional change from their point of view. Two outstanding Protestant Parlimentary leaders who worked for greater Irish independence at this time were Henry Grattan and Henry Flood.

These and other Irish Parliamentarians won greater freedom in the aftermath of the British defeat in America. Poynings' Law and other restrictive legislation were repealed. But British control continued to operate through the executive, and this part of the government could still dole out jobs, pensions and honors in exchange for votes in the Irish Parliament.

Catholics won some concessions at this time also. Many of the Volunteers thought that a true Irish nation would have to have free Catholics as well as free Protestants. In this spirit, the Irish Parliament repealed many of the Penal Laws. In another decade Catholics won the right to vote, but they still could not attain the right to sit in Parliament or hold government office. Making Catholics full citizens, which was called Catholic Emancipation, became an ongoing cause that lasted well into the next century.

The next great external event to jar Ireland was the

French Revolution, a very complex and confusing set of events, made even more so in the Irish context. Since the French Revolution attacked the power of the Catholic Church in France in the name of reason, many Catholic reformers in Ireland became negative towards it. Many more secular members of the Irish middle classes, Catholic and Protestant, supported it. Some of them formed the Society of United Irishmen which called for complete religious equality and for democracy, a doctrine regarded as dangerous and radical in the 18th century.

For decades Britain was locked in a desperate struggle throughout the world against revolutionary France. The British were apprehensive about Ireland because a French invasion might land on this island whose loyalty was undermined both by its own radical reform movement as well as by Roman Catholic peasant unrest. These fears were realistic. Some United Irishmen plotted insurrection, and under Wolfe Tone they conspired to bring in a large French invading force. At a most opportune time for invasion during 1796, a fog divided up a French invasion fleet, causing it to withdraw. Some of this fleet was poised to land troops along Bantry Bay when it was ordered out to sea again. Eventually Wolfe Tone was caught at sea in a French uniform and just before he was to be executed for treason, he committed suicide. Through these events, Wolfe Tone became a celebrated Protestant martyr for the cause of Irish nationalism.

Another botched attempt at insurrection took place in 1798, but this time sectarian violence flared to confuse the situation. Roman Catholic peasants rose in some places and fought the British army. The rebels were slaughtered savagely, but not before they had committed several ghastly atrocities against the Protestant population. Vinegar Hill in county Wexford was the scene of ferocious slaughter and fighting. All sorts of torture and numerous executions were perpetrated by British forces to get information to end a rebellion that they regarded as nothing more than barbarous savagery. They called the rebels "croppies" because of their short hair.

By the end of the 18th century the British government was convinced that something had to be done to make Ireland a less dangerous place. They could count on the cooperation of many Protestants in the ascendancy now, because many of them had been thoroughly frightened by the rising of 1798.

What Can Be Seen of the Ireland of the Protestant Ascendancy Today

Again, see the section on Dublin's Georgian heritage in Chapter One and the section on the interplay of history and architecture in Dublin in Chapter Four.

Since the Protestant Ascendancy idealized the ancient Greeks and Romans, it is no wonder that their architecture was classical. One of the last great classical buildings to be built in Dublin was the General Post Office, which was completed in the early 19th century. It became the focal point of the famous Rising of 1916.

Ireland has some grand 18th century mansions on country estates built by ascendancy landowners. Some have two or three stories and many windows, thereby indicating domestic security and confidence. Unlike landowners in Ireland during previous centuries, the

Protestant ascendancy of the 18th century did not make fortresses out of their habitations. One of the most noteworthy of these great houses of the 18th century open to the public today is Castletown in County Kildare, built in the 1720s in a style of classical architecture called Palladian. Such buildings fit into the lush landscape of eastern Ireland readily in the 18th century, since that part of the island comes closest to resembling the plains of England.

IRELAND IN THE 19TH CENTURY

From the Union with Britain to the Death of Queen Victoria, 1801–1901

To British statesmen locked in a desperate struggle with Napoleonic Europe, Ireland was a source of fear and frustration, a tumultuous and potentially treasonous island. It was vulnerable to a French invasion and therefore it had to be governed even more closely. Their solution was to amalgamate Ireland with Britain. An Act of Union came into effect in 1801, merging Ireland into Great Britain by dissolving the Irish Parliament and making space in the British Parliament for a hundred Irish members.

There were precedents for this move. Wales had been linked to England in the 16th century and Scotland had lost its Parliament when joined to England by an act of union in the 18th century. But Ireland was different because it was separated by salt water and had a majority of Catholics who once shared an ancient culture and language. Even so, British politicians were convinced that an amalgamation with their nation, which they perceived as obviously the most powerful, most prosperous and most enlightened nation in the world, would prove to be highly beneficial for the Irish. Protestants in Ireland generally favored the union but Catholics were against it because they would become a minority in the United Kingdom. Besides, Dublin would lose considerable influence and prestige and become more like other provincial British cities.

Before the Act of Union could come about, the Irish Parliament had to agree to its own demise. The decision was abetted by liberal doses of bribery, honors and awards. In other words, those who were *de facto* patrons of Irish Parliamentary seats were amply compensated for their loss. Most contemporaries expected that Ireland would now settle down and become another Wales or Scotland.

One rather pathetic rising occurred in Dublin a few years after the Act of Union. Robert Emmet, a Protestant inspired by the American and French Revolutions, led some rebels to seize Dublin Castle and proclaim a republic. The rising was put down rather quickly, but Emmett nevertheless made a very ringing and memorable patriotic declaration from the dock, saying that his epitaph should not be written until Ireland took her place among the independent nations of the world.

Catholics chafed under the union because they thought they had been promised emancipation, or equal political rights, to get them to go along with the union. This promise was not fulfilled by the British government. So Catholic Emancipation became the special crusade of the greatest hero of Irish nationalism in the early 19th century, Daniel O'Connell, a lawyer from the west of Ireland. Like Ghandi and Martin Luther King, Jr., later on, O'Connell believed in peaceful, nonviolent, mass demonstrations. He was the very first politician to look to the great mass of poor Catholics as the basis of a political movement. Close collaboration with the Catholic Church was the essence of his movement. He worked with priests to organize lay Catholics and bring them into the political arena for the first time in modern history. Under his guidance, Catholics learned how to use their numbers and public opinion to further their own interests.

The marches, huge meetings and demonstrations of peaceful, organized and disciplined Catholic masses alarmed the British government. Suppose this new movement was thwarted and became violent? A ghastly conflict might ensue. With these forebodings, British leaders gave in and granted Catholic Emancipation in 1828. Thereafter Daniel O'Connell and other Catholics could sit in Parliament and hold almost any government office. Catholics hailed O'Connell as the "Liberator" or the "Emancipator." He turned next to agitate for the repeal of the Act of Union. This would mean the restoration of a Parliament in Ireland, but now the majority of members would be Roman Catholics. This agitation for repeal failed to achieve its goals due to adamant British resistance and the onset of social turmoil in Ireland because of the Great Famine.

The Great Famine of the 1840s was a cataclysmic natural disaster. Before the famine, population growth had taken off in Ireland, leaping from approximately four million around the time of the American Revolution to over eight million in the early 1840s. This latter figure was the highest number of inhabitants ever to live on the island. Even in the 1980s, approximately three million fewer people lived there. Intense potato cultivation allowed early marriages for people who were willing to live on small plots. When blights destroyed successive potato harvests, outright starvation and disease made deadly by mass malnutrition resulted. The horrors observed in Ireland were comparable to those during the Black Plague of the 14th century.

The response of the landowners varied. Some helped their tenants and some carried out evictions all through the famine. The British government was overwhelmed and could not cope with a disaster on this scale. Governmental efforts were limited to public works, soup kitchens and some food distribution. Firm belief in capitalism and contracts assured the sad scenes of meat and grain being sold and exported from Ireland at the very time that hundreds of thousands of peasants died because they could not afford to buy food. This is a point many Irish nationalists underline by making the distinction between a famine, when there is a lack of food, and starvation, when people are denied food. Revisionist historians have hotly disputed this point, declaring that government sponsored imports of food far exceeded private exports.

The famine left a legacy of bitterness in rural Ireland. It also changed social patterns dramatically. Henceforth early marriages were frowned upon, and families arranged marriages for older offspring with great care in order to assure enough resources for their survival. To keep holdings from being overly subdivided, young people were encouraged to seek their fortunes abroad. Millions arrived to help develop America, while millions of others emigrated to Britain, where they supplied labor for Britain's dramatically expanding industrial revolution. The part of the island that is now the Republic did not experience a comparable economic transformation in the 19th century. It remained agrarian while Britain grew in numbers, wealth, urban development and power, altering the relative importance of the two islands on the world stage. After Ireland's disaster, the population dropped to half of what it had been, ironically at the same time that other European countries, including Britain, experienced population surges.

When the famine was over, the fundamental issue of Irish politics remained: How might the union with Britain be repealed or how might the union be made to work? Land was the key issue. Irish peasants had always viewed land ownership differently than landlords. Peasants felt that they had a share in the ownership because they lived on the land, worked it and improved it. Landlords, on the other hand, thought in terms of absolute private property and modern contracts. Bitter clashes resulted, often over evictions. Rural violence, consisting of burnings and assassinations, was met with vigorous coercion on the part of the government. Sometimes coercion included the suspension of the Bill of Rights for certain time periods in certain areas. The word "boycott" was added to the English language during these struggles. Captain Boycott was a landlord with a very bad local reputation, and so he was shunned by everyone, including his farm workers, in a tactic of passive resistance.

The British government became convinced that it was necessary to settle the land question in order to pacify Ireland and thereby make the union work. Concessions were offered to insure that rent was fixed and fair and that tenants were given security of long leases without evictions. The great British Liberal Prime Minister, William E. Goldstone, took up this matter as the keystone of his administration, declaring boldly: "My mission is to pacify Ireland."

The situation over land illustrated the old dictum that by the time the British got around to providing an answer to an Irish question, the Irish would change the question. By the time the peasants could assert their rights in dealing with their landlords, they objected to having any landlords at all. The transfer of ownership from the landlords to the tenants was the next great Irish demand. Eventually the government came around to agree to it, passing acts to set up funds enabling land transfers to take place with adequate compensation for landlords. But appreciation of these concessions was marred by the coincidental passage of tough new coercion acts to crack down on peasant violence. The British never wanted to appear, then or now, that they would ever give in to violence.

Gladstone had to deal with one of the toughest, most charismatic and strangest Irish politicians, Charles Stuart Parnell. He was the adamant leader of the Irish party in the Westminster Parliament, and therefore very important to British Prime Ministers because Irish votes might tip the balance between the two major British parties, the Liberals and the Conservatives, if election results were fairly close, as they usually were. Parnell was a very obstinate politician in Parliament, practicing tactics of obstruction to hold up legislation unless concessions were made to Ireland. Ironically, Parnell was a Protestant landowner who had been educated in England. His mannerisms and speech were very English, yet he nurtured a deep and abiding hatred for English rule in Ireland. Catholics recognized this and accepted him as their leader with enthusiasm.

Parnell and Gladstone struggled with one another and sometimes found themselves on the same side of a political issue. Both men came to the conclusion that the only way Ireland could achieve peace was through Irish Home Rule. This meant the restoration of the Irish Parliament and granting Ireland the status similar to that of Canada, Australia or New Zealand. These Dominions, as they were called, all controlled their own internal affairs, while the British government was responsible for their defense and external relations. Commitment to Home Rule meant the end of the dream of assimilating Ireland, making the island into another Wales or Scotland. In general, British Conservatives clung to maintaining the union and British Liberals followed Gladstone's call for Irish Home Rule. While Liberals could put together a majority in the House of Commons with Irish support, they were blocked by a Conservative majority in the House of Lords. By the early 20th century, this very question provoked a constitutional crisis that led to the curtailment of the power of the Lords to veto legislation. The Parliament Act of 1911 marked this change.

Gladstone's commitment to Home Rule for Ireland aroused the fears and fury of Protestants in Ulster. Ulster had been prospering on account of growing industrialism, particularly in the shipbuilding and linen industries. For the substantial Protestant minority thickly settled in the north, Home Rule meant subor-

dination to Catholics. Ulster Protestants resolved to resist at all costs.

Just as Daniel O'Connell was unable to achieve the
repeal of the union, Parnell and Gladstone were unable
to pass Home Rule. Parnell's leadership was derailed by
a sex scandal. He had lived furtively with a married
woman who was long separated from her husband. Her
name was Kitty O'Shea. What might seem ordinary today was condemned by the stern strictures of Victorian
sexual morality. Parnell died in disgrace shortly thereafter, when he was just over age forty.

The parties of Parnell and Gladstone pursued their
goals for Ireland through constitutional means. Simultaneously, smaller groups continued to pursue a new
destiny for Ireland by using revolutionary violence. In
1848, romantic middle class republicans led a rising in
the name of the "Young Ireland" movement, but were
easily put down. A longer lasting and much more violent group that was founded after the famine was the
Irish Republican Brotherhood, or the Fenians, a name
derived from that of a band of ancient Irish warriors.
The Fenian movement was based in Ireland and America. Many Irish immigrants had participated in the
American Civil War, and when it was over many
planned to fight for Ireland's independence.

Fenian escapades included an abortive invasion of
Canada, bombings in Britain, and a rising in Ireland in
which American Civil War veterans participated. In
Britain, Fenian became a term analogous to terrorist
today, and when Englishmen spoke of them, the word
'bastard' was likely to follow "Fenian." The Irish Republican Brotherhood is the forerunner of the Irish

Republican Army, and the famous Rising of 1916 can be interpreted as a second Fenian rising.

During the 19th century and beyond, the Catholic Church would not lend support to any violent schemes. It concentrated on specific issues, such as education, building churches and pressuring the government to disestablish the Church of Ireland so that Catholics would no longer have to pay for a Protestant establishment.

At the end of the 19th century, Ireland's future was a matter of intense debate. Some hoped that a permanent union could work and that the Irish would remain as one of the components of a united Great Britain. Others agitated for Home Rule, hoping that Ireland would become another self governing state like Canada. Still others plotted for a republic completely independent of Britain. Around 1900, the future as envisioned by the latter group seemed to most people to be the least likely to come about.

What Can Be Seen of the 19th Century Today

The Victorians were avid builders who favored using brick. In their era brick buildings replaced old wooden and sod buildings all over Ireland. Most towns and cities are still filled with Victorian structures, many of them now stuccoed and brightly painted. Large civil buildings were another Victorian specialty. The National Library and the National Museum in Dublin are fine examples that have counterparts in provincial cities.

Whole working class districts were built by the Victorians. So much of these neighborhoods survive that many films set in Victorian Britain are actually shot in

Ireland. The Dolphins Barn area of Dublin is a good example of an old working class district where the Victorian past is still very much in evidence.

Many Catholic churches and pro-cathedrals were constructed in the 19th century. Their massive grey pseudo-medievalism provides prime examples of a style called Victorian Gothic. Victorian country houses have their own distinct characteristics. They tend not to emphasize the lean classical proportions of the 18th century. Instead, they tend towards the elaborate or the romantic. One example of a country house built in the 19th century is Muckross House outside of Killarney. Closer to Dublin, in Bray, is Kilruddery House, a romantic imitation of an Elizabethan country house built in the early 19th century.

Last, the Victorians were notorious for redoing the past to make it correspond with their own romantic images. Should they rebuild part of a castle, such as the banqueting hall at Kilkenny Castle, for example, they would embellish it with designs and colors from their own vivid visions of the Middle Ages. Old churches and cathedrals suffered the same fate at their hands.

IRELAND IN THE EARLY 20TH CENTURY

Cultural Vitality and Political Crisis

Ireland's relative position to Britain changed dramatically from 1800 to 1900. Britain was only twice as populous as Ireland in 1800; in 1900, nine times as populous. The disparity in wealth between Britain and

Ireland had grown correspondingly. Both Dublin and Cork had lost their status as major cities in the British Empire by 1900 and largely Protestant Belfast, a comparatively insignifciant city of 20,000 in 1800, had grown to be larger than Dublin by 1900, a situation that would be reversed again later in the 20th century.

Relative significance in numbers and wealth in comparison to Britain aside, Ireland enjoyed a vitality in politics and culture in 1900. The Gaelic revival was in full swing. An organization called the Gaelic League attempted to revive many facets of old Irish culture including language, folklore, sports, dances, literature and the arts. The Gaelic revival stressed that Ireland was not simply an Anglicized, western part of Britain. Propping up the fast fading Irish language, enjoying ancient arts and stories, and playing Irish sports served the movement for Home Rule. Ireland's unique indigenous culture thus celebrated, justified a separate political entity for the island.

About the same time, a cluster of brilliant Irishmen dazzled the English speaking world with their talent, wit and creativity. Oscar Wilde and George Bernard Shaw dominated the English stage in the late 19th century. John Mellington Synge and William Butler Yeats celebrated Ireland with the most exciting poetry written in the world at the time. Yeats actually won the Nobel Prize for literature. The genius of James Joyce was at work in these years. His materpiece, *Ulysses,* looks back to a day in Dublin just after the turn of the century. Most of this rich creative activity was carried out in English and not in Irish. It had to be in English to have such an impact on the wider world.

Irish politics in the early 20th century focused on Home Rule. Since British Liberals were finally able to break the power of the Conservative dominated House of Lords, a limited Home Rule bill was enacted. It was supposed to become law in September, 1914, but the outbreak of World War I in August, 1914, shelved Home Rule until peace returned. The actual outbreak of World War I came as a surprise to Britain and Ireland because attention had been so fixed upon the possible outbreak of civil war in Ireland. Ulster Protestants were resolved to defy Parliament over Home Rule, proclaiming as their slogan: "Ulster will fight and Ulster will be right." Ulster Protestants signed a solemn pledge called the Covenant to defend themselves to the last against Home Rule. Their Covenant was supposed to be similar to the Covenants in the Bible which bound communities together. To back it up, Ulster Protestants created their own private army, the Ulster Volunteers. Sir Edward Carson, a tough, humorless Protestant born in Dublin, became the determined leader of the movement. Some have characterized him as a forerunner to today's leader of unyielding northern Protestants, Ian Paisley. Conservative leaders in Parliament expressed support for the Ulster resistance and many officers in the British army declared they would resign their commissions before they would try to put Ulsterman down by force.

Meanwhile Catholics in the south armed themselves also. The National Volunteers was formed, drawing heavily upon members of the Irish Republican Brotherhood and the Gaelic League. Both private armies, north and south, were armed with weapons smuggled in from Germany. One schoolgirl watching an unloading at

Howth was surprised to see her angular, bespectacled mathematics teacher helping in the work. He was Eamon de Valera, the Republic's future leader.

Once the great war in Europe began, the question of whether or not Ireland should participate was raised. John Redmond, the leader of the Irish Parliamentary party, decided to cast Ireland's lot on the side of Britain in the war, hoping that this loyalty would demonstrate how worthy of Home Rule Ireland was. A minority of Irish Volunteers disagreed with this decision, and the dissenting group would eventually evolve into the Irish Republican Army. The majority of the Irish Volunteers supported the war effort, however, and many of them fought and died as volunteers in British uniforms. The Ulster Volunteers eagerly joined the British army as a unit and were subsequently cut to pieces on the western front.

The Rising of 1916

Heroic Irish support for Britain in World War I was overshadowed by a destructive, hopeless uprising that occurred in Dublin in 1916, the famous Easter Rising. It is an event as important to the Irish nation as the fall of the Bastille is to France or the Declaration of Independence to the United States. It set in motion a series of dramatic, bloody events which eventually created a sovereign, independent Irish Republic for 26 of the island's 32 counties.

The small group that rose in 1916 had little faith in the promise of Home Rule or they regarded it as a sellout to Britain. Some shared the melodramatic conviction that the Republic could never become a reality unless there was a heroic blood sacrifice to absolve the sins of a long collaboration with Britain. Some were old Fenians, like Patrick Pearse and Tome Clarke, who worked with the dissident Irish Volunteers. Some were union organizers and socialists, such as James Conolly, who enrolled workers in the new Irish Citizen Army.

After some bungling and confusion, fewer than 2000 participated in the rising, including almost 30 women. They took up strategic positions in Dublin, including Boland's Mills and the General Post Office. In front of the General Post Office the leaders proclaimed an Irish Republic in gripping, patriotic language. Poorly equipped and hopelessly outnumbered from the start, the rebels never had much of a chance. Once the shooting started, the British brought in heavy reinforcements and bombarded the rebel positions, causing severe destruction in the heart of Dublin. Before it was over, close to 500 people had been killed, including hundreds of civilians, and many more were wounded.

From all appearance, the rebels were an unpopular minority. They were hooted and jeered as they took up positions. When the British reinforcements arrived they were warmly welcomed along the way by Irish people. The destruction that ensued from putting the rebels down was generally blamed on the instigators rather than on the British forces. What is more, the war against Germany and Austria-Hungary was in full swing in 1916, and many Irish families had sons in British uniform. So to many Irish people, the rising looked like a cowardly and treasonous stab in the back that might jeopardize Home Rule.

Perceptions changed once the British authorities began to exact retribution. The captured rebels were packed into Kilmainham Prison and given swift trials by court-martial. Several leaders were taken into a narrow execution yard and shot. Thousands more were arrested, and who was to know at the time how many more of them would be shot. Actually, most were detained in England and Wales without trial and released fairly soon. Somewhat inexplicably, this was the fate of de Valera. By acting so impulsively toward some leaders, the British military inadvertently made martyrs out of some rebels. Now they are great national heroes. The British just did not take them and their aims seriously enough, and did not regard their uprising as anything but foolish. In the minds of many, once British prosecution began, their futile sacrifice did become noble and heroic, because it served to rekindle the dream of the Irish Republic. The flag of the Irish Republic had flown, and the rebels had given memorable patriotic speeches on the eve of death. Due to this doomed, hopeless and heroic uprising Home Rule was no longer the goal of zealous Irish patriots. The idea of an independent republic had become their goal. Or, in the words of the poet Yeats, a "terrible beauty" had been born.

The Anglio-Irish War and the Irish Civil War, 1919–1923

Impatience grew towards the Irish Parliamentary party sitting in the Westminster Parliament. A militant nationalistic party called *Sinn Féin*, or "ourselves alone," began to draw support from most Irish voters. *Sinn Féin* advocated withdrawing from the British Parliament and forming an Irish Parliament to sit in Dublin. In the important general election of 1918, *Sinn Féin* gained almost three quarters of the Irish seats. They pulled out of the Westminster delegation and organized their own Irish Parliament in Dublin, the *Dáil*. When the British government ignored them, Irish republicans began a general state of disorder which soon degenerated into a civil war, called either the Anglo-Irish War or the Irish War of Independence. By either name, it lasted from 1919 to 1921.

It was a nasty struggle that has been poignantly etched on the memories of older Irish people, becoming part of the oral history of many areas. The British recruited tough ex-soldiers for mercenary military service against the republicans. They came to be called the "Black and Tans" because of the color of their uniforms. They soon acquired a reputation to rival that of Cromwell's troopers on account of their violence. The Irish Republican Army was ill-equipped compared to the Black and Tans and their paramilitary police allies, and had to rely upon hit and run guerilla tactics. During this time, Ireland was rife with undercover agents, double agents, spies, informers and assassins. Michael Collins emerged as the clever, audacious intelligence leader of the I.R.A., a man whose career spawned legends.

When both sides were exhausted by war and by long, difficult negotiations, they came to an agreement, the Anglo-Irish Treaty of December, 1921. David Lloyd George, the wiley Welsh Prime Minister, was deliberately vague about the final status and border of the north. Ireland became a "Free State," a name chosen to get around the British delegation's objection to calling it a republic. Thus partitioned, the Free State became a self-governing part of the British Commonwealth, a status not unlike that of Canada. Nevertheless, with this treaty,

800 years of British rule in southern Ireland came to an end.

Unfortunately those who had fought against the British were split by the treaty. Some did not want to stop fighting until all of Ireland, north and south, enjoyed a republic entirely free from Britain. Others saw the treaty as a major step forward and believed that the rest would come in time. Pro-and anti-treaty forces drifted into a nasty continuation of the war, only now it was exclusively among the Irish. Like the British government before them, Free State authorities imprisoned and executed rebels for treason, actually killing more Irishmen on that charge than the British had done in the Anglo-Irish war, which is another striking irony of Irish history. The Irish vs. Irish civil war lasted from 1922 to 1923, and during it one of the leaders of the 1916 Rising, Eamon de Valera, desperately resisted the pro-treaty forces until he was imprisoned by Free State authorities. Michael Collins, the hero of the Anglo-Irish War, led Free State forces against the anti-treaty I.R.A. until he was gunned down in an ambush.

By the time the pro-treaty forces finally gained a victory, British objectives appeared to have been achieved. Northern Ireland was saved from being subordinated to a Catholic majority through partition and the Free State was still in the British Empire. Part of the achievement proved to be temporary, however, because Irish nationalism was running at full tide. Irish history was being reinterpreted, emphasizing the episodes of resistance to Britain. No matter how squalid or relatively unimportant previous violent uprisings may have been, they were now transformed into noble chapters on a long road to republican freedom. Thus the Fenian rising of 1867, Young Ireland's episode of 1848, Emmet's rising of 1803, the rebellion of 1798, the struggle against William III, 1689–1690, and the rebellion of 1641 all became glorious chapters in a story leading to 1916 and the Republic. Retrospectively, the use of violence against Britain was glorified in the rewriting of Irish history for the purposes of republican nationalism.

What Can Be Seen of the Early 20th Century Today

Much of the Dublin of James Joyce still exists. During the tourist season, walks through scenes immortalized in *Ulysses* are regularly held. The martello tower at Sandycove, mentioned in the chapter on travel, houses the James Joyce Museum. Many of the pubs of Dublin, including several described by Joyce, still evoke the atmosphere of the turn of the century. Kilmainham Jail, described as an 'Irish Alamo' in Chapter One, has become a shrine to the martyrs of 1916. Extensive, richly detailed exhibits highlight the theme of retrospective glorification of violence against Britain. Kilmainham also houses the ketch *Asgard,* which brought German arms to Howth harbor. The place of disembarkation is marked by a plaque on a jetty wall within the harbor itself. Elsewhere in Dublin there are many sights associated with the Rising of 1916 and the wars of 1919 to 1921 and 1922 to 1923. Many remain unmarked since this is such recent history and, for many people, still in living, painful memory. Boland's Mill is still a bakery and the General Post Office, rebuilt from its destruction in the Rising, still functions in its original capacity, although a statue and plaque commemorate the dramatic events that took place there. The Garden of

Remembrance, at the north end of O'Connell Street, near the Municipal Gallery of Modern Art, has gigantic, heroic statuary of almost Soviet proportions to commemorate those who died for Irish nationalism. Glasnevin Cemetery, properly called Prospect Cemetery, is where many of the heroes lie in rest.

Outside of Dublin, local municipalities have sponsored patriotic remembrance of the Rising of 1916, particularly commemoration of local people who participated. Plaques and statutes honoring 1916 are found in many locations.

IRELAND'S HISTORY SINCE 1923

The Irish Civil War of 1922–1923 has retained considerable significance since both major modern political parties trace their origins to the two opposing sides in the contest. Eamon de Valera emerged from it to become the most important political figure in Ireland for fifty years, ranking with Daniel O'Connell and Charles Stuart Parnell as towering figures in Irish history. He was born in New York of a Cuban father and an Irish mother, and arrived in Ireland as a young child. De Valera was educated to be a schoolteacher. He became a member of the Irish Republican Brotherhood and the dissident Irish Volunteers. He was very lucky not to have been shot for his leading part in the 1916 uprising. After his release from British detention, he became a staunch anti-treaty *Fianna Fáil* leader. It took some time before he could accept the minimum requirements for participation in Free State politics, but once he did, he commanded a nationalistic party that regularly returned him to the office of *Taoiseach*.

Despite Ireland's hardships in the 1930s and 1940s, de Valera was always popular. To some he was a mystical leader, or the living personification of Irish ideals. To his bitterest critics he was the "tall, lanky misery." He remains a figure of controversy. Today younger Irish intellectuals are revising estimations of his greatness downward, but his importance can never be denied, no matter how sharp the criticism. De Valera's main priority was to shape Ireland into a pure, austere nation with a special, spiritual quality. He idealized a frugal, anti-materialistic, self-sufficient, predominently rural Ireland. De Valera was a puritan in his own personal life and a firm Catholic. In many ways, he became a stern father figure for the nation, often cold, hard, authoritarian and aloof.

Although his fame originated through his brave leadership in 1916, in power de Valera was a staunch constitutionalist and centerist, having no patience with extremism. Moreover, he would not allow any discrimination against Irish Protestants. He was determined to eradicate all religious strife in the Republic. It is noteworthy in this regard that two of the Republic's presidents were Protestants at the time that de Valera served as *Taoiseach*.

De Valera's political career was actually longer than that of Stalin or Franco. He became the chief executive in 1932 and stayed in power most of the time until he was kicked upstairs to the largely ceremonial President's office in 1959. During his long period of power he brought the nation out of the deliriums of civil war, broke the last links with Britain and the British Empire and kept Ireland neutral during World War Two. The Free State became, under his leadership, the sovereign state of Eire in 1937 and the Republic of Ireland in 1948.

Success did not crown all of his policies and programs. His passion for using the Irish language was never shared by a majority. His keenness to revise or get rid of the border with Northern Ireland proved fruitless. Furthermore, a big economic upswing did not happen while he was in office. Of course, much of de Valera's time as Taoiseach coincided with the Great Depression, but his economic policies of protectionism and trade wars with Britain were costly.

De Valera's economic policies were abruptly changed when Sean Lemass introduced new men and women and new ideas when he became *Taoiseach* and leader of *Fianna Fáil* in 1959. He opened Ireland as a base for foreign firms. In the 1960s, new hope for a brighter future took hold in Ireland, manifested in rising employment and standards of living.

During the 60s, the traditional life of Ireland so admired by American tourists was coming to an end rapidly in many parts of the country. Frugal, rural Ireland ceased to be the environment of most Irish people as urban population grew at the expense of the countryside. Ribbon sprawl stretched around towns as new cottages and bungalows went up. Western style materialism became increasingly characteristic of Irish life as radios, television sets, cars, refrigerators and other consumer goods became available to an expanding population. Education and social services experienced massive growth simultaneously with the growth of social problems taken up in detail in Chapter Four. Television, the paperback revolution, the greater liberalization of the Roman Catholic Church and the easing of censorship all have had a bearing upon the in-complete process of transforming Ireland into a modern European state.

In foreign affairs as well as in economic matters, Ireland after de Valera reached outwards to a wider world by joining the European Economic Community. Irish leaders look forward to even closer economic integration in 1992 and beyond. Ireland's neutrality has been maintained at the same time that Irish military forces have served with distinction in United Nations peacekeeping efforts.

The issues from partition in 1922 have never gone away. The border and relations with Britain have continued to preoccupy politicians in the Republic. Some signs of hope glimmer in the quagmire of hatred and violence, the worst legacy of the long, troubled and often ironic history of Ireland.

INDEX

Other Companion Guides from Hippocrene

These are books written by American professors for Americans who wish to enrich the travel experience through an understanding of the history and culture of vacation destinations.

COMPANION GUIDE TO PORTUGAL
by T. Kubiak

Describing the sights, sounds and smells which the visitor will encounter, Kubiak evokes the rich texture of Portuguese life, while presenting a comprehensive review of the nation's history and traditions. The author is a professor of geography at Eastern Kentucky University.

260 pages   ISBN 0-87052-554-9 $14.95 paper

AN AMERICAN'S GUIDE TO THE SOVIET UNION (Rev. Ed.)
by Lydle Brinkle

Covering all the Soviet cities which can receive visitors from the West, this guide gives a taste of the great diversity of flavors and rhythms of life in a country with over 130 ethnic groups. This new edition contains a chapter on the Crimea, just recently opened to foreign tourists. The author is professor of geography at Gannon University, Erie, PA.

314 pages   ISBN 0-87052-554-9 $14.95 paper

COMPANION GUIDE TO ROMANIA
by *Lydle Brinkle*

In the only up-to-date guide to the heart of Eastern Europe, the author of the guide to the Soviet Union now unveils the colorful history and great natural beauty of the country chiefly known as the home of Count Dracula.

xxx pages   ISBN 0-87052-634-0 $14.95 paper

Also by Henry Weisser
UNDERSTANDING THE U.K.: A Short Guide to British Culture, Politics, Geography, Economics and History

265 pages   ISBN 0-87052-428-3 $11.95 paper